CONTEMPORARY IDEALISM
IN AMERICA

CONTEMPORARY IDEALISM
IN AMERICA

CONTRIBUTORS

George Herbert Palmer   R. F. Alfred Hoernlé
Charles M. Bakewell   Joseph A. Leighton
Wilbur M. Urban   John E. Boodin
Edgar S. Brightman   Charles W. Hendel
G. Watts Cunningham   Radoslav A. Tsanoff
William E. Hocking

Edited by

CLIFFORD BARRETT

NEW YORK
RUSSELL & RUSSELL · INC
1964

FIRST PUBLISHED IN 1932
REISSUED, 1964, BY RUSSELL & RUSSELL, INC.
BY ARRANGEMENT WITH CLIFFORD BARRETT
L. C. CATALOG CARD NO: 64—11850

141
B27c

49,678
Apr., 1965

———————

To the memory of
JOSIAH ROYCE
who proclaimed the dignity
of the human spirit

———————

PREFACE

The philosopher is first and above all else, an inquirer. In each age, the representatives of historical attitudes are confronted with new data, if not with new problems. The richest legacy bequeathed by the classic philosopher to his successors is not a doctrine to be proclaimed, but a method and spirit for furthering the enlargement of human understanding. In general it may be said that the modern idealist is the disciple of Plato and of Kant, but this does not mean that he would merely reiterate their conclusions. While knowledge remains incomplete, and the conquest of mind continues, new issues will require new interpretations, and new ideas will be gained at the cost of old.

Scientific investigation as well as realistic and pragmatic criticism have shown inadequacies in certain conclusions of the older idealists. In so doing they have proven valuable friends, making clear the points at which further analysis is needed and at which the light of recent thought may make possible more satisfactory interpretation. Idealism, with its profound trust in the supremacy of reason over the irrational, must greet with utmost cordiality, any alteration of doctrinal statement which arises from deepened insight. But in view of more recent inquiry and criticism, what precisely is the position of the idealist? In the thought of critics, and to some degree of friends, the answer very often appears to be a confused one.

In the following discussions, it is the purpose of the writers to consider problems of fundamental human interest, in the light of contemporary thought and in the spirit of idealistic interpretation. In the attitude which these interpretations express, they are united, but no claim of unanimity is made for all of the specific conclusions reached. Idealism is regarded as a philosophical attitude, primarily, and not a rigid dogma. The writers present no doctrinal creed, and attach no claim of finality to their conclusions. To hold views concerning what is ultimate and absolute in the universal order is one thing, but to suppose that one's *views* regarding these things are either ultimate or absolute is a very different thing,—yet the two have often been strangely confused by the critics of Idealism. Confidence in the ultimacy of value and rationality in the universe inspires enthusiasm in the prospect of what has and what may be achieved by human thought, but also, it inspires a sincere modesty in the philosopher who considers the fragmentariness of his own insight.

The editor desires gratefully to acknowledge indebtedness to the writers of the following pages. Their generous cooperation and cordial interest have been given unsparingly, rendering the task of preparation in the fullest sense a mutual one. In addition to those whose contributions appear, the association and valuable assistance of the late Mary Whiton Calkins, Professor in Wellesley College, and of the late Charles Andrew Armstrong Bennett, Professor in Yale University, are remembered with deep appreciation. The true philosopher's concern that inquiry shall be carried forward as earnestly and fruitfully from other points of view as from his own, has been demonstrated again in the generous encouragement and assistance of Provost Ernest Carroll Moore of the University of California at Los Angeles. The wise counsel and constant support of Dean Charles Henry Rieber of the same university, place upon us a debt which is very gratefully acknowledged. Professor Robert Scoon of Princeton University has contributed highly valuable suggestions and criticism. For courteous permission to quote from publications, the authors are grateful to *Philosophy*, *The Journal of Philosophy*, The Open Court Publishing Company, the Harvard University Press, and The Macmillan Company. It is remembered with appreciation that, in formulating plans for the volume, large profit was derived from the wise advice and interest of Professor Archibald Bowman of the University of Glasgow, and of Professor John Henry Muirhead of the University of Birmingham.

CLIFFORD BARRETT

CONTENTS

I

In Dedication:

JOSIAH ROYCE

<small>GEORGE HERBERT PALMER</small>

Harvard University

JOSIAH ROYCE [1]

George Herbert Palmer

Josiah Royce was one of the glories of three universities—California, Johns Hopkins, Harvard. His thought is already absorbed into the mind of the race. To depict the great philosopher in due proportions is the work of another time, place, and writer. The present paper has a narrower and more personal aim. We teachers work in a way unlike the members of other professions. We constitute a family, which meets each week, and feels its mutual dependence; our successes and failures are interlocked, ourselves enriched by the supplemental traits of one another. When one of us dies, his colleagues mourn more for their own than for the public loss, each sharing with each such bits of remembrance as illustrate the beauty and excellence of the absent friend. In the history of Harvard I would record in a fragmentary and intimate way the affection which thirty-four years bred in me for Royce. He was a picturesque figure, a prodigious scholar, a stimulating teacher, a heroic character, a playful and widely loved friend.

His appearance was strange. His short stocky figure was surmounted by a gigantic round head well sunk in his shoulders. The top of it was sprinkled with red hair, while the strongly freckled face seemed to himself and to every stranger unparalleled in homeliness. The resemblance without and within to Socrates was striking. But no one who knew him well could wish a line of that face changed. Every inch of it expressed wisdom, modesty, humor. In our hearts we called it beautiful, though those who knew him less could go no further than "distinguished" or "original." His clothes, of no particular fashion, seemed to have as little to

[1] Through the courtesy of Professor Morison, Professor Palmer arranged for the printing of this paper here as well as in *The Development of Harvard University*, Harvard University Press.

do with him as matter with mind. His slowly sauntering gait was characteristic. And if you were short of time, it was not safe to ask him a question, however simple; for you received a lecture from which you at least gathered that truth was never fragmentary but had meaning only through its place in the system of the universe.

Early he was remarkable. We know the poverty and isolation of his boyhood years, and have heard that he moved through those hardships with the same unflinching cheerfulness with which in later years he met public attack, domestic affliction, and failing health. Such hardships would have quenched a less resolute spirit. His parents, of slender means, lived in an obscure valley of California in 1855, a time when that state was more cut off from the rest of the world than any other of our Union has ever been. Things of the mind were little regarded by the seekers for gold. The State University did not begin instruction at Berkeley till 1873, but it had Royce already among its students, he taking his bachelor's degree in 1875. Tuition was free, but for "a timid and ineffective boy," as he afterwards called himself, discomforts abounded. "My comrades," he writes, "very generally found me disagreeably striking in my appearance, by reason of the fact that I was countrified, quaint, and unable to play boys' games." To such exuberant and unimaginative youths Royce's perpetual inclination to ask questions and accumulate knowledge seemed as queer as his appearance; but undisturbed, he gathered needed instruction in social customs from those who laughed, moral and mental stimulus from the books of Mill and Spencer, and still more from two great teachers, Edward Rowland Sill, the lucid poet and Professor of English, and Joseph Le Conte, the philosophic geologist. His graduation thesis, on the theology of Aeschylus' Prometheus, was so remarkable that it was printed by the University, and it prompted a group of gentlemen to offer the means for his further study in Germany, a welcome aid afterwards scrupulously repaid. At several German universities he received profound influences from Kant and his Romantic followers, from Schopenhauer, from Lotze. Acquaintance with Hegel came many years later. Just as his resources were coming to an end, Johns Hopkins University was founded, and offered Royce one of its four earliest fellowships. He returned to this country and took his doctor's degree at Baltimore in 1878, immediately afterwards accepting an instructorship in rhetoric and logic at the University of California.

Those who know only his later writings may wonder at this appointment. One does not easily imagine Royce correcting compositions. The style we think of as his was not neat and exemplary. Its sentences were usually long and tangled, with a good deal of repetition, and little assistive rhythm. Condensed, brilliant, epigrammatic writing was never his. He needed considerable sea room. His papers seem composed rather for the clarification of his own mind than for that of his reader. In short, his style was rich rather than formal, that of one on whom thoughts were ever crowding, and to whom beauty of phrasing made but a slight appeal. A peculiarly genuine style it was, therefore, convinced and convincing. No one can submit himself to its massive flow without feeling that he is under the guidance of a master—competent, candid, large-thoughted, as large in heart as in brain.

Now it is interesting to see that this volume and rush of style came to Royce through the deepening experience of life. In the beginning his sentences were brief and conformable to pattern. In his third year of teaching he printed a small *Primer of Logical Analysis for the Use of Composition Students*. It is admirably written, academic in its clearness, conciseness, and attention to the user's needs. I name it to mark the contrast between Royce's early and later styles. But it well illustrates something still more important, which I may call the tenacity of his intellectual growth. He was ever changing, ever constant. In this his first book he treats of a subject on which his thoughts were largely engaged at the time of his death. But how differently the subject was conceived! That was always his mode of progress. He carried his past with him, not dropping early conceptions, but evolving them continually into richer significance. Few minds were more progressive; few more steadfast.

Royce's departure from California gives us our first view of that easy courage which was one of his central traits. The year 1882–83 William James was to spend abroad. He and I reported to President Eliot that we wished Royce to take his place. We had hardly more knowledge of him than a few published papers afforded. As the appointment was only temporary, President Eliot consented, and we invited Royce, offering a thousand dollars for salary and nothing afterwards. James was to return at the close of the year. A poor man, and with a wife and baby, Royce resigned a permanent position and brought his family across the continent. When in later life I asked him how he had dared, he said that risks of this sort were inevitable for one who would go on to power, and were safer the earlier in life they came. In that first year he showed his quality so fully that I offered to provide him a second opportunity by taking the sabbatical absence which had been for some time due me. After two years the entire University was convinced that he could not be spared. He became an Instructor for a third year and in 1885 an Assistant Professor.

But something happened in that third year which showed the moral sensitiveness and heroism of the man. Knowing Royce's slender means, President Eliot suggested to Augustus Lowell that Royce be offered a course of Lowell Lectures, with a fee of a thousand dollars. Royce was summoned to a conference. I met him as he returned. He had refused. Mr. Lowell, probably feeling some misgivings over the strange youth, had told him that the founder's will contained a statement of religious belief to which it was necessary each lecturer should assent. To this Royce demurred. He could accept no creed as a condition of receiving money, nor could he be sure that his own understanding of these doctrines was in accord with that of the founder. Uncomplainingly he returned to poverty, and I do not think ever mentioned the matter to half a dozen persons. We who knew persuaded him to give to the University in public lectures the material he had intended for the Lowell Institute. This was the origin of his *Religious Aspect of Philosophy* published in 1885, a book whose freshness, force, and devout spirit gave him a commanding position throughout the country.

Then followed a period of enormous productivity. Benjamin Rand enumerates twenty-three volumes and ninety-four articles written by Royce, and his oral product was hardly less astonishing. For college work he taught more hours than any other member of his department, saying he preferred to do so because in contact with the minds of others he could best formulate his own. Every year he gave numerous lectures, often whole courses, at other colleges and cities. At Aberdeen he gave the Gifford Lectures, at Manchester College, Oxford, the Hibbert Lectures, and from both universities received honorary degrees. For several years he taught in our Summer School. He took but one sabbatical year and few vacations, in the early years seldom went to bed till after midnight, smoked incessantly, and allowed himself little exercise. Feeble as he was left by a serious illness four years before he died, it was during those four years that some of his strongest books were written, a striking instance of scholarly hardihood. To himself he was ever a stern taskmaster, and while perhaps overconsiderate in dealing with earnest students of middling powers, he was exacting with men of capacity, impatient with pretenders, and scornful in exposing careless ignorance. Perhaps his classes did not always follow the intricacy of his lectures, but they knew that something big was going on above them, and were all duly elevated. Each gained his own vista into an unsuspected world, many having their minds and characters re-created in the process, and every year a sufficient number stood ready to elect courses known to be severe.

His large tolerance of those who differed with him had in it nothing of that negative indifferentism which, having no convictions of its own, counts one belief as good as another. He was ever a believer, precise, insistent, and inquiring, his

temper constructive and not merely critical. Strikingly original in thought and speech, he never ceased to build, each
bit of truth captured being firmly bound up with what had
gone before, till one was equally astonished at the range and
exactitude of his knowledge. Indeed, whoever talked with
him hardly thought of what he knew as knowledge. It was
rather a unified outlook on life—spacious, detailed, conse-
crated, amusing, inexhaustible. All knowledge was his
province. Among his specialties were psychology, logic,
ethics, metaphysics, the philosophies of nature and religion;
he knew—none better—the course which philosophy had
taken since its rise; had elaborate acquaintance with mathematics, biology, and most of the natural sciences which relate to man; he wrote a novel and History of California;
music and poetry were the arts that moved him, and he was
at home in the literature of England, Germany, France, and
Italy. Yet the living man was never lost in the great scholar.
The same intellectual impulse which carried him over such
vast scholastic fields sent him just as eagerly into the common affairs of the day. His belief in the crimes of Germany,
the land of his spiritual birth, pursued him day and night
and had considerable influence in bringing about his death.
When the quiet scholar stepped on the public platform to
speak of the war, his moral passion swayed the entire
audience and much of the world outside.

But that moral passion deserves a higher name. It was,
indeed, religion, a feeling not merely reverential toward law,
but addressed to a person manifested wherever order appears
and needing our concurrence to complete that order. In
his all-embracing Absolute, Royce found room for our individual existence here and hereafter, for our sins, repentance,
atonement, and salvation. Loyalty to this sovereign Person made him one of the most unshakably religious men I
have ever known. From organized religion he held aloof,
partly because it was his disposition in all things to go his
own way, partly, too, through reaction from certain rigidi-
ties of his boyhood. But he acknowledged to me that there
was something childish in such aversion, and twice in his

later years he conducted prayers in Appleton Chapel. Personally he fairly lived with the Eternal, the affairs of time being still counted worth while because in them too can be seen "bright shoots of everlastingness." To his happy home came many sorrows, "afflictions sorted, anguish of all sizes." And he suffered. Who that knew that tender heart could doubt it. But at the center of him there was peace. "Shall not the judge of all the earth do right?" he always seemed to say. Through every experience he walked unperturbed, no fear, no clouded intellect, no check of philosophic humor. I do not believe he was ever known to complain. At one time he was bitterly attacked by a man whose book he had scathingly reviewed. Abusive articles were sent broadcast through the country and the Harvard Corporation was petitioned to remove him. Just at this time his mother died. When I said to him that it was hard to meet two such blows at once, he answered, "No. Each is bad, but there is a gain in having them together. They lean up against each other, and when I become sore over one, the other gives change." So did he travel on earth's common way in cheerful godliness. That elfin figure with the unconventional dress and slouching step, that face which blended the infant and the sage, that total personality, as amused, amusing, and intent on righteousness as Socrates himself—happy the University that had for a long time so vitalizing a presence!

II

INTRODUCTION

CLIFFORD BARRETT

Princeton University

INTRODUCTION

Clifford Barrett

Half a century ago clear lines differentiated well-established philosophical positions in America. Subsequently those lines became blurred and broken at many points. The dominance of Idealism, which had been conceded in earlier days, came to be protested. If the protestants did not succeed in winning an equal authority for their own positions, at least they were able to stir a widespread suspicion that Idealism had its eyes fixed worshipfully upon its past prophets, and was incapable of dealing adequately with the problems of an expanding intellectual world. During these years, investigations of the physical sciences have shaken traditional cosmologies and disturbed metaphysical assumptions. Objective psychology has undermined familiar theories of the *self*,—body and soul; it has raised doubts as to the possibility of a justifiable non-naturalistic account of *mind*. Realism has directed its most determined attacks against the method of "speculative philosophy." Pragmatism has reiterated with finality, the relative character of all human thought and standards. Important changes of social structure on its political and economic sides, with a notable shift of emphasis toward economic interest, have suggested a dubious fate for established theories of obligation. Widespread effort in the direction of reëvaluation of moral and religious attitudes, marked by a sense of tragedy or of inconsequentiality in human life, has shaken confidence in "eternal values." More subtle has been a shift not merely of opinions about philosophical subjects, but of the very subjects which we trouble to have opinions about. The massive dramatic themes,—God, Freedom, Human Destiny,—no longer hold the center in philosophical controversies. The extensiveness of these changes places upon all philosophers the necessity of redefining issues and positions, and for Idealism, the need is particularly urgent. There is little excuse for mere reiteration of the systems of Berkeley or Hegel, but there is profound need for reconstruction which brings to present problems the insight of each of the great philosophical attitudes.

Even learned critics have tended to identify Idealism with some one or a sum of idealistic systems of the past. The very age and brilliance of its history, indeed, render this attitude especially liable to such misunderstanding. But it is an error which is impoverishing, imprisoning in systems constructed in the environment of other ages, the universal genius of a major philosophical interpretation. The experiences of each age are limited, and its interpretations are fragmentary. Each must make its own intellectual adventures, and bear for itself the hazards of philosophical conquest. The welfare of any generation requires that its problems be surveyed from each of the great philosophical vantage points. Idealism, like Naturalism, is to be regarded as such a primary point of view. It is an attitude, not a creed. It is a way of interpreting human experience, not the conclusions of a specific interpreter. It is a living tradition, not a religious veneration of accumulated philosophical dogmas. Its classic expressions contain much that is of profound universal significance, yet it lives as an insight, in new situations enlightening the minds of successive interpreters.

It is the purpose of the present book to offer interpretations of issues of fundamental consequence in the present order of thought and action. The interpretations are founded on the postulates and principles of Idealism, as understood by the writers. What these postulates and principles are can be made more clearly evident in the later discussions than would be possible in any brief definition here. Yet it is a fair question which asks at the beginning of any discussion for some preliminary indication of the significance of a central term. In the present intellectual world, what are the characteristic marks of an *idealistic* philosophy? By way of reply, certain typical aspects of idealistic interpretation may be illustrated from fields of philosophical inquiry. If we turn to the field of metaphysics, for example, it is clear that with disavowal of older conceptions of "matter," the clarity of line which characterized the age-long dispute between "idealism" and "materialism" has been lost. Scientific and metaphysical interests have shifted the foci of their attention from problems of "substance" to problems of "structure." For metaphysics, the pertinent inquiry is that as to the ultimate order of a world which "naturalist" and "idealist" agree in describing for scientific purposes in terms of *energy-structures* or *events*. The fundamental difference between "naturalism" and "idealism" is philosophical and not scientific. It has to do, not with descriptions of physical processes as such, but with their significance and final order,—a problem which at once, leads to questions of *meaning* and *value* in their systematic relations to cosmic structure. The only fruitful "philosophy of science" is that which keeps clearly in mind that its interpretations, both in aim and method, are of a different kind than the activities of the physical scientist which provided their data, and that they are subject to quite different tests. The idealist is deeply interested in the attitudes and results of the physical and social sciences. He is ready to respect any serious philosophical account of the physical world. But he cannot take seriously the borrowed glory which any interpretation appropriates to its conclusions from the scientific-demonstrability of the data which it endeavors to synthesize and explain.

It is an extreme form of "naturalism" but rarely taken seriously by even its professed adherents, which asserts, in Mr. Russell's popular phraseology, that "the universe is all spots and jumps, without unity, without coherence or orderliness, . . . that the external world may be illusion, but if it exists, it consists of events short, small, and haphazard. Order, unity, and continuity are human inventions just as truly as are catalogues and encyclopaedias." As if these cataloguing minds were not themselves parts of nature! Aside from so "short and simple" a metaphysical creed, there remain possibilities for accounts of cosmic structure in terms of "mechanical" and of "organic" systems of relationships. Of these, the idealist prefers the latter as a basis for descriptive analogy, emphasizing as it does, the dependence of the part upon the unity of the whole, or more accurately, of the specific functioning upon the system of the whole. This grounding of particularity within a larger and finally within a universal and self-sufficient order which incorporates and gives meaning to its fragmentariness, constitutes a primary insight of idealistic philosophy, variously expressed in historic systems under concepts of "God," "Reason," the "Supreme Idea," the "Infinite," the "Causa Sui," the "Absolute," and the "Blessed Community." The idealist does not question the genuineness of the items of his experience of the world, but their genuine separateness and self-sufficiency. Out of that which the particular is, in common with what is not exclusively its own, must arise not only any claim to consideration as a participant in a world order, but also the claim for any significance vested within its particularity. The emergence of greater from less, however described, requires the miracle of creation *ex nihilo*. But the partial expression of the greater in the less is by no means incomprehensible or *unnatural*.

The idealist, dealing with the metaphysics of structure, presses a step further. It is clear that no adequate account of the world can neglect so important a datum as "spirit." Here the definitive characteristic of Idealism is evident, for more than in anything else, as Professor Bakewell points out in later pages, the continuity of the idealist tradition is to be found in the recognition of the primacy of "spirit" in the world. The world is intelligible to man because and to the extent that its order is also the order of his rational life. The only form in which consciousness can exist as Kant showed, is that of synthetic interpretation. The interpretations and syntheses of man's thoughts are of consequence for knowledge only so far as the evaluative order on which they are based also possesses a regulative status in the world which they are taken to represent.

Idealistic philosophy is no opponent of physiological psychology, nor of the objective method in experimental investigation. It does oppose philosophical constructions which blur the distinction between genetic physical relations of psychological activities and their normative relations to structures of meaning and value. Participating in a system of physical relations, the structure of a specific thought-activity presents problems for physiological psychology; participating also in a system of meanings and values, it may present problems for ethics and logic. In general the newer forms of Naturalism have been pleased with a "biological" account of human life in its entirety. Purposes are mechanically explicable responses arising from the primary urge toward adjustment to environment. Advances in physics have tended to discredit thoroughly mechanistic presuppositions, but these linger on in the work of numerous psychologists. The idealist has no cause to argue whether this type of explanation provides a valid account of certain aspects of rational life, but he denies that it can offer a complete or adequate account of all aspects. To insist that all knowledge is to be adequately explained in terms of "events in nature" is to destroy the possibility of any knowledge of nature. If thought activity is only an occurrence in nature, it can be judged in no other way than any natural occurrence, that is, as existing or not existing. To a physical event as such, no test of validity or of moral quality is applicable. "It would be as meaningless to ascribe truth to a judgment as to the fall of a meteor if both are wholly the outcome of matter-of-fact occurrence." [1] Even *meaningless* then loses its significance as a descriptive term, and becomes inapplicable. Spirit and mechanics are not genuine antagonists, for it is only in the service of purposes and values that the "mechanical" may win significance.

The effort to isolate *values* and to regard them as constituting a field for independent investigation has been characterized as "probably the greatest philosophical achievement of the nineteenth century." [2] In even so superlative a

---

[1] G. P. Adams, *Idealism and the Modern Age.*   [2] F. C. S. Schiller.

statement, many realists and idealists, as well as pragmatists, would concur. But their investigations in this field lead to widely varied conclusions. On one side of the "great divide in philosophy," are those who regard human experiences of value as resting back upon limited value-systems, which themselves occur in an order of nature over which values hold no regulative power. For them, values are human creations, arising out of physiological processes, or emerging from the valueless. On the other side are those who look upon human experiences of values as arising out of man's participation in the order of the universe, of which he is a part. Values are not his creation, but his discovery. He is aware of values because he has the capacity to realize in intelligent life, the order of universal nature. As its physical processes participate in his bodily life, so its regulative order is further discovered and expressed in his activities of reason, appreciation, evaluation. The idealist, accepting the latter general position, may view individuality as primordial and the world in its ultimate structure as pluralistic, or he may regard individuality as applying to the limited expressions of a single universal nature. In either case, man's interpretative activities may be based upon a system of meanings and values which in kind are one with the regulative principles of the cosmic order out of which they arise and to which they provide man's key of knowledge. It is in the significance which they attribute to values in human knowledge that Pragmatism and Idealism draw closest together. In their metaphysical assumptions as to the nature of these values, they are separated.

Constructive activity may express as penetrating insight as analytical reflection. The philosopher-king may be as wise a man as the hermit. Enthusiasm for intelligent social ends may be as honorable a philosophical condition as cloistered retirement from concerns of human welfare. The idealist, with the sincerity of his emphasis upon the necessity of understanding the partial in its relations to larger units than itself, and finally to the whole, is committed to the consideration of aspects of thought and life in terms of the individual as a totality. The individual person, in turn, with his purposes and activities, he must seek to understand within the order of society, and human society as in some way realizing the order of the universe. Of deep interest to idealistic interpretation, therefore, is the present widespread effort toward clearer understanding of social relations and toward reëvaluation of social standards and institutions.

Eras of economic and political readjustment are likely to be alert to problems of ethical theory. In some instances, the desire for intelligent guidance, in others, desire for intellectual justification, leads to exertions of effort to a degree unknown in more complacent times. Out of the disillusionment of the recent past, old faiths gave way to skepticism, and men came to question not only their own and others' purposes, which might have been profitable enough, but they came to doubt the worth of purpose itself. This was to doubt the worth of intelligent living, and to leave social obligations without support. But the gloom of general disillusionment seems now to have begun to cast its shadow over disillusionment itself. That, too, proves futile, and we must look for something more positive. It is clear that freedom is not mere antagonism, but the wholehearted pursuit of well-examined and coördinated ends.

Here the idealist feels the need of extending the boundaries of ethical judgments. The horizons of an immediate situation are too narrow for intelligent choice. Practical decisions based upon their limited perspectives need to be corrected and supplemented in the light of farther ends and more inclusive purposes,—ultimately, indeed, so far as possible, they are to be viewed in terms of their coherence with the whole of life and the whole of nature. That this *whole* is not directly apparent does not alter the fact that situations enjoy no atomic independence, but present aspects of larger situations, and can be dealt with intelligently only in the light of the fullest understanding of their universal aspects, as well as of their limitations. To view the particular situation in the larger field of its far-reaching relationships requires the accumulated experience of other situations, but it requires also the analytic ability to discover the universal within the particular; the lines of the complete within a present incomplete expression. It requires, too, the synthetic ability which can see the present activity in terms of distant ends. Idealism would reiterate that rational direction of individual and social conduct must always be in terms of purposes and ends, and that it follows that the most inclusive organization of purposes should provide the basis for the most intelligent and moral life. In turning its attention to farther purposes and distant ends, philosophy need not deal, as is often charged, in vague speculations. Rather, it will be its aim to discover in more immediate situations, principles which by their coherence and stability, reveal not only a basis for an experimental assumption of probability, but a foundation for wholehearted reliance upon their trustworthiness.

So much may be said in an introductory suggestion, by way of pointing out characteristics of idealistic interpretation, as they appear in its application to contemporary fields of inquiry. Whether in the considerations of metaphysics or logic or ethics, or elsewhere, the idealist finds the immediate and partial incapable of rendering a full account of itself, but discovers that its essential nature is to be understood only as it is viewed in relation to the more inclusive order which it articulates in nature and behavior. The physical world and the physical body abound in analogies which it is unnecessary to mention. The immediate datum is not isolated, but appears within a situation including other factors than its presence. This situation, as Pragmatism has argued convincingly, itself rests upon constructive activities motivated by the desire to realize certain purposes or values. The idealist would press farther, however, and maintain that the purposes and values which dominate in the viewing or controlling of a definite situation lose their character except as they, too, are viewed as related within larger structures of purpose and value, and ultimately, within a cosmic order of purpose and value. Thus, within the specific situations of life, purposes, meanings, and values constitute the basis of organization and control, and within cosmic structure, they hold a regulative position. In part, at least, this is the idealist's meaning when he speaks of the *primacy of spirit* in the world. To the objection that purposes, meanings and values are possessions of human minds, he replies that these possessions are discovered and not created by man, who, as a part of the cosmos, expresses its structure within himself.

It is with such a basis of systematic interpretation, rather than detailed conclusions in which all necessarily concur, that the present writers unite as idealists. Their purpose is neither defense nor propaganda, but the presentation of a view of fundamental issues in contemporary thought.

III

CONTINUITY OF THE IDEALIST TRADITION

CHARLES M. BAKEWELL

Yale University

CONTINUITY OF THE IDEALIST TRADITION

Charles M. Bakewell

Back of all differences that characterize the great systems of speculative thought, differences in method, differences in problems singled out for emphasis—a matter largely determined by the spirit of the age—differences in conclusions reached regarding specific problems that fall properly within the scope of philosophy, lies a common fund of agreement which is apt to be lost sight of just because it is taken for granted, and because philosophers spend their time in discussing their differences, which is, of course, as it should be, for these are the live issues. One may even say that these discussions of differences are keen and bitter in proportion to the extent of basic agreement. We go together so far; why can we not go together the whole way? Aristotle was a severe critic of the Platonic theory of ideas just because he had so much in common with Plato. We do not argue with those with whom we totally disagree; we pass by on the other side. All this is especially true of those philosophies generally regarded as idealistic. The agreements are far more profound and more important than the differences, and they give continuity to the idealist tradition.

It is well at the start to emphasize the fact that idealism is not, in any of its significant expressions, to be identified with mentalism. That is, it is not a doctrine that resolves physical objects into mental states; a doctrine that holds that the things that you see out there in space are in reality just bundles of feelings, groups of sensations, states of consciousness, within the mind. We cannot even state such a doctrine without assuming that we do, to begin with, know things as distinct from our impressions. No idealist, at least in the Western world, not even the much maligned Berkeley, has defended a doctrine so patently absurd.[1] The idealist keeps intact the distinction between subjective and objective, and views spatial experiences as the experiences of real objects in space, and not as feelings or sensations having their being in some mysterious way out of space altogether and in the mind. He holds that Nature's laws and ways and processes are what they are, and not what we in our ignorance may fancy them to be; that things do not come into being in coming to be known; that Nature is not created anew with every revolutionary discovery in science; that we must obey Nature to conquer her, must patiently interpret and not impatiently anticipate her, to use Bacon's phrases. It is indeed part of his task to show that if, and insofar as, the material world is viewed as unreal, the mental order becomes itself unreal. One can only fix one's meanings, and distinguish thinking from dreaming, by tying up to the physical order. The old Hindu thinker who had persuaded himself of the unreality of the world of physical phenomena drew the only proper inference when he proceeded to deny the reality of the mental as well, and to teach the "fourfold nothingness" in the words: "I am nowhere anything for anybody nor is anybody anywhere anything for me." In short, the idealist accepts the well attested results of science with as much docility as the most "tough minded" thinker. It is true that some idealists have attempted to twist the facts in order that they might the better conform to their theories, as, for example, Hegel did in his Philosophy of Nature. This, however, is a human failing by no means confined to representatives of any one school.

Further confusion arises from the tendency to regard idealism as defined by contrast with realism. Modern realism has found many expressions, and it is hard to reconcile them with one another. In some of its forms it makes heavy drafts on Platonic idealism, in others it appears as a sort of attenuated materialism. Insofar as realism is a protest

---

[1] The nearest approach to a defense of mentalism is to be found in the writings of Karl Pearson, who can hardly be regarded as a representative idealist.

against subjectivism, insofar as it is an insistence upon respect for the facts of experience in all their stubbornness,
and upon the humble acceptance of the teachings of science,
we are all realists. If realism means to affirm the existence
of independent reals outside the realm of experience, and
therefore wholly independent of consciousness, it is the old
hypothetical realism whose absurdities have so often been
shown up in the history of philosophy. If it means to affirm
the existence of independent reals which are none the less
wholly accessible to experience, directly experienced or
known, it is hard to see how this doctrine conflicts with
idealism, except that the idealist would be constrained to
point out that the word "independent" is not strictly taken
in such usage. It is merely a name, and a rather unfortunate
one, for a problem,—the problem how one and the same
empirical content can be viewed in one context as part of a
private individual experience, and in another context as
part of the universal realm of experience. The conflict becomes irrepressible and absolute only when the knower is
identified with the physical organism and one's realism is
tied up, as it is by some of its American defenders, to a behavioristic metaphysics.

Again, there is no conflict between idealism and pragmatism insofar as the latter is voluntaristic, emphasizing the
practical and insisting that thinking is determined and directed by human needs. The conflict only becomes serious
when pragmatism is identified with "radical empiricism,"
and the latter is taken as meaning that the categories are
simply felt conjunctions within the stream of consciousness.
This the idealist must regard as a confusion of the logical
with the psychological which inevitably leads to subjectivism and skepticism. Professor James himself escapes this
consequence by falling back upon faith, by an affirmation
of over-beliefs, which provide for the guidance of life. The
conflict with instrumentalism is more serious. We can all
readily agree that the pursuit of truth is the quest for means
of controlling experience, and that the good is that which
carries one forward in the direction in which one desires to

go; that reason's task is to see that scientific criteria are applied to inventions as they affect the lives of human beings here and now, and that it is a misuse of reason to employ it in the endeavor to escape from the world and find refuge from its insecurities by conjuring up the picture of a "heaven of pure delight where saints immortal reign." Nevertheless, the idealist is constrained to point out that not only in ancient times but in modern classical physics as well, forming a picture of reality has served as a means for securing control of events; that the concept of the fixed, both in science and in philosophy, has served the same purpose; and that even in modern physics the doctrine of relativity is very far from being a return to the view of the old "flowing philosophers" for whom all was changing and relative. The old absolutes of Newtonian physics have but given way to new absolutes which more successfully eliminate the "observer," and thus give more precise and accurate instruments of measurement. Furthermore, ability to control events is of little use except as determined by some standard, some value that is decisive. If one is to use knowledge so as to affect the lives of human beings, it must be so as to affect them in ways which, antecedent to and exterior to your determination, human beings are intrinsically entitled to be affected. Now this end or measure of value is, the instrumentalist tells us, not to be determined, after the usual fashion of empiricism, by identifying it with what satisfies or is enjoyed. Professor Dewey himself has no doubts as to what this end is, and presumably the end, as he conceives it, represents the direction in which every one really desires to go though he may know it not: the manifold purposes and meanings of life must be "interconnected"; we must recognize the "solidarity of human interests," and work for an "abundant and significant experience participated in by all." It is implied that it is the duty of all to seek to further these ends. These ends may be vague, but they represent the instrumentalist's substitute for what appears in idealism as the categorical imperative or as the principle of loyalty to loyalty or as the essential form of the good. In other words, when the instrumentalist turns social reformer he trails an absolute unawares.

The one fundamental and persistent conflict is that between idealism and materialism with its attendant mechanism [1] and consequent subjectivism. The first thoroughgoing materialist of the ancient world, Democritus, found himself compelled to represent the secondary qualities as subjective but still believed that a finer organ of thought gave a direct knowledge of the atoms and their mathematical qualities. His fellow-townsman, Protagoras, rightly saw that the primary and secondary qualities were in the same case, and that if one group were subjective the other must be subjective also, and so he proclaimed a thoroughgoing relativity under the doctrine that man is the measure of all things. The philosophy of Socrates and Plato may, from one point of view, be described as simply an attempt to escape from this subjectivism while at the same time accepting the *homo mensura* doctrine. They found in the doctrine that man is the measure, not the last word of skepticism, but rather the only hope of reaching certainty. If man did not measure for himself he could never know whether he was being deceived or not. In working out their position they laid down certain principles which have been characteristic of idealism from that day to this. Knowledge involves spontaneity. The soul or knower is self-dependent and creative. Nevertheless, the individual thinker, insofar as he observes the rules of correct thinking, may reach results that are valid for all minds. They saw clearly that when the object is taken to be an immediate impression, the-thing-as-immediately-apprehended, it turns out to be tantalizingly subjective. Objectivity proves to be not something handed over as a gift in the direct impression, but rather,

[1] Modern scientific theory has so changed our conception of the nature of physical reality as to make it difficult to define mechanism in positive terms. The most comprehensive definition that can be given is—mechanistic is any interpretation of experience which excludes purpose as a true cause. An attempt is sometimes made to escape from the antithesis, mechanism versus purpose, by means of the currently popular doctrine of emergent evolution, explaining purpose as a certain set, configuration, or propensity in the physical organism. This is, however, in truth, a denial of the effectiveness of purpose in its only significant meaning. See McDougall, *Modern Materialism and Emergent Evolution*, for a searching criticism of all such attempts.

a characteristic which the impression acquires in being thought.

There has been in recent years a revival of materialism which has captured a considerable, and voluble, group of men and women of the rising generation, sometimes with a dash of Freudianism thrown in. They not infrequently exploit this view with an amusing cocksureness; but with a commendable frankness they draw the inevitable conclusions: the wisdom of the past is hoary folly, religion is foolishness, morality (or what has hitherto passed for such) an illusion. This modern materialism does not begin with atoms and empty space, but with the physical organism, and it would avoid the perplexing problem of knowledge as the ancients confronted it by simply throwing out consciousness altogether. It might be called the new dogmatic philosophy of "nothing but," with its attendant mythology, of which Mr. Watson is the high priest. According to this view, the mind is nothing but a complex of word habits, "thinking is nothing but talking to ourselves," personality is nothing but the "end product of our habit systems," and so on. Is this conclusion justified by evidence? No, but this is the only way in which mind and mental behavior, or what has passed for such, can be viewed as things tangible, observable and measurable, and the only way in which thought can be described in terms of natural science. In a word, it accords with our initial dogma. But alas, this view that would be ultra-objective turns out to be ultra-subjective— just Watson's way of working his muscles. The word meaning itself must, we are told, be tossed overboard as nothing but a "literary expression"—whatever that may mean in behavioristic terms. The thinker, or what passes for the thinker, is chasing around like the rat in the maze, looking for the satisfying verbal pattern and, having found it, pounces upon it like the rat upon the cheese; its word-hunger appeased, it looks no further. The words true and false have, however, no application to the result. How childish then is our interest in one another's views; just idly watching the wheels go round in some man machine.

As Aristotle put it, philosophers may be divided into two classes, those who begin with chaos and those who begin with Zeus. For the former the problem is to account for the amount of order and rationality that has resulted; for the latter the problem is to account for the amount of disorder and irrationality that seems clearly to exist. Now the idealists, from Plato and Aristotle through to Kant, Fichte and Royce, "begin with Zeus," which means that they begin with the soul, for as Aristotle is frank to admit, the only positive meaning we can put into the idea of God is found by ascribing to Him what we are "in our best brief moments." [1]

The point of departure for idealism is then the reality, the existence, the spontaneity, the hegemony, of the soul. I use the word soul, in spite of the psychologists, without apology. It is fully as respectable a term as matter, and certainly no more elusive in meaning. When the soul dons academic garb and puts on its dignity its *nom de guerre* is mind, but since it is not merely knower, but the determiner of all other values as well as truth values, both individual and social, the old-fashioned term is the more fitting. The more sophisticated call it the self; those primarily interested in religion prefer the term spirit.

The initial ground for our belief in the existence of the soul is found in the ontological argument—"when me they fly I am the wings." Its reality is affirmed the more certainly the more stoutly it is denied. It is affirmed in every conscious purpose, presupposed in all rational intercourse. This argument could only apply to supersensible realities. Perhaps it is misleading to call it an argument. It is, in fact, immediate knowledge, corresponding, where noumenal reality is concerned, to awareness of objects in the phenomenal order. Belief in the existence of the soul is as instinctive as my belief in the existence of yonder table which I see. But it may be an illusion, as may be the table. The only test reason can then apply is, does the recognition of its existence help to explain the facts of experience? Kant, to be sure, while

[1] And, we may add, what is implied in the possibility of those "best brief moments."

virtually accepting this argument in the case of practical reason, denied it in theoretical, but, because of this denial, he created an impassable gulf between theoretical and practical reason, and left the soul helpless and useless in the interpretation of experience. This was due to the dogma, which his own philosophy should have freed him from, that for theoretical reason existence must be given in a presentation. Obviously, the soul cannot be presented as an object to itself. Kant's argument (the supposed paralogism) consists merely in pointing out the fact that the soul cannot be found as what the soul is not. If the soul is real it must actually function in the determination of the facts of experience; if belief in its reality is to be justified it can only be because its activity supplies principles which are needed to explain those facts.

The drive of philosophy is the homing instinct, as Plato called it; the desire to be at home in the world of nature as science teaches us to interpret it, and in the world of the spirit as the saints and seers have taught us to interpret that; and through the knowledge thus attained to build a better and more homelike world. The aim is vision in the light of the whole. Could one attain that vision one would no doubt be able to " run up and down the dialectical ladder," needing no outside support, for the whole would be self-supporting. But this remains an ideal of reason. Science itself, however, similarly aims at wholeness of vision, but within the field definitely marked off from other fields by the presuppositions and the point of view of the particular science in question. The method of philosophy is, like that of science, both empirical and rational. It must, of course, begin with experience, with accurate observation and description; but its aim is explanation, and this means finding the principle or the law which links all facts together and reveals the pattern of the whole.

Let me give an illustration. Plato was in the habit of giving his pupils problems, and one in particular that greatly exercised the Academy was that of the motion of the planets. They seemed to wander to and fro in a most irrational man-

ner. But the world must be orderly and intelligible. That is
the primal demand of reason. And so the problem was, to
"save the appearances." This the Platonists did by means
of cycle, epicycle and eccentric, and presumably drew a
fairly accurate pattern of planetary motion. But it was
still merely a description. The explanation came with the
discovery of the law of gravitation. Here was a principle
that tied all bodies in the universe together and enabled
one not only to describe the movements of the planets but
to show why they must be as they are; enabled one to move
forward to fresh discoveries (Uranus and Neptune), and
really "save the appearances."

Similarly, in the early part of the nineteenth century
science was almost wholly descriptive, card-indexing the
facts in chemistry, botany, geology, biology. But the principle of the conservation of energy, of elimination by natural
selection, and perhaps we should add the theory of cellular
tissue, changed all this. These principles enabled the scientist to box the compass of reality within the limits of his
subject matter and swing full circle. Description became a
stepping-stone to explanation, and the laboratory super-
seded the museum. The appearances were saved. One begins by wondering that things should be as they are, but in
the end, with the right thread in hand, one would wonder
should things be other than as they are.[1]

Philosophy differs from science simply in comprehensiveness. It takes all experience for its province. It must be
judged, as science is, by its success in discovering the principle or principles that link all the facts of experience in a rational and orderly whole.

There are three distinct steps in the development of philosophy as an interpretation of experience. As is well known,
the Greeks, in the age of mythology, and before the rise of
philosophy, while explaining experience by reference to the
Gods as powers behind the scenes, had been forced, in order
to explain *their* behavior, to set up a further principle,—
necessity, fate, or destiny,—which kept them within their

[1] Cf. Aristotle, *Metaph.*, Bk. I.

proper bounds. It was taking this idea of fate from the background of Olympus and placing it in the actual world of experienced objects that gave the concept of nature that started philosophy and science on their way. We should find the key, the bond of fate, if we could only discover what nature abidingly and steadfastly is. The changing could then be interpreted in terms of the changeless, and this seemed to be what reason demanded. Zeno, once for all, showed the insufficiency of this principle. His puzzles of motion are unanswerable, *if* you let him state his case, and for the simple reason that he is stating motion in terms of rest. The *solvitur ambulando* of Diogenes is the plain man's sufficient answer. There is something wrong with your premise if it forces you, in trying to explain experience, to explain it away.

The second step is to start with motion, with an ever-changing world, and see if we fare any better in finding the permanent in the changing; and as a matter of fact we do. The permanent is found in form rather than in matter, in the law and the logos. This is the view that still dominates science. In the practical reference, it dominated the thinking of the Stoics, of Augustine and of Calvin. But there are two things that give us pause in accepting this principle as adequate. It may be true that man's search for permanence in this way has created the world of physics. But this method of interpretation gives universals and identities, not the unique, the individual. Furthermore, the explanation is too simple to account for the facts. The world as ordered in accordance with this principle is shot through with disorder, and most clearly so where the deliberate actions of men are in evidence. Here are physical happenings that do not fit into this conception of rationality. They are more troublesome than Plato's errant planets. They present a "problem," and the problem is again, to "save the appearances." Finally, this method of explanation represents the story of the world as a tale that is told. One is still caught in the toils of fate, and the significant human values are lost. The plain man's sufficient answer is, like that of

Diogenes to Zeno, *Solvitur volendo, solvitur agendo, solvitur intelligendo.* There is something wrong with your premise if it forces you, in trying to explain these experiences, to explain them away.

And this brings us to the third step, which is the position of idealism. What we need is another dimension of reality, another type of order. Into a world bound by fate you cannot squeeze freedom, any more than you can translate motion into rest. But if we start with freedom we can perhaps account for fate. So the idealist starts with freedom, with spontaneity, creativity, that is, with soul or spirit. We come nearest to a description of reality when we regard it as a community of self-active creative spirits; [1] and the test of the validity of this view can only be, does it enable us to explain, better than otherwise appears possible, both the stubbornness and independence of the physical order as science describes it, and also the effectiveness of ideas and ideals in determining events in that order, while at the same time preserving the significance of human values. When one speaks of the soul as existent or real, one must mean that it is actually effective in determining facts in the common realm of experience. The universal form that this activity takes is the creation of wholes, in which the whole is always more than the mere sum of the parts.

If Driesch is right, this is a factor in all living organisms. It is as if the end were present as a determining factor throughout the process. (Aristotle's τὸ τί ἦν εἶναι.) And although the great majority of biologists, especially in America, refuse to follow him, their chief reason for not doing so seems to be that they cannot put meaning into the principle he invokes; that is, they cannot interpret this third stage of knowledge in terms of the second, which of course they cannot. But in any case the principle here, in plant and animal, is implicit, and confined to the individual organism. In

[1] I do not mean to imply by this statement that all idealists are pluralists. Socrates in one of the Dialogues is made to remark, in effect, "If I could find any one who could solve the problem of the one and the many I would follow in his footsteps as in those of a god." And this is still the central problem in idealism. Professor Royce devoted the better part of his time in his riper years to its solution, seeking in his conception of the "beloved community" to transcend the antithesis, monism versus pluralism.

man, the principle is, at times, more or less explicit and over-individual. But it still manifests itself in making who'es, piecing together the fragments of experience into a whole, a single realm of experience; or, in creative art and enlightened conduct, seeking to create wholes that do not yet exist.

In the first stage in the development of philosophy reality is viewed primarily as stuff, in the second as form, in the third, through emphasis of end or purpose, as spirit (soul or entelechy).

A word of caution in passing. The soul, as the term is used in this paper, is not an existent of the same order as physical existents, nor is it that curious metaphysical hybrid, a disembodied spirit, external to the body, and stepping into the body and out again as a man might step in and out of a boat. The relation is one of inclusion. The soul in its essence, or taken absolutely, is no where and no when, for all wheres and whens are by intention present in it. But the soul as just this unique individual soul, with definite knowledge and definite tasks, has its ποῦ στῶ in the physical order precisely in the body, and, through the body its specific time and place and history. Thus the soul is the life of the body, but it is more than that, for it is also transcendent of bodily limitations; and the body is the expression in the physical order of the nature of this soul, of this soul made flesh, but it is less than that, for at best it could only represent the soul to date, and that most inadequately. Now the body is, more or less, under the control of the nervous system. And nervous tissue has the peculiar property of being, under limitations, sensitive and directly and immediately responsive to the desire and volition of the knower, to the creativity that is the soul. This seems to be an ultimate fact of experience.

The continuity of the idealist tradition is manifest in that all idealisms deserving the name undertake to explain experience from the standpoint of what I have called the third stage of knowing. This does not mean abandoning the principles employed in the second stage, but, rather, a restriction of their use, and a re-interpretation of their meaning from the point of view of the third stage. The categories employed under the second stage in the interpretation of nature are inadequate for the interpretation of the realm of the spirit, for describing the relations of persons as persons. Nevertheless the physical world as thus interpreted is the manifestation of one aspect of the universal nature of spirit.

The continuity of the idealist tradition may be illustrated by comparing Plato and Kant, two thinkers who are often by superficial students of philosophy supposed to be so far apart that the word idealist is not fittingly applied to both. Both begin with the conception of the soul as self-active, creative. Socrates is only interested in fertile, creative minds. With the barren, the unthinking, he can do nothing but send them off to Prodicus or some other "inspired Sophist" to be pumped full of sham wisdom. Truth is not truth for you until you have created it for yourself. The most fundamental difference is the method of approach. Plato, like a true Greek, is object-minded. He looks out rather than in, but is led by inevitable steps to the interpretation of the real world as the world that reason makes. Kant, a true modern, begins with the subject, the knower, but, in order to interpret him is led by inevitable steps to interpret the known world in objective, realistic, fashion. The clearest statement of Plato's idealism is found in the sixth and seventh books of the *Republic*. There are four degrees of reality, and four corresponding stages of knowledge: shadows (guesswork), things of sense (opinion), mathematical or scientific truths (discursive reasoning), and ideas or philosophic vision (wisdom). The first pair taken together comprise "things that come and go," *i.e.*, transient realities; the second pair, things that abide, permanent realities. But it is clear from the interpretation given that there is no absolute separation of these groups. One and the same object may appear in all four divisions. It depends on the degree of knowledge attained. Knowing consists in fixing the object in an ever-enlarging setting. The thing, anything you please, is what it is experienced *and known as*. Things are unstable and unreal in proportion to our ignorance. All of us live part of the time in the shadow world, in a world of unrealities, giving the prize to the best guesser of the shadow that is coming next. Often we rise to the "thing" view, occasionally to scientific truth, rarely, if ever, to that completed insight which is our goal and guiding principle. That vision attained, we should see things as they truly are in the light of the "idea of the good," and find in it the source both of truth and of reality. The real world is the world that reason makes, starting from the confused facts of sense.

The activity of the soul Plato represents (again because he is object-minded) as desire, whose true object is the whole, the perfect, the complete. "The fiend that us harries is love of the best." In knowledge, it is desire for completed wisdom, vision in the light of the whole. But this same activity expresses itself in passion (eros). And there are gradations in the love bond corresponding to the stages in the development of knowledge, from the shadow world of brutish craving where there is no reverence for the object of desire up to the ideal, where alone true beauty is found, and "the better part of the soul is victorious" leading to "an ordered life and to philosophy." It is beauty that "fills the soul with warmth and relieves it of the rigidity that had kept its wings from growing." The quest of the soul is like the Faust quest for the experience to which he could say "*verweile doch du bist so shön*," but with this difference, that it is not enjoyment that the soul seeks, but creation, "possession and birth in beauty absolute."

Again in the will, the "spirited element," under the guidance of reason, the soul is seeking to create the perfect, the completely integrated life. This is the "royal art" of justice. All the activities of the soul are good when they function in coöperation for the welfare of the whole; any one is bad when it seeks its own interest at the expense of the rest. But since man cannot live alone the "royal art of justice" finds its fullest expression in the social order, in the ideal, and only real, state, where each is performing the task for which he is best fitted in the interest of the whole.

There is an element of mysticism in Plato's idealism. One lives always ahead of the actual, molding the actual in conformity with the ideal, and there is a sense in which one is even now at the goal that one is seeking.

When we turn to Kant certain striking contrasts are indeed evident. The mysticism is lacking, though there are not wanting hints that point in that direction, especially in the *Critique of Judgment*. And the exuberance of Plato's imagination in describing the gradations of the love bond would make the austere and thrifty old Königsberg bachelor blush to the roots of his old gray wig. This was something he never could understand—and probably a case for the censor. But when we turn to their ethical interpretations these two men have more in common than is generally supposed. To be sure, the puritan in Kant led him to make central the concept of duty, a word not found in Plato's vocabulary, and to regard the pure will, and not desire, as the true measure of moral value. It is, however, just this that makes Kant's moral law so formal that it is all but impossible to translate it into precepts applicable in the determination of concrete moral issues. But Plato distinguishes sharply between what one may think one desires, and what one really desires. The real desire is for the complete good, and this is just a more concrete interpretation of the Kantian good will. Moreover Kant himself finds that in the conception of the complete good virtue and happiness are conjoined. And the Platonic conception of the ideal (and real) state from which selfishness, the desire for self-aggrandizement at the expense of others, has been completely eliminated, is in effect just a more concrete picture of the Kantian Kingdom of Ends.

But it is in the theoretical region that the fundamental agreement is most striking. Even the fourfold division of the line representing stages of knowledge and degrees of reality finds a parallel in the Critique. There is first the "raw manifold of sense perception," corresponding to the shadow world, where thought is at a minimum; then the world of things dated and placed, and named; then the same world as interpreted by the principles of science, and finally the same world unified through the ideals of reason.

But Kant's point of approach is from the subject, the knower, as active, creative, and the form of his problem is how can man with just his human categories and human fashions of thinking determine the nature of real objects; and what must we mean by objects that can be so determined. This brings us at once to the problem of the categories. Plato had, indeed, in one of the later dialogues recognized this problem, but apparently he did not make much of it. Aristotle gives us a table of ten categories, the so-called predicaments, which is an attempt to discover the points of view implicit in significant predication, in the definite determination of an object. It may be described as the first attempt to discover the logic underlying grammar. Kant attempts to discover the points of view implicit, not in the determination of an object considered by itself, but in the determination of an object in its relation to all other objects of possible experience. In other words, it is an attempt to discover the logic underlying science.

Now if the mind is active, creative, in knowing, it follows of necessity that its activity must have its own dependable structure, must function in definite ways, else would all be confusion,—no mind at one with itself, and no coherent or objective world. The categories are just the structure of self-active reason, but, being such, they are also structural in the world that reason knows, for it is reason's world. Growth in the unity of self-consciousness runs *pari passu* with growth in knowledge of an objective world. Should one doubt one's sanity the last thing to do would be to look within. One must look out, link fact to fact in the world of experience and in discovering its unity recover one's own. The transcendental ego is not another ego, but my own. The world of nature is both dependent and independent; dependent on the universal knower, but independent of just this finite and most imperfect knower; except insofar as through his particular center of activity in the space-time order, that is, his body, he can effect changes in its history.

The soul discovers further what its nature is in the unified world of science that it constructs from the fragments of experience; as also in creative art, and in righteous living, in living the integrated life, individual and social.

The physical world is, and can be, understood only in terms of experience and possible experience. This does not mean that it is made up of the sum of our several experiences. It is infinitely more than that. It contains innumerable facts that no one has experienced or ever will. There is a single realm of experience, and our individual experiences have their being therein. My experience fixed in its place in the space-time and in the causal order is no more mine than thine, though it may mean many things to me that it does not to you because of the different private context into which it is received, for, for each of us life is, after all, a fresh adventure.

When I perceive an object, yonder table, for example, I do not perceive some shadowy copy, in my mind or in my brain, of an existent object. It is the existent object itself in the common world that I am directly and immediately conscious of, for the knower is on the object as well as the subject side of the subject-object relation, as Kant clearly saw. Subject and object, inner and outer, are strictly correlative. Now, if it is fatal to regard these as separate and then to draw the object into the subject, it is equally fatal, having once separated them, to draw the subject into the object. If the former gives solipsism, the latter may be said to give solistism, or what Professor Lovejoy has called "solipsism of the object." Thus a realistic interpretation of nature is not only consistent with, but demanded by idealism.

But because the knower always views the world from his particular station therein, his body, there is a foreground of more or less distinct experiences, and a background that fades away into the distance. Yet the background is one and continuous with the foreground, and every whit as real, and I can penetrate that hidden background and discover what it contains just insofar as I find indications in the foreground, in facts that I can only weave into the contexture of unified experience by inferring the reality of such un-experienced things.

I have illustrated the continuity of the idealist tradition by comparing Plato and Kant, but might equally well have taken almost any of the other great idealists, such as Leibniz, Ward and Howison, Hegel and Royce, Green and Bosanquet. It would be more difficult, I confess, to fit Bradley into this picture, and yet perhaps not wholly impossible.

In what has been said above there has been no intention to disparage logic and technique, or to minimize the importance of the differences that separate idealists, or to make light of the issues that are still in dispute. But it is well, once in a while, to overlook these things and to attempt to describe the common bond that brings idealists together in a single fold. If we fought less we might understand more, and more hopefully coöperate in constructive effort.

IV

THE ONTOLOGICAL ARGUMENT IN ROYCE AND OTHERS

WILLIAM ERNEST HOCKING

Harvard University

THE ONTOLOGICAL ARGUMENT IN ROYCE AND OTHERS

William Ernest Hocking

I

In his last course of lectures on metaphysics, that of the year 1915–16, Josiah Royce brings forward the ontological argument as containing in some form the central doctrine of idealism. In his lecture of February 29, 1916, he said:

> Sooner or later, if you are going to take any position about metaphysical questions, you find it necessary to face this matter. There is no more important issue between realism and idealism than this. I don't think you get a fair view of idealism if you think of its issue with realism merely in terms of Professor Perry's egocentric predicament. It is not the most important feature of idealism that it appears to be committed to an insistence . . . that the being of things, whether of God or man or the physical world, is a being in the mind of some thinker. . . . The really most important feature is exactly the issue here concerned: does the existence of anything make any difference to its existence? is it any part of the essence of a thing that it exists? [1]

During the course of these lectures, he repeatedly recurs to this theme,—the misconception of idealism involved in Professor Perry's exposition with its emphasis on the egocentric predicament; the fact that idealistic metaphysics, like all metaphysics, is concerned with the nature of the objective world, the world of reality; that any approach to reality, however completely it moves in the realm of objects, however "realistic" if you like,—if it is capable of reaching the truth at all, will bring the thinker to the result that the world of the reals is a world of spirit. Royce himself stood for no one way of reaching his result: indeed, this last course of

[1] By remarkable good fortune two students in this course (Philosophy 9) during this year took fairly full stenographic notes. Transcriptions from these notes are deposited in the libraries of Harvard and of the University of California at Los Angeles.

lectures was divided into two parts, which were entitled "The social approach" and "The logical approach," in neither of which is there any trace of that subjectivity suggested by the phrase, "The world is my representation." To emphasize this fact, he makes his "logical approach" by way of Santayana.

Santayana's thought is resolutely objective with that well-limned outline which comes from a carefully personal choice of lighting. His discriminations readily appear as persuasively final partitions among the reals; it appears both ungracious and impious for man to unite what Mr. Santayana has put asunder. It is this adventitious clarity of Santayana which makes him an excellent text from which to initiate any discussion of the radical relations of essence and existence. Royce lights for this purpose upon one of his charming *obiter dicta*, put out in the course of a paper on "Some Meanings of the Word 'Is.'" [1] The verb "to be" as copula, says Santayana, has two meanings which belong purely to the realm of essence, viz., *identity* and *property*. "A is A," "business is business," "This is Odysseus" exemplify the first use: "Wine is red" the second. This same word is used, however, to express something quite different, namely, *existence*. Here Santayana takes pains to exhibit the complete disparity between this and the prior meanings which language perversely conveys by this same most-used word.

> Existence adds no new character to the essence it hypostatizes, since the essence of any existing thing is its full character; but the hypostasis is temporal and caught in a mesh of natural relations to which the essence is impervious. . . . Existence exhibits things in a situation and with an emphasis (shock?) which their mere essence could never have had. Things generate one another, and their flux, by catching the dye now of one essence and now of another, becomes varied and describable. Something *is*, in the sense of *exists*, when it figures in this changeful and selective illustration of essences. . . . (Existence has to be determined by exploration; it) can never be determined by analyzing the essence of what is said to exist.

Nothing could be clearer; Kant's "existence (Sein) is evidently no real predicate" [2] becomes "existence adds no new

character, since the essence of anything is its full character";
and with this admirably adroit phrasing of the case, the
ontological argument appears, as Santayana later terms it,
"an obvious fallacy."

In expounding this passage, Royce merely raises the question whether a distinction so evident can remain an absolute
gulf, without "mediation"; perhaps, he suggests, "to understand the distinction between essence and existence means
to find a certain inadequacy in it." For how could we
understand that essence is not existence without knowing
what we mean by existence? And to find a meaning for
existence, is this not to find its essence? I interpose these
questions, which do not appear in the report of Royce's
lecture; for they seem to convey the situation which Royce
then designates by the remark, "Here Santayana relieves
one of mere polemic." For his success in making the distinction between existence and essence an *understood* distinction,
is the substance of his failure. Essence, which was to remain
on one side of the gulf, appears on both sides!

With this suggestion of Royce's I take leave for the moment of his argument. It is characteristic of contemporary
realistic thinkers to adopt in some form or other Santayana's
distinction between the realm of essence and the realm of
existence. The former is an infinite world of eternal and
changeless subsistence, in which each essence is not only
eternally self-identical but also eternally distinct from every
other essence. The latter is a world of flux and causal connection, a world of variety but of mutual invadedness, a
world of passing spatial-temporal events. There is however
this unsymmetry in the relation; the essences are not per-
turbed by the existences, they are "impervious" to these
natural relations; but the existences are visited by the
essences, as mortals who cannot pass into heaven are nevertheless visited by the angels,—they "catch the dye" now of
one essence, now of another. Perhaps it would be more accurate to say—not "they" but the web of becoming catches
the varying dyes, and by this impregnation the existences
are constituted. For after all, when a "thing" exists, *it* is a

group of essences that has become momentarily—I will not
say entangled in the flux,—but exemplified there. Realism
still labors with the problem of Plato, what is meant by
this exemplification, this "participation," this dye-catching
process? No one suggests that the process is accidental, or
managed by some *deus ex machina:* it is assumed to be a
regular character of the cosmos. And this, without further
ado, would imply that essences and existences, so far from
being disparate types of entity, have a natural adjustment
and mutual reference.

II

Now the ontological argument, in its traditional forms,
undertakes to define a bridge between essence and existence;
but only in a special case, that of the essence of God. The
idea of God, it avers, is peculiar in this, that its essence contains the essence of existence, that essence which neo-realism
would feign non-extant, while giving it careful definition.
Because of this peculiarity, it cannot be the idea of a non-
existing thing. To suppose it so, to suppose it to have mere
esse in intellectu, as may well be the case with every concept
of imagination, would be to admit the contradiction, "My
idea of the real may possibly be my idea of a non-real." It
becomes a case of the identity of essences, and of my ability
to know what my own essences mean.

Two things are evident at once. First, that this argument
does not cover the whole scope of the traffic between essence
and existence, as we have just described it. Either the property of becoming existent, when the appropriate signal is
given from the heart of the flux, is common to all the possible
essences, or else there is a general principle of ingerence,
which manages the emergence in the flux of now this and
now that essence. It is possible to extend the conception of
God, so that God includes this general principle of ingerence.
It may be possible, with Professor Whitehead, to identify
God with the principle of ingerence alone (ingression, realization, concretion). But this aspect of God's nature was not
explicit in the minds of St. Anselm and his followers. In

their theological language they might have commented that this function of passage from the ideal to the actual realm was allocated to the Second Person of the Trinity; and perhaps that a special form of the argument might be stated for that Person. Since if one's idea of the "Word becoming flesh" were supposed to be a "mere idea," it would not refer to that which it does in fact mean, the general agency or principle by which eternally perfect essences are perpetually being born into the world of becoming and perishing, but without surrendering their immortal nature. In any case, they were not attempting in their ontological argument to deal with the whole problem of the relation between essence and existence.

In the second place, it is evident that the present statement of the argument does not correspond precisely with any traditional form. Anselm does not say of God's essence that it includes the essence of existence: he says simply that it is the idea of "the greatest," "aliquid, quo nihil majus cogitari possit"; and he argues that by logical necessity, this "greatest" must include objective as well as subjective being. In his reply to Gaunilo he changes his ground: God is defined not as "the greatest," but as "the necessary" being. And if we mean by necessary being, an essence such that it cannot help existing, the definition begs the question: it is requisite that the essence be alleged in other terms if the argument is to avoid circularity. If there is any necessary being, that being surely exists. But is there?

Here the formulation of Spinoza and one of the formulations of Descartes mark a distinct advance in cogency by making an advance in metaphysical perception. It is no longer the "greatest" that must exist, it is the "perfect." And with the radical premise that it is necessary to assign a reason for non-existence as well as for existence, Spinoza isssues the bold doctrine that nothing can prevent a good thing from coming into existence except a better thing:— it is the inherent nature of the valuable to realize itself. With this premise, the perfect would necessarily be without

effective opposition in the supermundane struggle for existence: if the good and only the good tends to be, the perfect
necessarily is.

It would be inviting to inquire at this point whether the
concept of "the perfect," or of "the most perfect," is a true
essence, or only a pseudo-essence. I shall adopt however a
more technical line of comment, namely, that this advance
in cogency is gained by leaving the strict ground of the ontological argument. It is not from the very essence of the
perfect that its being is seen: it is from the additional metaphysical thesis—restated in recent years by Mr. L. T. Hob-
house,—that the only reason that can be alleged for existence is value.

The criticisms of Hume and of Kant were necessary, not
to demolish the argument, but to prepare the way for a
valid statement.

III

Hume is not interested in the ontological argument. It is
not for the sake of disposing of it that he reiterates his doctrine that all questions of existence are questions of fact. He
would approve Mr. Santayana's view; the proper method of
verifying existence is exploration. There can be no necessary
existence; for anything whatever can be supposed, without
contradiction, not to exist. If this is true, the ontological
argument is swept away; for whatever its form, it proposes,
at one point at least, to abandon empirical humility in regard to existence: "*This* essence, we know *a priori*, is to be
found in the realm of the real."

Now Hume himself supplies a mode of reasoning from idea
to existence. For since all ideas, in his system, come either
from impressions or from derivations thereof, every underivable idea evidences an impression, ergo an experience of its
object. A hippogriff is an ingeniously derived idea; no experience is implied: the idea of color, supposing it to be underivable from other sense-impressions, evidences the experience and therefore the existence of color. It is precisely
because he rejects the possibility of innate ideas that he is

compelled to trace the essence *in intellectu* to the essence *in existentia* or *in re*. There is for Hume no ingression of essences into existence; there is an egression from existence to essence, from impression to idea: in the moment of impression, essence and existence are in contact; and because of this origin, no essence is ever wholly mine,—it bears upon it a trait of reference to its source in experience, sometimes in the distinct form of memory. Thus every primary and underivable essence may be said to be twofold; itself plus an accent—in turn an essence—denoting "My original is or was in existence." To put it otherwise, the essence, as merely *in intellectu*, is known as an abstraction: one is *always* safe in arguing from a primary essence to an existence *via* an experience! Thus in place of a single *a priori* argument from essence to existence, Hume presents us in effect with an undetermined plurality of such arguments *a posteriori*.

In contrast with Hume, Kant has a lively interest in the ontological argument. He begins by accepting it (Nova Dilucidatio, II, vii); he continues by distinguishing two forms, of which he accepts one and rejects one (Einzig mögliche Beweisgrund, III); he ends by rejecting one cartesian form, without reference to the form he has earlier judged valid, and leaves this sole negative impression on the minds of posterity. And this famous refutation, which to those who are satisfied with the hundred-dollar illustration is conclusive, is based upon the erroneous ground that existence is in no case a predicate.

But like Hume, Kant replaces the ontological argument by a series of inferences from essence to existence, though of a far more intimate and inescapable sort than Hume's.

The proper evidence for the existence of a particular thing Kant would say, quite in agreement with Hume, is discovery, *Wahrnehmung*, together with inferences from what we observe, along the lines of the known laws of nature. But the evidence for the existence of things-in-general is of another sort. The shock of givenness belongs to the crude stuff of experience; but if one asks *what* is experienced, one has to answer in terms of essences some of which experience cannot furnish, nor yet evade. The existent is not an "object" until it is formed according to the categories; and the categories are so many essences, conditions of the possibility of any experience at all, and yet integral constituents of existing things, and of the order of nature in which things are found.

To generalize somewhat the Kantian doctrine, experience cannot present itself, the realm of existence cannot tell its own tale, without our coöperation. It comes as a dumb stuff which requires to be interpreted; we must help it up into meaning by supplying it with a language. It cannot resist the categories we supply, for it has no others; it cannot belie them, for in order to reject or deny, it must first become vocal. On the other hand, we cannot change "the facts"; our help, rendered to the voiceless, cannot exceed the minimum requisite to lend it the power of assertion. The categories are the elements of this minimal language. Whatever these categories may turn out to be, whether the Kantian list or some other, we may say of these essences that they "exist,"—that is, they characterize existence, if there is any existence at all. They cannot be *in intellectu* without being also *in re*.

Thus, on Kantian grounds, one would be prepared to erect an ontological argument for the existence of space, of time, of the various categories of quantity and quality, of substance, of causality, of the reciprocal interplay of events in nature. And it lay within the scheme of Kant's philosophy, though he failed to explore the psychological and social categories, to inquire whether there were here also interpretative essences as of selfhood or of deity, which the stuff of experience demanded in order that it should become a significant realm of existence.

Much of Santayana's language is Kantian; but Kant could never wittingly have subscribed to Santayana's easy and complete severance between essence and existence, for the whole labor of the deduction of the categories is but a majestic attempt to unravel the essence of existence.

IV

We are now prepared to return to Royce's argument with a better appreciation of its setting. It is concerned, not primarily with the proof of the existence of God, but with the general argument from essence to existence. For "it is an essential feature of idealism (a difficult thesis, and not the one most commonly made explicit) that there is a connection between essence and reality, such as Santayana doesn't recognize."

Royce appreciates to the full the plausibility of the ordinary refutation of Anselm, and characteristically supplies certain apt illustrations of his own.

> Whoever fills out a check writes out the essence of the thing so far as he can express it. The problem of the contrast between essence and existence is closely analogous to the problem about the relation between the check and the account. . . . If it were possible to define the *greatest possible amount* that one could write out on a check, that would hardly guarantee that the check would be honored. . . . The ontological argument appears to have this fundamental absurdity about it, and has been repeatedly thrown out as utterly insignificant, yet it has a fashion of returning.

He adds an incident which had remained in his memory as further illustrating the absurdity in question. A Maine farmer, having been induced to exchange his greenbacks for counterfeit gold, remarked pathetically "I thought gold was so precious that it couldn't be counterfeited": wherever you had the essence you must, in so precious a metal, have the existence also! But

> Over against these obvious objections, we are using something like the ontological proof all the time. Aren't you using at the moment something like an ontological argument for supposing *that there is a real world*, and answering the question why there isn't rather nothing at all? You reply that something has to exist . . . you know there is a world *from the nature of the case*, from the very definition of the world.

Likewise with the time categories, the past, the future,— why not regard them as "all some sort of dream"? Any particular memory may be in error, any particular historical proposition false, any particular expectation misleading.

Even the results of scientific induction, as they apply to the future, are merely probable. Nevertheless, past and future must have some reality: we cannot be mistaken in thinking there was a past and will be a future, though we have at hand only their essences. "If the question arises, 'Why anything at all in the place where tomorrow will be if it comes? why not suppose that there is nothing whatever there?' your answer is that somehow the nature of the case seems to forbid this. It is of the essence of the past that it was; it is of the essence of the future that it will be."

The same is to be said of those general principles of the structure of existence which lie at the basis of induction. There is a "coherence of past and present which we verify neither in the past nor in the present, but only by interpreting our relations to a past and a present." Prior to discovering the particular laws of nature we believe in the lawfulness of nature: the conception of a law, its essence as a universal, removes it from the possibility of direct observation; one cannot by the method of "exploration" determine whether a law, or law, exists in the world. It lies in the nature of a universal that it cannot be discovered by inspection, by Wahrnehmung; nevertheless the realm of existence cannot be defined without reference to law. It belongs to the essence of law to form an element in existence.

Santayana's method of learning of existence is "only by exploration, through experience or evidence, or the flux of nature." By "evidence" we extend our knowledge beyond the limit of immediate perception: this is Kant's method of tracing outward from present Wahrnehmungen along the lines of natural sequence.[1] Royce illustrates:

> You go out doors in the morning and see in the snow the foot-tracks of a human being, a cat, dog or whatever it is, and thereupon you make an existential judgment: A cat or dog or man has been finding its or his way through the snow. . . . Owing to the laws of nature or to something known about the world, it is the essence of foot-tracks to imply, not the existence of foot-tracks, but the existence of some animal adequate to make them.[2]

[1] K d r V, *Postulate des empirischen Denkens ueberhaupt*, 2 Aufl., 273.
[2] Lecture of March 7, 1916.

It is not the particular meaning of the footprints, but the underlying basis of all such inferences, namely, this *relational form* which we assume; and to say that we assume rather than perceive it is to give it a primary status as essence, but as an essence which we so spontaneously refer to existence that we fail to observe that we are doing so.

My whole point is this: Whenever one existent is supposed to give you ground for inferring another existent, then the ontological proof is used, in so far as this relational system, of which the evidence and that of which it is the evidence form parts, is a system such that the world cannot but contain it.[1]

Royce designates this a "relational form of the ontological proof."

In this connection Royce makes effective use of his doctrine that individuals are not objects of direct perception. One is certain, let us say, that his brother is a part of the world of existence; his evidence is that he has seen him this morning. In presence of the skeptical questions regarding the possibility of absolute identification, one is driven to one's conviction of the uniqueness of the personal quality of the brother.

If common sense is asked, But what evidence have you that this is your brother and not merely somebody who looks like him? you would have to answer, The evidence I have certainly goes beyond experience: this is very like my brother, and there *can't be anybody else* who looks so like my brother. . . .

Whoever says that, concludes . . . that there is some essence or nature such that the world cannot give it any embodiment unless an individual embodiment, and that the world does give it this individual embodiment.[2]

In brief, there is here, and in all personal relations a union, of observation with belief—a continuous use, in interpreting experience, of a conception of personality which is not derived from existent facts, but contributed to them. "Whoever appeals to *evidence* for existence is using some form of the ontological proof."

There are dogmas about existence which can have no

support at all unless by an ontological argument, as that the world of existents consists of individual entities. The realistic tendency to place the realm of essence apart from the realm of existence often goes with a tendency to take it as "inevitably necessary" that all existents shall be individuals. What is the basis of the view of the nominalist, who rejects the existence of universals "as a matter of common sense"? It is certainly not an exhaustive enumeration of particulars! He has not encountered "courage" nor "leoninity" nor "the community" in the flesh: but it is not on account of this merely negative aspect of experience that he issues his denial. It is on account of a preliminary assurance of what the world must be like, an essence which must be existent. Hence

> Nominalism is a doctrine depending on its own form of the ontological proof. The only ground which you can give for the assertion that this world consists of individual beings depends on saying it couldn't be otherwise; it is of the essence of existence that the existents should be individual. The world of the Platonic ideas may have its own shadow of reality, but the world of existents must consist of individuals . . . because it is of the essence of an existent to be individual.[1]

Without attributing this sort of nominalism to Santayana, Royce finds that

> Santayana gives you his own carefully shaded version of the ontological proof: "It is idle to say that a thing exists or does not exist if we do not say when or where." That is, you couldn't mean anything unless you were ready to add the time and place. This is to say something about the whatness of the that:—nothing can exist unless its space and time have this determinate character . . . because it is the *nature* of existence to reject existents not determinate by time and space.[2]

Royce has thus given good account of his view that "the ontological proof underlies all your notions of all reality," even to the extent that its severest critics unwittingly employ it. It is the central problem of metaphysics whether reality is such that we can understand it. Those who make a clean break between essence and existence impose a final negative at the outset. Anselm's route is indeed not tenable:

[1] Lecture of March 9, 1916.   [2] *Ibid.*

You cannot get the ontological proof to apply to the divine being in Anselm's way, nor to the counterfeit gold; but unless there is somewhere an ontological proof which holds, then indeed we have no logical proof for any existence, and there need be no real world at all.[1]

Royce regards this result as confirming an idealistic view of the world:

Giving the realistic doctrine of Santayana its fullest scope, it forced upon us a problem as to what instances of reality are determined by the nature of the essences. . . . It was not by retiring from Santayana's clear and cool and objective view of the world into some mystery of romantic consideration of our own inner states of mind that we were led to idealism. It was by endeavoring to find out what evidence there could be for asserting the existence of anything. If there is any such evidence, there is a what such that in a certain context it demands . . . existence.[2]

The direct bearing of this discussion on idealism remains, in these lectures, suggested rather than fully stated; but the purport is clear. The world of existence is a world whose character is ascertained by a process of "interpretation," whose whole concern is with essences: that which distinguishes existence from essence, the actual from the merely ideal, turns out to be itself ideal. The object is shown to be—not subjective, God forbid—but shot through with categorial essences: to those which Kant mentions, Royce adds certain categories from the personal and social order. To be real is to fulfill certain rational purposes.

There are important differences between the positions of Royce and of Kant on this point. For Kant it is only a part of the objectivity of the object that is constituted by the categories: there remains the brute givenness of the material of experience.[3] Royce implies that the entire fabric of the object is derived from the world of the essences. He does not use the word "category" in this connection; nor does he use the freer terms "hypothesis," "postulate." The word "interpretation," which he prefers, suggests a tenta-

[1] Lecture of March 7, 1916.
[2] Lecture of May 25, 1916.
[3] "Die Wahrnehmung aber, die den Stoff zum Begriff hergiebt, ist der einzige Character der Wirklichkeit." K d r V 2 Aufl., 272.

tive rather than a necessary essence; since it is in general true of an interpretation that it admits a re-interpretation. Nevertheless, it is clear that Royce aims to establish such a relation between certain essences and the existents that one may say, If there is any world at all, it must be of this sort,—an element of invariance in our interpretation of the world for which the term category would be appropriate. And he aims also to eliminate in the end that "if" which distinguishes his ontological arguments from the classical form; for he holds that there can be in the end no "if" about the existence of the world. The essence, world, is such that it must exist.

V

Let us briefly estimate the effect of Royce's discussion.

Royce has established his general thesis that there is a close connection between essence and existence. The central element of logical force in his discussion is the dialectical showing that whoever undertakes to make a rational distinction between essence and existence unites them, precisely in proportion to the vigor and definition of his thought. Existence, for such a thinker, must be thought, and thus taken up into essence.

Royce has also fairly disposed of the assumption that idealism is wrapped up in egocentricity. The ontological argument is the fit weapon for this work; for the ontological argument is precisely *the escape from egocentricity*. It is the demonstration of the essence or essences which cannot be in the mind without being also in the thing. If there is any answer to solipsism on the logical plane, its kernel will be found in what the ontological argument essays to state. It thus deserves the particular attention of the realistic school; for in their characteristic assurance that in knowledge we are dealing with a world "outside of the self," they are either relying dogmatically on natural intuition, or else on a bit of submerged logic which it is greatly to their interest to bring forward. The rifts in the realistic school indicate the pertinence of this comment.

Instead of an egocentric idealism, Royce presents a logocentric idealism. Nothing can escape the net of essence; nothing which can enter into experience or thought can evade the fate of being known as essence.

Royce has no intention of ignoring the value of the actual distinction between essence and existence: he distinguishes throughout between the "conceptual essences" which may be and commonly are *in intellectu* without being *in re* from those essences (which I have called categorial) which must also be *in re*.

Of these categorial essences, Royce does not undertake to demonstrate severally their necessary objectivity. His appeal here is to individual acknowledgment: we are, indeed, "using an ontological argument all the time." Time we regard as such that "in the nature of the case it must be true of existence." If we undertake to defend this habit of reference in any special case, we are reminded that the nominalist is presented as using the same form of objective attribution for his view that the world of existence must consist of individuals, and as using it erroneously. For the completion of the argument there would be required either a separate showing for each of the categories that its essence is such that it cannot not be, or else a deduction of the categories from a single essence which has this demonstrable objectivity. This logical completion lies beyond the scope of Royce's effort in these lectures.[1] He here confines himself to the general thesis, existence has an essence, and to its ample exemplification.

It is perhaps an incident of this fruitful generalization of the ontological argument that the logical keystone of the arch should have been assumed rather than rendered salient. Let us now consider for ourselves the relation between these general connections of essence and existence and the central motif of the ontological argument.

[1] His essay on "Principles of Logic" in *Encyclopedia of Philosophical Science* indicates that his thought would take the latter direction; perhaps appealing to the conception of "order" as the essence which most fundamentally must characterize existence.

VI

The field of eventual connection between essence and existence is twofold: the passing over of existence into essence and the passing over of essence into existence.

1. There is nothing in experience which cannot be taken up into essence. Insofar as existence appears in experience, this proposition holds for existence also.

We are obviously dealing here with the processes of retention and analysis which form the basis of Hume's system as a psychological picture. Its logical substratum is the postulate, whatever is experiencable is thinkable.

But psychology here gives an admonition to logic in requiring us to allow for a "residuum" which is not "thinkable" in the usual way of conceptual analysis. It is this kernel of unformed "stuff," the "given," which thinkers from Plato and Aristotle to Kant, and to Santayana, have attempted to preserve as diverse from the achieved categorial essences. This residuum continues to give off "characters" as the history of speculation proceeds, which suggests that it may ultimately be resolved into essences; but this resolution has not been effected. Spencer's discrimination of "vivid" from "faint" manifestations, Santayana's "emphasis" and "shock," and the like, attempt to give it a characterization in terms of energy. It has something to do with an external "activity" to which we are "passive" or "receptive." It has something to do with our ontological dependence, our *being-made* from moment to moment in what we call "experience." It has much to do with that imposition of a not-self upon the self, conveyed by the term "experience," which implies a cognitive reaching out of self into the not-self. It occasions, and enters into, the meaning of the essence "not-self," which is one of the fundamental essences.

2. There is nothing in essence, so far as it is apprehended by mind, which does not tend toward existence. It belongs to the essence of the world of apprehended essences to have a nisus toward existence. This aspect of the connection be-

tween essence and existence is prominent in Spinoza and in Hegel. Its anthropological aspect is *will:* its logical substratum is the postulate, Whatever is desirable is possible (I do not say realizable); the existence of desire is itself a highly general union of essence and existence.

Hegel is especially interested in what we might call this active version of the ontological relationship. He first attributes to the Notion (*Begriff*) a self-objectifying character. When we conceive Begriff as a merely subjective essence, we at the same time conceive something more complete, namely, the embodied Begriff: this is to appreciate, as it were, the tug of the Begriff toward existence. Hegel, following his habit of giving in his language a quasi-personal life to his logical characters, has it that "Begriff differentiates itself from Sein, and sublates the difference between them." Now if the self can be regarded as a focus of Begriffe, the will may be regarded as a resultant of their several tendencies to being: for according to Hegel, life is of the same stuff as Begriff, and the "soul" is not something which we merely have or make, it is our grasp of a universal process. Hence, "No man is at peace with his pure Selfhood; that self-being must give itself Existence; the activity of Begriff is not merely dialectic, it is also (in the field of anthropology) impulse." When we thus survey the processes of the world, we see that

> There is nothing of which everything is *so Beispiel* as the overcoming of this opposition between subjective and objective.[1]

When Kant said that we cannot claw out the Sein from the Begriff he was thinking, Hegel remarks, not of Begriffe at all, but of finite conceptions such as we deliberately set off from actuality.

Apart from Hegel's effortful and figurative language, it is clear that he has in mind an actual trait of the interplay between essence and existence. This interplay is circular. In perception we take outer objects up into essence. If we are interested in them, we improve our concepts until we

[1] Lectures on the Proofs of the Existence of God.

have the "real essence" of the thing. The test of having this conceptual mastery is that we can make or reproduce the object; we cannot be sure of the adequacy of our essence until we can thus realize it in existence.

Existence, then, is to be conceived, *inter alia*, as the *field for the realization of essence*. It is at least possible that "existence" has no other meaning: its distinctive character is entirely contained in the relation "realization of": our problem then centers in the nature of this relation.

VII

Thus these generalizations again lead us to look to the center of the traffic between existence and essence. For the scholastics, this center was the being of God: for Descartes and Malebranche it was the necessary objectivity of the God-idea that guaranteed the objectivity of the rest of our experience, which objectivity has suddenly fallen into suspicion. Descartes particularly needed an ontological argument of some kind as a rescue from the artificial subjectivism which his own meditations had imposed on the whole field of experience. In losing sight for the moment of the scholastic interest in the being of God, we have run the danger of missing the unity which that interest confers on the whole problem. And in his wholly justified concern for showing the relative unimportance of the egocentric predicament for the case of idealism, Royce, I am inclined to think, unduly subordinated the element of truth in the Cartesian insight which is essential to the point of the ontological argument.

Normally speaking, it is in our own experience that we "realize" our desires; *i.e.*, "realization" is something which happens to essences of ours within experience. If the question arises whether our experience is "real," we must counter with the question, What is our standard of reality? If you doubt whether experience provides that standard, are you assuming that the standard itself is a wholly *a prior* essence? Then are you yourself assuming an essence of such sort that it must be realized? These are the questions which lead us to the center of the ontological problem, and which are rendered inescapable by the tremendous force of the Cartesian subjective reflection.

In this respect Hegel is thoroughly justified when in his *Lectures on the History of Philosophy* he discusses the ontological argument in immediate connection with Descartes' "I think; I exist," itself an assertion of a union between essence and existence.

> Das "Ich denke" enthält unmittelbar mein Sein: dies, sagt Cartesius, ist das absolute Fundament aller Philosophie. Die Bestimmung des Seins ist in meinem Ich.—When I say "I," I am saying implicitly what I mean by Being.

For at least a part of what I mean by Being, he elsewhere asserts, is "immediacy." Then, he continues,

> Kant has objected that Being is not contained in Thinking, that it is different from Thinking. That is true. But still they are inseparable, constituting a single identity: their unity is not a prejudice to their difference (nor their difference to their unity). The idea of God is an idea of *an idea* (or subject) with which existence is bound up. The very notion of existence is that of a negative to self-consciousness: nevertheless, not "out of thought," but the thought of the "out of thought."

The problem and its solution are bound up with self-consciousness and the self-transcending habit of self-consciousness.

The inevitableness of this course of thought is confirmed in an interesting way when a competent thinker, out of a quite independent background, strays into this field of speculation. Mr. Eddington, to indicate the difference between theoretical and experimental physics, is obliged to inquire into the meaning of the terms "real," "existent," "actual." "Actuality," he says,

> is that distinctive property of the world A—the world around us which we study experimentally—which is not possessed by the other worlds which might have occurred consistently with all the laws of nature. . . . It does not appear in the scheme of the theoretical physicist. . . . The experimental physicist, for whom actuality is vitally important, has to turn elsewhere, and he turns to consciousness. He simply accepts as actual that which the mind recognizes as actual.[1]

[1] This phrasing is from Eddington's essay in *Science, Religion and Reality*, Joseph Needham, editor. Similar doctrine will be found in *The Nature of the Physical World*. Quoted by permission of The Macmillan Company, publishers.

According to Hegel and Eddington, then, the essence of existence cannot be completely described without bringing "immediacy" into the picture. Neither, I think, can it be completely described without bringing in something very opposite from immediacy. I can be only as actual as the things I am at any time dealing with; I get my reality in part from what is over against me. On the other hand, nothing can be more real than the self: that which is over against me gets its actuality from the fact that I am dealing with it. Reality implies an intercourse between self and not-self; it lies, as it were, on both sides of the line between them. When I speak of "realizing" my self or my ideas, I am lending the standard to the not-self: when I speak of "realizing" the purport of an event, I am taking the standard of reality into my own world of meanings. The meaning of reality involves this reciprocity: the other realizes itself in me, in my essences; I realize myself in the other, in its existences.

Let us recur to that "residuum" in the meaning of existence toward which, we said, we hold a truce of logical analysis, and at the same time find a sense of personal dependence as of something by which we are being made. This non-ego is no doubt something which I apprehend: I have a thought of the "out of thought"; it is something meant by me and placed among my categories. But it is mere dogma to say that this or any other category I may apply to it is *imposed by me*, Kantian fashion, on a non-vocal stuff. Let us adopt a radically opposite view, which, as I see it, experience requires. Let us say that reality *interprets itself;* that the categories, the fundamental essences, are given with the stuff, the nature or essence of reality being revealed with the fact of reality. There is no use grubbing for a dumb datum, as a sort of inarticulate minimum of experience, as if all the interpretation were a gift of the individual knower. Such "contributions to the given," as the fate of Kantianism shows, cannot escape the odor of subjectivism, even though they constitute for us the very meaning of existence. Experience is of universals and not merely of the here-and-now.

Which ones of the received essences are necessary we learn as we distinguish within our propositions those existential elements which experience can have no tendency to revise. But at least this is necessary, that selfhood is not limited to one side of the line between ego and non-ego in experience. As with "reality," the entertaining of essences, which *is* selfhood, is reciprocal.

Consider now that by the term God we shall mean, whatever else may come to belong to its essence, this reciprocal of self, inseparable from self and from self-consciousness, the external factor in a single reality which consists in the intercourse of both. By the essence of God I here mean not primarily "the infinite," "the perfect," nor merely "the real": the ontological argument does not consist in the tautology. The essence of "the real" is real. The ontological argument is the answer to the question, May the idea of God be merely subjective? That answer is, In forming the essence "merely subjective" you have at the same time formed the essence "not merely subjective" as in contrast thereto; and "God" as essence belongs to the "not merely subjective." Whatever artificiality there is in the argument hails entirely from the artificiality of the question. The natural situation may be stated thus: the essence of God must be real, because it is an essence inseparable from my continuous consciousness or experience of reality.[1]

There is a phrase in one of Descartes' discussions of this argument which reaches beyond any statement which he developed: it is that the notion of the infinite precedes that of the finite. The ontological argument has to do with this question of logical precedence. The whole precedes in our thought and in experience the two partial aspects of ego and non-ego; the necessary precedes the possible, the probable and the actual,—a strand of consideration dwelt on by Leibniz and the earlier Kant; the real, as self and other-self, precedes the distinction of essence and existence. For that

---

[1] It is a terminological error to regard the ontological argument as an argument that God "exists." God does not exist as an object placed in space and time,—in Santayana's third sense. Both God and self are factors of reality which span the distinction between existence and essence.

by which we distinguish essence and existence is more completely present and known than either. To be aware, as the common man is aware, of the lack of finality in the mode of being possessed by essence and by existence, is to possess in a negative form the heart of the metaphysical problem.

V

ON THE MEANING–SITUATION

G. WATTS CUNNINGHAM

Cornell University

ON THE MEANING–SITUATION

G. *Watts Cunningham*

The notion of meaning is frightfully ambiguous, and yet no term is more frequently used in discussion. It is indispensable, despite its ambiguity. Particularly is it important for philosophical discussion; not only must it be continuously employed in such discussion, but many issues in philosophical construction turn around it and in some of these at least it is basal. The purpose of the present essay is to enter upon some preliminary considerations with reference to its empirical setting.

This study is avowedly introductory. It aims to focus attention upon what I shall call the "meaning-situation" and to inquire concerning its main characteristics. All larger questions about the meaning of meaning and its implications will be rigidly excluded from consideration, though it is assumed that what is here said is logically fundamental to such larger issues. Whatever meaning may in the end mean and whatever in the end its implications may be, it is in any event first of all observable in meaning-situations, which deserve to be studied on their own account and without prejudice to these later questions; indeed, such a study is an indispensable prerequisite to such further inquiries.

The method to be followed is partly analytical and partly synoptical. The attempt is made, first, to analyze the meaning-situation into its more obvious components; and, second, to sharpen the analysis by refining and enlarging it. I call this second step "synoptical," because as we shall see it necesarily involves an appeal to the larger context within which the components of the situation severally stand. If such an appeal is admitted as a step of analysis (as

I think it generally is, in practice at least), then the method may be called analytical without qualification.

By the meaning-situation I understand any empirical situation of which one may significantly say, "This situation is meaningful." And the analysis here undertaken will proceed primarily with reference to the situation viewed from within. The question to be answered is, What are the characteristics of the meaning-situation thus viewed? This limitation of the inquiry is to be borne in mind throughout. It has the disadvantage of excluding from consideration many issues of importance of philosophical construction; but, on the other side, it has the advantage of bringing to the fore certain preliminary matters that need saying. And, in any event, it is made necessary by the limitations of space here available.

Nothing which will be disclosed by the analysis is, I think, in principle novel; but it all seems to me quite important, and so far as I am aware it has nowhere been brought together explicitly and with special emphasis. I cannot hope, however, to claim universal acceptance of it, though much of it has been presented in varying contexts by others. No effort will be made to trace agreements or differences with other thinkers, since the purpose of the analysis is primarily constructive and would hardly be forwarded by raising troublesome questions about the historical attribution of views. It presumably should go without saying that no dogmatism is intended by this procedure, or that the writer is not over-confident of the positions advanced.

I

Of the meaning-situation there are five *prima facie* distinguishable types. Whether these may be permitted to stand as distinct in the end, they are in the beginning apparently so and should be distinguished. They may be classified as follows: (1) the perceptual-situation, (2) the conventional-situation, (3) the conceptual-situation, (4) the affective-situation, and (5) the evaluative-situation. What these several types of the meaning-situation are, and what are the subtypes falling under them, the following analysis may serve roughly to indicate.

1. Any meaning-situation which focalizes around the "here-now," broadly understood as a "this-here" with meaning attached, is what I understand by a perceptual-meaning-situation or, more shortly, a perceptual-situation.[1] "This means" may be said to be the general formula for this type. And of this there are at least two subtypes. In the first place, there is the perceptual-situation exemplified in pointing and, when verbalized, describable in some such phrase as "I mean this" or "this is meant." Such a perceptual-situation we may conveniently call the *direct* perceptual-situation, since it is in some sense immediate and self-contained. In the second place, there is the type of perceptual-situation, verbalized in the phrase "this means that," where both the "this" and the "that" are natural things or events. Concrete examples of this type are: "the glow in the sky means fair weather," "the sound from the street means an automobile," and the like perceptual experiences. Clearly, this is essentially the same sort of situation as the preceding, only more complicated. It may therefore be distinguished as the *indirect* perceptual-situation. In it immediacy tends to become more comprehensive and the "here-now" aspect of the situation correspondingly expands both spatially and temporally.

2. The second general type of meaning-situation I have called the conventional-meaning-situation or, more briefly, the conventional-situation, because "conventions" are focal within it. And by conventions I understand products of human ingenuity which may on occasion bear meaning. In this type, the "this" in "this means" is a convention, not a natural thing or event taken as such; and herein lies the chief difference between this type and the one just described. And here, again, two subtypes are distinguishable, namely, the verbal and the symbolic. The verbal may be expressed

---

[1] There is no intention of asserting here that all perceptual situations are meaningful, but only that some are. These alone are to be understood as designated by the hyphenated "perceptual-situation." Perceptual-situations that lack meaning, if there be such, are not under consideration. Whether there are such is a question left open.

in the phrase "it means," where the meaning is of some statement whether oral or written or pictographic. In this case,
the meaning is the meaning of statements in this broad sense.
The symbolic finds its expression in traffic-lights, flags of
countries, ceremonial artefacts, and the like human con-
trivances that function as signs and symbols. Here the
meaning is the meaning of artificial things set with design.
Of course there is no difference in principle between the
two subtypes of the conventional-situation here distinguished; but there is a difference between them sufficiently
important to justify at least a preliminary differentiation of
them.

3. By the conceptual-meaning-situation, or the conceptual-situation, is to be understood any meaning-situation
exemplified in an ideational or inferential structure, such as a
scientific system. Such structures are, of course, numerous;
and so, consequently, are the situations of this type. But they
seem conveniently to fall into two main groups which I shall
call the categorial and the postulated respectively. The categorial are those meaning-situations centering around the
sundry conceptual systems of common sense and science—
tables, electrons, organisms, evolution, society, God—in
which the body of our so-called knowledge about existence
is presumably more or less precisely, and more or less truly,
formulated.   The postulated-conceptual-situation includes
within its scope all of those ideational structures which are
founded on more or less arbitrarily chosen initial assumptions—such structures as are exemplified in the systems of
pure mathematics, for example, or in any system of logic
avowedly built on definitions and postulates.   Between
these two types of the conceptual-situation there is a difference that apparently runs quite deep.   The postulated-
situations appear to be arbitrary in a sense in which the
categorial-situations are not, involving as they do a sort of
necessity which is not "factual" (as it is in the categorial-
situations) but which seems to spring from internal consistency alone and to be completely determinable by the
abstract law of contradiction.

4. By the affective-meaning-situation, or the affective-situation, I understand any meaning-situation in which impulsion to action or to gratification of desire plays an important rôle.[1] This situation is broadly identical with a plan of behavior in the larger sense which includes also satisfaction of interest. And here, once more, one may distinguish two subtypes: the purposive and the desiderative. The purposive is exemplified in overt conduct directed towards the attainment of an end. The end may be immediate or remote, simple or complex; but in any case it is something which is sought through purposive behavior, and which stands as in some sense the goal of the behavior. The desiderative-situation may be merely desiderative, as in the case of "A wants (or does not want) this" where "want" is equivalent to a desire or interest and the "this" stands, so to say, alone without a competitor. Or the desiderative-situation may involve election or choice, as in "A prefers (or does not prefer) this" where "this" is the object of desire standing in competition with other objects of desire.

5. Finally, by the evaluative-situation is to be understood any meaning-situation in which evaluation is involved. And by "evaluation" is intended the process of appraisal, both positive and negative. Here the more obvious subdivisions correspond with the traditional distinctions among truth, goodness, and beauty—the ancient trinity of values. The first type of evaluative-situation, then, we may call the logical; here the situation is that in which "X is true (or false)." The second we may name the ethical, in which "X is good (or evil)." And the third is the aesthetic, in which the meaning is that of "X is beautiful (or ugly)." To these should be added a fourth, however, which falls broadly under the heading of the economic and in which the general notion of utility is dominant. Here the meaning is that of "X is useful (or useless)," its worth being measured primarily in terms of more or less immediate wants. Analy-

---

[1] In terminology, I am following Spinoza here. But in taking over his term "affect," I am adapting it to my own use; with the term I do not intend to adopt the implications attaching to it in Spinoza's system, or to burden him with any responsibility in connection with my use of it.

sis of each of these subdivisions of the evaluative-situations might readily be carried to greater length, but for the purposes of the present survey this is hardly worth while—though it would appear to be an oversight of significance not to include the type above called the "economic" in the list with the traditional three. And it should also not be overlooked that empirically the "X" in any of the types may vary widely in nature.

We have then, in sum, the following types of the meaning-situation: the meaning of "this is meant," where the "this" may be fairly indicated by pointing (direct-perceptual); the meaning of "this means that," where the "this" is more immediate in the situation and the "that" more remote (indirect-perceptual); the meaning of "this means," where the "this" is a statement broadly interpreted so as to include pictographic representations (verbal-conventional); the meaning of "this means," where the "this" is some sort of perceptual artefact (symbolic-conventional); the meaning of "X means," where X is some more or less complex conceptual system ultimately connected inferentially with some perceptual occasion (categorial-conceptual); the meaning of "X means," where X is either itself a postulate or linked implicatively with a postulate (postulated-conceptual); the meaning of "A purposes," where overt behavior is directed towards the attainment of a consciously entertained end (purposive-affective); the meaning of "A wants" or "A prefers," where the want or the preference is definitely expressed (desiderative-affective); the meaning of "this is true (or false)," where the "this" is anything of which truth or falsity may be predicated (logical-evaluative); the meaning of "this is good (or evil)," the adjectives having a moral reference (ethical-evaluative); the meaning of "this is beautiful (or ugly)," the situation being interpreted broadly to include passive enjoyment, active and critical appreciation, or creative construction (aesthetic-evaluative); and, finally, the meaning of "this is useful (or not)," the notion of utility being broadly construed but without direct moral reference (economic-evaluative). These several types, taken in their appropriate groupings, constitute five major types of the meaning-situation. No brief is held for the names used to designate them, and doubtless the terms could be improved upon; but, terminology apart, the types appear to be important and to need delimitation.

It may be questioned whether this classification exhausts the denotation of the meaning-situation. And one may specifically suggest that there should at least be added what might be called the memory-situation—the situation, that is, where "this-now" means "that-then." I should have no fixed objection to making such an addition; but, on the other hand, I see no special reason for it. The memory-situation seems to be involved in principle in every meaning-situation. Its chief claim to separate classification would appear to lie in the fact that it uniquely stresses the temporal process and its part in experience; but all of the types of the meaning-situation mentioned above overflow the limits of the "now," if not in both directions, at least backwards. And, if this is true, not only is there no positive reason why the memory-situation should be separately classified, but there is positive reason why it should not be; separate classification of it might tend to lend support to the assumption that it is not basically involved in the other types, and this would be very unfortunate.

I do not myself at present see what additions to the list should be made to make it exhaustive, and I am assuming that it is at least roughly so. But whether it is so or not, it is sufficient for the purpose of the present discussion so long as it is admitted to traverse an important segment of the denotation of the meaning-situation. Only in the event it can be shown to be incomplete and to leave out of account types of the meaning-situation which are negative instances with reference to the conclusions of the present discussion, is its incompleteness logically significant in respect of those conclusions. Any limitation of them necessitated by the possibility that this can be shown is hereby acknowledged.

Two other questions about the classification remain. Do not the divisions in it, both major and minor divisions,

overlap in various directions? And is there any justfication
for including (4) and (5) in the denotation of the meaning-
situation, in fact, does not one beg some quite important
issues by so doing? These two questions undoubtedly raise
issues that are basal—so basal, indeed, that they cannot be
discussed here with any degree of adequacy.

The first question readily resolves itself into several problems. Are perceptual- and conceptual-situations separable
from each other, or are perceptual-situations also ideational
structures? Can postulates and categories in the end be
kept apart, or are postulates also categories and run somewhere ultimately to ground? Is postulated necessity in
principle different from categorial necessity and determinable by the law of contradiction alone? Such are some of the
more fundamental issues raised by the first question. The
second question raises specifically the issue concerning the
relation between "thought" and "will," or meaning and
value—an issue, once more, of profound significance.

Whatever may be the final solution of these problems, they
are inescapable for a theory of knowledge. Indeed, one would
hardly go wrong in saying that a theory of knowledge is just
a solution of them. I can here make no pretense of dealing
with them, since they lie beyond the scope of the present
inquiry—which is concerned with matters that are preliminary to them. One or two observations, however, must be
set down.

The classification of meaning-situations I have given does
seem to me to violate the formal rules of logical division,
since the several divisions appear to overlap in various directions. Precisely why this is so cannot be stated until the
results of our further analysis of the meaning-situation are
developed. Nor can one intelligently inquire into the significance of the fact until after these results are obtained.
Hence further discussion of the matter would at this point
be premature. I wish to observe, however, that this admission of the formal inadequacy of the classification does
not negate its importance, either with reference to the use
made of it in the later analysis or with reference to its in-

trinsic significance. For it will here be used merely as a preliminary basis for the later analytical study; and its intrinsic significance lies primarily in the fact that it forces into the clear precisely those issues that turn about the question of its own formal adequacy.

I am compelled to admit, further, that in classifying (4) and (5) among meaning-situations, I have in some sense prejudged the question whether they should be called meanings at all. This is partly a question about terminology, but I am not blind to the fact that the issue runs deeper—that in this instance, at any rate, terminology is of material significance. Whether I am right in the position implicitly taken is, once more, a question that lies on before. It should be noted, however, that the inclusion of (4) and (5) among meaning-situations involves nothing more than the assumption that they are types of the meaning-situation among other types. In this there is no implication that they are identical in every respect with the other types, of course, or that the other types are of a kind with them; in other words, there is no implication that values are simply meanings (in the cognitive sense), or that meanings (in the cognitive sense) are simply values. All of this is subject matter for later study; and this special issue is in no way prejudged by the classification itself. And I wish to urge, with respect to the use I am here making of the classification, that, even if the inclusion of (4) and (5) should in the end turn out to be unwarranted, its significance for the present purpose would be unimpaired. For the conclusion later to be advanced is not bottomed on the assumption that this inclusion is essential. This conclusion is to hold merely of the meaning-situation; and if (4) and (5) are not types of this sort of situation, then they are simply irrelevant. The only admission that this conclusion involves is that the classification includes at least genuine types of the meaning-situation, and does not exclude instances that are negative relative to the conclusion advanced.

Proceeding, then, with the analysis, I wish next to emphasize the complexity of the meaning-situation and to state in what respects it seems to me to be complex. And I shall first note the more obvious points.

II

The *prima facie* components of any meaning-situation are two. They are: (1) that which means, and (2) that which is meant. Each of these is, at first glance at any rate, distinguishable from the other; and they call for separate consideration.

1. "That which means," it is first to be noted, is itself complex. There is that which means, in the sense of entertaining meaning; and there is that which means, in the sense of bearing meaning. Where "this is meant," for example, there is that "for" which the meaning is and that "to" which the meaning somehow directly attaches. And these components seem to be present throughout the several types of the meaning-situation. Neither of them taken alone is, at least on first look, fully equivalent to "that which means" within the situation; only the two taken together seem adequately to meet the empirical demands. In further exposition I shall employ the term "mind" to refer to that "for" which the meaning is, and the term "content" to refer to that in which the meaning seems somehow directly to inhere. In the case of the direct perceptual-situation, "mind" is that in respect of which the "this" appears as meaningful and "content" is the "this" which so appears.[1]

[1] In making use of the term "mind," in this or in any context, one of course plays with fire. One thereby exposes oneself to a grave danger, which is inherent in the very term and against which I myself am most anxious to be on guard—the danger, namely, of begging the quite important question concerning the nature of the "agent" in the meaning-situation. But what other term, as adequate and yet less objectionable, is here available? Meinong's "act," or any term like it in respect of its reference to a specific event or happening at a given time, certainly will not do. As I have tried to show elsewhere (*Five Lectures on the Problem of Mind*, Appendix I), it inevitably leads, through the logic for example of Mr. Russell, into a blind alley from which there is no exit except backwards. Such an "act" or similar event cannot serve to function in the rôle of the element of "that which means" here under consideration; and I think much confusion has arisen from the attempt to make it do so. "Organism" is hardly acceptable, because it even more definitely tends to beg the question we are wanting to save from such a tragedy. "Psycho-physical organism" would come nearer to meeting the demands of the situation, since its very indefiniteness is in its favor. And I should have no objection to using this term, save for its cumbersomeness. I prefer to use the shorter term, largely because it is more convenient. I beg the reader, then, in what follows to understand that "mind" is used in the very loose sense in which it is generally equivalent to the psychophysical organism. And I should also beg him to remember that the question concerning what more specifically the term is to mean is a

Any analysis of the meaning-situation which fails to note this distinction within "that which means" is simply unfaithful to what apparently are the facts in the case. For in all types of the meaning-situation this duality indisputably appears to be present, as a survey of the several types will show. In the perceptual-situation, both direct and indirect, mind and content plainly appear to be distinguishable aspects of "that which means." The "this," in "this is meant" or "I mean this" where the experience is essentially that of pointing, discloses on analysis that in one aspect at least it is the bearer of the meaning in the situation, while the passive form of the verb in the first formulation of the situation, or the "I" in the second, implicates that with reference to which the meaning is a meaning and which is another distinguishable aspect of what means; and the two conjointly taken seem to be necessary empirically to equal "that which means," neither alone will suffice. Likewise, in the indirect perceptual-situation, where "this means that" and where "this" and "that" are both natural things, what means is not only the "this" but also something to which the "this" as the immediate bearer of meaning refers for support; apparently, "this" alone does not mean, but "this" in conjunction with some center of reference "for" which or "to" which the meaning "appears." Again, the conventional-situation seems to exemplify the same dual nature of "that which means." In the verbal type of this situation, the statement of course means but it is somebody's statement, and "that which means" is neither the statement nor the somebody taken by itself alone; while in the symbolic form, that which means is at once the thing set with design and the designer.[1] The conceptual-situation,

question the answer to which must be approached through some such analysis as we are here engaged upon. I will venture the suggestion that, as a result of such analysis, the term in all probability would have to be variously described in different types of meaning-situation.

The term "content" is perhaps colorless enough to be used without serious risk, though of course it too involves ambiguities that threaten. At the moment I can think of none better, and there seems no reason why it should lead into thoughtless assumptions.

[1] If an interpreter is introduced into the conventional-situation, "that which means" is even more complex; then there are two minds and a correspondently dual content. The same in principle holds of the other situations, of course, where two minds are trying to share meanings.

also, in each of its types exemplifies the same duality: in the categorial, there are the category itself and its context, both of which mean and only when taken in conjunction; in the postulated, there are the postulatum and the ground of it, again both together being apparently necessary to constitute "that which means." In the affective-situation, once more, there is something which immediately initiates the act or desire or choice, about which the act or desire or choice focusses as its immediate content, and there is also, apparently implicated in these, the agent or desirer or chooser; and, insofar as meaning may be said to be involved in the situation, each of these is indispensable to "that which means." And, finally, the same bipolar relationship is manifest in all types of the evaluative-situation. Where "this" is true or good or beautiful or useful, if such statements are empirically meaningful, "that which means" is both the "this" which is true or good or beautiful or useful and that "to" which or "for" which the "this" is thus true or good or beautiful or useful.

Thus, in all of these several types of the meaning-situation (and I am frankly assuming in all others, if there be others) "that which means" is a major component and is everywhere complex, involving both mind and content in inseparable union.

Before passing on I wish to recall to the reader's attention the limitation within which the present analysis is moving. This limitation must be borne in mind, or the conclusion here stated may be misinterpreted. For one may be disposed to ask whether the conclusion is supposed to imply that all meanings are riveted to "mind," and whether this implication is being lugged in as opening an easy road to idealism. But the limitation of the present analysis is that it has to do with meaning-situations—empirical situations, that is, which are meaningful. And all that has been said so far concerns only such situations. The conclusion, then, is that empirical meaning-situations, when viewed from within, involve a complex component ("that which means") which on analysis discloses itself to be composed of mind and content, both of which seem to be fundamental. Whether both of these are indispensable within the structure of "that which means" is a question yet to be considered. Whether, if so, meanings are riveted to mind and whether, granting this for empirical situations, we are committed to some form of idealism—these are questions that cannot in the present context be raised. It is clear, however, that the present analysis of the empirical situation is preliminary to a consideration of them. And we now proceed with the analysis.

2. The second *prima facie* major component of the meaning-situation, we have said, is "that which is meant." This component has traditionally been called the "object" within the meaning-situation, and I propose to adopt this term in further discussion. Like "mind," "object" is ambiguous; and in using it one runs a risk of being misunderstood and (which is worse) of misunderstanding oneself. But, once again, it is the commonly accepted term for the referent here in question, and there is no other clearly preferable. And, when properly guarded, it need not lead into blind assumptions. As used in the present analysis, it refers simply to that within the meaning-situation which is what is meant. And it is so used without prejudice to the question concerning the detailed nature of the "that"—which rather obviously varies with different types of situations.

In all types, however, the object in some sense is clearly present; there is always something which is meant. This is commonly acknowledged, the chief debate turning about the question of the relation between content and object. Before entering upon this question, however, it is important to observe that content and object are everywhere *prima facie* distinguishable within the meaning-situation.

In the direct perceptual-situation, the "this" which is meant is apparently not at one with the "this" which functions as the content within "that which means": the only alternative would be to hold that what is meant is the bare datum, and there is no evidence for holding this—on the contrary, the evidence seems to lie against it since what is immediately given in the situation is never quite identical with what is intended. In the indirect perceptual-situation, clearly "this" and "that" appear to be different; the glow in the sky is not fair weather, nor is the sound from the street an automobile. Again, in the conventional-situation, the object is always distinguishable from the content; the statement does not mean itself, and the symbol is not a symbol of itself. Categories, too, have meaning only within a context which somehow reaches beyond them and which in some important sense appears to remain constant despite the more or less radical variations in the categories themselves; while postulates and definitions fall within a system of some sort, which apparently is significantly different from them as the background with reference to which they are posited and in terms of which their full meaning is to be defined. Purposes and preferences, again, are selective, and the focus around which the selection converges is not the totality of the situation within which the selection is made; there is always a broader context which is not immediately involved in the purpose or preference, but which would appear to be basal to the meaning of the purpose or preference. And, finally, in the sundry types of the evaluative-situation the same distinction would seem to be apparent: the trueness or goodness or beauty or utility intended in the several cases outruns that which is true or good or beautiful or useful, and such predicates are apparently meaningful only with reference to this larger context.

Thus throughout the various types of the meaning-situation content and object apparently do not fall together into a precise identity. Everywhere the two seem to be significantly distinguishable. Such is the general conclusion to which we are driven by an analytical survey of empirical situations which are meaningful.

In general summary, then, we may say that a first analysis of the several types of the meaning-situation discloses: that the meaning-situation is primarily made up of something which means and something which is meant; that the first of these seems to be complex, and on analysis resolves into mind and content; that the second major component, the object, is everywhere present and everywhere *prima facie* distinguishable from the content. The meaning-situation is therefore apparently a relationship involving three distinguishable aspects; the words ("mind," "content," and "object") used to indicate these aspects are used without prejudice to any later issues that may arise concerning the nature of each.

III

The general direction of further analysis is pointed by the questions that spring directly from the results we have thus far obtained. Are the three aspects apparently embedded in the meaning-situation severally to stand in the end? If so, how is their interrelationship empirically to be described? With these questions we come to the parting of the ways, at which important differences among epistemological theories begin to emerge.

1. The first question, whether the three aspects may be permitted to stand, naturally divides itself into three separate questions under the headings of (a) mind, (b) content, and (c) object. What is to be said of the claims of each of these? A full consideration of any one set of claims involves the others, of course, but their interconnection may for the moment be neglected.

(a) The historical fortunes of "mind" have indeed been very hard. In its history it has been forced to assume sundry forms—the full-blooded "soul" of the earlier tradition, the "bundle of perceptions" or the "transcendental unity of apperception" or "subject" or "consciousness" or whatever other "echoes of the full-blooded soul" there are in the later periods, and the stirring of the guts or the movements of the mechanisms of breathing and vocalization with which some of our later enthusiasms have identified it. But with these historical details, fortunately, we are not here immediately concerned. And I wish to turn at once to the main issue: Let mind be what in detail it may be, must it in some sense be left standing as an integral element within the meaning-situation?

I confess that the answer to this question seems to me plain, and it is an affirmative one. If mind, in any and every sense, be utterly abstracted from the meaning-situation, what is left? Certainly not a meaning-situation: the meaning-situation is thereby irremediably disrupted. There seems to be no significance whatever in the statement that something specifically means, or is meaningful, unless there is a mind as some sort of center of reference "for" which it means. I at least can see no other possible reading of the meaning-situation, so long as one sticks to empirically verifiable considerations. Everywhere, as we have already seen, mind is present in the meaning-situation; to abstract it from the situation is quite arbitrary and indefensible.

Nor do I find that any philosopher has ever consistently maintained, or even intended to maintain, that mind can be wholly abstracted from the meaning-situation. Those who apparently do so, or who openly avow an intention to do so and suppose they have proved their case, are always thinking of mind in some peculiar sense which is distasteful to them, and in that peculiar interpretation of it they deny its existence both generally and specifically. But, as I read them, for mind in the sense denied they invariably substitute mind in some other sense. If mind as "soul" no longer appeals, they in this sense negate it and substitute mind as "subject" or "consciousness" or "act" or "psycho-physical organism"; or, if mind as in any sense non-bodily is unacceptable, the physiological organism robbed of its "psyche" is made to play the rôle. In any case, if mind is denied, some substitute is provided whereby its function in the meaning-situation is carried on. And this substitution is plainly necessary, since that function is indispensable: to neglect it utterly is at once empirically without warrant and theoretically intolerable. Mind in some sense must remain.

Of course, I am not blind to the crucial issue here, which indeed lies close at hand. It concerns the precise sense in which mind is to be taken if permitted to remain. This is precisely the issue that underlies widely divergent constructions. Since the issue leads beyond the limits of the present analysis, however, it cannot be considered here in any detail. But I will venture to make a general observation which falls within the purview of this analysis. And this observation is that, whatever other characteristics mind may have, it at any rate is complex and systematic in respect of the meaning-situation. Its constituents are not joined together agglutinatively, so as to compose a mere bundle or aggregate. On the contrary, they interpenetrate in such a manner as to form a systematic whole—a whole, that is, within which the constituents are so linked and merged as to fall into a unity. There is here, of course, no reference to mind's unity taken as a whole or in general; in what sense the mind of an individual from birth to death is unitary is a question with which we are not here concerned. The thesis is, simply, that a given mind in a given meaning-situation is complex and focalized: its multiplicity goes beyond the immediate situation, but it also converges significantly upon the immediate situation. Mind always over-reaches the given situation, and this is the reason why mind in the meaning-situation can never be identified with an "act" however defined; but mind also significantly includes the given situation within its multiplicity as a constituent part, otherwise the situation would not be meaningful. And this significant inclusion of the situation within a multiplicity which reaches beyond is precisely the exemplification of the mind's systematic nature within that situation. Mind is a biographical history; this history is not a rope of separate strands, but of interwoven and interweaving strands; and the given meaning-situation is a set of these.

And from this follows a consideration of importance, which because it frequently is neglected needs emphasis. Any analysis of the meaning-situation which proceeds as if its connection with a biographical history were of no significance to the analysis is *ab initio* caught in a vicious abstraction and can hardly obtain anything but abstractions in the end. The plain empirical truth seems to be that every meaning-situation is somebody's, and the "somebody" is no mere "act" but an historical process. And the process is deeply involved in the meaning-situation that finds its place within it. This is the truth at the bottom of the "egocentric predicament," if one chooses to call it so—a predicament, be it noted, which is inescapable, so far at least as empirical meanings are concerned. To read the meaning-situation as if it had no part in such a biographical process is to misread it: taken thus it is taken abstractly, and viciously so.

(b) Though varying in nature with different types of situations, the content seems to be present in them all as empirical observation discloses. This we have already seen, and it now remains to inquire whether content is logically indispensable.

The only alternative to acceptance of content as basal within the meaning-situation is the identification of it with object. Such an identification has been attempted, but the attempt seems definitely to have ended in failure. Insuperable difficulties stand in the way of it. If the content is to be identified with object, how are we to account for the discrepancies in perceptual-situations that arise from the finite velocity of light (as in the instance where this ray of light means an extinct star, for example) or from the variation between public and private spaces (as in mirror images, perspectives, and the like)? What is to be done with dreams and hallucinations? How, above all and comprehensively, are we to understand our "mistaken" meanings—indeed, how could there be any such meanings? The plain implication seems to be that, once we merge the content with the object and are willing to be consistent, error in all its forms defies us. How could erroneous meanings then arise; or, having arisen, how could they possibly be corrected? It strains credulity to hold that objects are erroneous, and it is even more fanciful to suppose that one object could correct another. All of this would appear to be nonsensical: objects are not erroneous, they simply are; and if they could be erroneous, they would not be corrigible. But if content and object are to be identified, then objects must be erroneous or erroneous meanings must be denied. The identification of content with object, thus, leads to an impasse: it renders the existence of erroneous meanings unintelligible; and, once admitted, such meanings remain on the hypothesis intractable.

It is sometimes urged that, if the content is permitted to stand as distinct from object, we are thereby committed to a dualism the logical result of which is solipsism. This is the consideration that motivates recent attacks on the status of the content. If this consideration is well-founded, I see no way of escape; in any event, the distinction between content and object is indubitably characteristic of the meaning-situation and whatever consequences the distinction entails must be accepted. Whether the consideration is well-founded is a question which remains open to debate, and some observations in connection with it will emerge from our further analysis.

(c) The object has not infrequently been supposed to be the most important term in the meaning-situation. Whether it is so or not, it certainly is an indispensable one. To say that it may be utterly abstracted is equivalent to saying that the meaning-situation is a situation in which there is nothing meant; and this, on the face of it, appears to be an absurdity. Abstract the object, and the meaning-situation is thereby hopelessly truncated and rendered nugatory. The status of the object within the meaning-situation must be accepted as ultimate for that situation.

An alternative to this position is the identification of object with content. The attempt to identify object with content, however, is doomed to failure; it is logically on a par with the attempt to persuade the content to perform the office of the object, of which attempt indeed it is but the reverse error. The emphases in the two cases are, of course, different; and so are the detailed consequences following from them. But in the end both come to the same thing: the discrepancies between the immediate and the more remote aspects of the meaning-situation are left unexplained and inexplicable. Both alike do violence to the complexity of the meaning-situation by eliminating from it one or the other of two components, both of which are essential to the situation in its full character as meaningful.

Some philosophers have made the attempt, however, and their failure to carry it through consistently is particularly instructive with reference to the logical considerations involved. Hume and Kant, each in his own way, have come nearer accomplishing the identification of object with content than have any other thinkers with whom I am acquainted; but each in his own way is inconsistent with his basal principles, and his inconsistency is inescapable. Hume, in his very attempt to derive all ideas (especially ideas of relation) from "impressions," is compelled to assume a definite context for the impressions—a context which in his system cannot logically attach to them but which, as in some sense including them, plays an indispensable rôle in his genetic account. And in his description of the function of belief and judgment in experience he constantly appeals (at times explicitly, though more often implicitly) to the object. In fact, it would perhaps not be an exaggeration to say that there is no crucially important step taken in Hume's analysis at which the object as distinct from the impression is not functioning in the background and rendering necessary aid in the analytical procedure. Likewise, Kant's phenomenalism exemplifies the same point, though naturally with important differences in detail. In his more subjectivist moods Kant does indeed identify object with content, though even here he is forced to supply a context beyond the mere "given" which he reads in terms of his *a priori* forms. But when he raises the inevitable issue concerning the "objects" thus constructed (phenomena), he finds himself driven on to some admission into his scheme of the functional office of "things-in-themselves" in order to account for the "objectivity" and the peculiar sort of "necessity" which belong to his phenomenal objects. Objects, he in the end agrees, are more than data, even as organized through the instrumentality of the *a priori* forms; for, as thus organized, they are also in some sense noumenal in reference. Thus Kant, like Hume, is at last forced into a position which is inconsistent with any thoroughgoing identification of object with content. And to those who would uphold this identification the suggestion may not irrelevantly be made that they give careful attention to the analyses of these two protagonists of the thesis and indicate precisely at what points their arguments may be reconstructed so as to remove the inherent inconsistencies. The upshot of such a study, I dare say, will be the conclusion that either a distinction between object and content must be admitted or the meaning-situation is logically intractable.

It has at times been suggested that historical idealism, on its side, has been disposed to deny the object, and this is occasionally advanced as a very damaging criticism of it. I wish in passing to make a remark on this accusation.

That this accusation, if true, would be a very damaging criticism of historical idealism, I thoroughly agree; in fact, I should hold it to be a wholly damning criticism. But that the accusation is not true seems to me certain. It does not apply, without important qualification, to any of the systems of idealism with which I happen to have acquaintance. I know of none in which such a denial is affirmed; and, on the contrary, all seem to me to place emphasis precisely on the object.[1] Even Berkeley, who is traditionally supposed to be the arch-offender here, is hardly open to the charge— if, that is, one is willing to judge him on the basis of his system taken as a whole. His initial assumption, I think, is that object and content must be identified; and, so far, he is guilty of denying the object. By this assumption he is logically committed to solipsism, since in the circle of his own presuppositions public objects are non-existent. But, of course, he admits public objects; not only does he admit them, but he bottoms his arguments for his theistic metaphysics (in whose fortunes, be it remembered, he was chiefly interested) directly on them. The "choir of heaven and the

[1] I must exempt from the above statement that type of idealism represented by such thinkers as Croce and Gentile and sometimes called "neo-idealism." I except this type of idealism, not primarily because I positively think it is open to the charge under discussion, but because I am unable to see (from inability to understand, no doubt) what position on the point its exponents wish in the end to maintain. I may refer to a brief comment I have elsewhere made on the view as I understand it (*Five Lectures on the Problem of Mind*, Appendix II).

furniture of the earth," as different from ideas in the sense in which ideas function in empirical situations, play an indispensable rôle in his construction; and in this sense, at least, he certainly does not wish to deny them. This may be inconsistent with his basal assumption, and I think it is; but precisely on that account it emphasizes all the more the indispensable character of the object in meaning-situations. The post-Kantian idealisms, one and all so far as I am aware and without inconsistency (with the possible exception of certain phases of Fichte's system), lay great stress on the object. This is particularly true of the so-called "absolute" idealism which derives from Hegel, who, despite the common assumption of his critics to the contrary, finds the drive of his dialectic precisely in the object; and in this emphasis at least the later formulations of "absolute" idealism are at one with Hegel. But into these historical matters there is here no space to enter, and they are largely irrelevant to the present purpose. In any context, however, insistence on accurate interpretation of philosophical systems is not entirely irrelevant.

Presumably there is no need of the warning that the immediately preceding observations are not supposed to be in any sense a proof of idealism. They are concerned with the historical formulations of idealism only in respect of their treatment of the object. And the assertion is simply that in them the object has not been denied, either in intention or in principle. That idealists have insisted on a peculiar reading of the nature of the object is, of course, historically true; that they have negated it or that they have thought that its negation is of importance to their ultimate thesis is, equally certainly, historically false. The assumption that they have done so is an unsupported prejudice.

But, historical considerations apart, what is one to say about the object in such meaning-situations as those concerned with Humpty Dumptys, golden mountains, round squares, and the like? Or what about those postulated-situations, in which the postulata are apparently quite arbitrary? Here if anywhere, it would seem, objects fall into identity with content. Even in such cases, however, content and object remain distinct, and the object functions. In so far as Humpty Dumpty or a golden mountain or a round square is meaningful, there is the universe of discourse within which it means; and the meaning of postulata, however arbitrary, involves their larger implications which, on being drawn out, constitute systems of greater or less significance and complete their meaning. And it is clear that the universe of discourse is not identical with Humpty Dumpty or the golden mountain or the round square in the sense in which these are the immediate content of the meaning-situation; nor is the system of its implications literally identical with the postulatum. In such imaginary or arbitrary situations, object and content remain distinguishable: the object is always in some sense beyond the content and is inextricably linked, in the background at least, with the meaning of that which in the particular instance means. Of course, in such situations object tends definitely to break away from "existence" and somehow to float free; and one may suspect that just in this fact is the root of the difficulty most of us feel with reference to the object in such cases. It is not to be forgotten, however, that the question whether all objects "exist" is an open one and should not be begged by tacit assumptions burdened with ambiguities.

While any consideration of the nature of the object, like that of the nature of mind, lies beyond the limits of this analysis, it must be noted that the object, like mind, viewed as an aspect of the meaning-situation, is complex and systematic. It is no mere aggregate of loosely related constituents lying, as it were, side by side; it is no bare summative manifold. Like mind, the object too is a history—a history of causally connected occasions or events, among which is the immediate occasion that constitutes the meaning-situation. Or, if the situation be of the postulated type, the object is an ideational structure rather than a history strictly so-called; but, as such, it still centers about the situation, even though it reaches beyond, and includes it as one of its integral elements. In either case, it is a systematic whole—a whole, that is, within which inference may move prosperously from constituent to constituent, at least within limits, without running against the "unintelligible." There is within it a sort of necessity which is implicative or inferential, never merely additive: what is merely additive is not regarded as a constituent of the object at all, but is looked upon as simply belonging to another object. Within the meaning-situation in which it functions, thus, the object is a systematic complex in which implication and inference hold. This, indeed, is only another way of saying that the object is meaningful; and herein, I think, is to be sought and found what justification there is for Kant's dictum that "the understanding makes nature."

This systematic complexity of the object, like that of mind, is also of profound significance with reference to the meaning-situation; and any analysis which proceeds in forgetfulness of it is intolerable. Such analysis truncates the meaning-situation *ab initio*, and is consequently ruinous. To neglect this characteristic of the object is to overlook one of the outstanding features of the meaning-situation; for, whatever other characteristics may belong to the meaning-situation, it certainly is characterized by this reference beyond the merely immediate. And the significance of this reference is that it is the Ariadne-thread which saves us from the subjectivity and solipsism with which the "egocentric predicament," if abstracted from it, must surely engulf us. The complexity of the object, thus, like the complexity of mind, cannot with impunity be overlooked. If either is denied, explicitly or implicitly, the situation is thereby disrupted and falsified. And the consequences of such an oversight are disastrous: neglecting the complexity of the object, we are in imminent danger of being lost in the fog of a romantic sentimentalism or of an irresponsible phenomenalism; neglecting the complexity of mind, we are only too likely to indulge ourselves with imaginary "absolutes."

To summarize the results of this discussion of the separate claims *prima facie* presented by the three aspects of the meaning-situation, the conclusion is that each in the end must be left standing as integral to the situation. Analysis cannot take any one of them away; or, if it does so, the relational complex which bears meaning is by such analysis destroyed. Mind cannot be identified either with content or with object, for neither will perform its function in the situation; and the object cannot perform the function of the content, nor can the content perform the function of the object. Mind, content, and object are all alike in some important sense ultimate within the meaning-situation; each has its unique office which neither of the others can fill.

2. But are the three to be left standing, each, so to speak, on its own ground? With this question we are brought to our second problem and to the verge, be it added, of even more debatable territory.

That mind and object are everywhere separate and distinct entities seems quite clear. And this is so, whatever view one may hold of either of them. Where the object is an existent in the temporal order, as in the perceptual-situation for example, the distinction between it and mind is presumably not open to serious question. Where the object is not an existent in the temporal order, as in the postulated-situation, the matter is somewhat more involved; but the distinction still quite evidently holds. Everywhere throughout the different types of the meaning-situation, the biographical history within which the situation falls is plainly other than the object which functions in the situation. This, I think, may be taken for granted. But what is one to say of the content? Is it a separate entity in its own right, a "third thing" between mind and object?

Of course, there is always an existential aspect of the content. There is always some specific happening within mind which serves as the immediate focus around which the meaning-situation centers. Let us call this the eventual content, or the content as eventual. Thus taken, the content is literally "in" mind as a part of it—a perceptual image, a memory image, a statement, or what-not. But, thus taken, the content does not belong to the object and can in no sense be said to be "of" the object. There is no

element of identity between what existentially is "in" mind
and what belongs to the object; the two are always numeri-
cally distinct, and distinct in every detail. They are in different places and different times, if the object is spatial and
temporal; and, if the object is non-spatial and non-temporal,
that very fact makes it non-identifiable with the eventual
content which is *eo ipso* both spatial and temporal. And it
should be clear (though it is not always so) that this epistemological dualism cannot be avoided by the expedient of
denying the "mentality" of mind and identifying it with the
organism biologically conceived. Identify mind with the
central nervous system and set it plumptly in "nature" as
you will, the epistemological dualism remains; organic behavior is not the object and has no element of identity with
it. The chasm cannot be bridged in this manner. Nor can it
be bridged in any manner, so long as mind and its object
are held to be distinct entities—so long, that is, as the integrity of the meaning-situation is respected.

It should be noted, in passing, that any analysis which
seeks to find the content exclusively in its eventual character
is logically doomed to skepticism. This, I think, is clearly
enough illustrated by the procedure and the logic of the
older representative theory. If the content is merely an
event "in" mind as an "idea" or an "impression," then the
object is a mere unknowable entity, so far at least as cogni-
tion is concerned. And the principle holds, if organic processes are substituted for "ideas" and "impressions."

But the eventual content is not the content which functions in the meaning-situation. Of course, the two are intimately connected; and presumably the functional content
is dependent on what takes place in mind. But the two are
by no means identical. A descriptive statement of the one
is not at all adequate as a descriptive statement of the other.
The eventual "this," where "this means star" for example,
is what the psychologist would describe as belonging to
mind (however defined) at the moment—the percipient event
with whatever qualities an analytical survey might disclose
as characteristic of it. But the "this" which actually func-

tions in the meaning-situation has other features which do not belong to the eventual content. It is much more complex, involving as it does a whole body of more or less competent knowledge (or so-called knowledge) concerning physical and astronomical phenomena—the velocity of light and the motions of stars as well as the more commonplace knowledge derived from experiences with stellar appearances. And this distinction between the functional and the eventual content would appear to be of basal importance in epistemological theory.

There are two characteristics of the functional content which, in conclusion, I wish to note. These are (a) its complexity and (b) its relational character. And each of these is essential to the logical function which the content performs in the meaning-situation.

(a) It has at times been held that the content is simple, or an aggregate of simples. But I am not convinced that it is ever so. On the contrary, the complexity of the content seems to me everywhere empirically present and theoretically necessary.

Those who are inclined to hold that the content is simple suggest that it is empirically so found in perceptual-situations where the "this" is a mere datum or an aggregate of mere data. What they have in mind in such a statement is the eventual content, the content as a given color or shape or image. Whether the eventual content is simple or not, the functional content at least is never simple. It is always characterized by a complexity, which of course is amenable to analysis but which by such analysis is disjointed and broken into aspects abstractly taken. This is true of the content in perceptual-situations; it is even more clearly true of contents in other types of meaning-situations. The chief difference between contents functioning in the other types of situations and those functioning in perceptual-situations is the difference, broadly speaking and without reference to possible exceptions in detail, between relatively more and relatively less complex contents, and not the difference between contents that are complex and contents that are simple. And in some of the other situations, notably in conceptual-situations, the complexity of the content is so involved that it lies beyond the reach of many minds: certainly, not to every mind may scientific categories or mathematical and logical postulates be "given," and some of them can be "given" only to a relatively few even among the experts. This holds in a greater or less degree of all contents that pass beyond the relative simplicity of those commonly accepted as common sense notions—a simplicity which, in its turn, is never quite simple but involves at least the degree of complexity characteristic of spatial and temporal patterns.

The complexity of the content manifests itself in a peculiar characteristic which I may call its elasticity. It is not hard and fixed, but elastic and a thing of degrees. This is true of the content in what one may loosely call the same situation—the "this," for instance, in the case of two perceivers confronted by what may vaguely be said to be the same object. Here the "this" is by no means fixed, but varies within rather wide limits, as is evident when one compares the botanist's perception of the flower with that of the layman or that of the layman at one time with a later and more instructed observation by him. The same point is perhaps even more clearly illustrated by comparing different types of content—the "this" in "this means table," for instance, and the "this" in "this means electron" or "this means a denial of the axiom of parallels." The first of these is complex and varies within limits, and to take it as simple is to mistake it; but as compared with the others, it is relatively simple since its inner structure is much less involved and intricate. Of course, any content is always unitary; it is also in some sense immediate and, for the occasion, must be accepted with "natural piety." This is true of even the most arbitrary postulated contents. But this characteristic of the content should not blind us to the fact that it is also mediate, and that the degree of mediation involved may be greater or less according to circumstances. As Dewey has well urged, the "given" is also a "taken."

And to this observation should be added the emphasis that its "taking" is in varying degrees, but always in some degree, inferential; it is never quite a hard atomic datum, but is ever complex and inherently expansive.

(b) The essentially relational character of the functional content is manifest in its dual reference. It is at once "in" mind and "of" object. As "in" mind, it is logically linked with a biographical history to which in some important sense (not here considered) it is relative and with reference to which it must be understood. As "of" object, it is characterized by an "objective reference"—a reference, that is, beyond itself to a nexus of events or implications. This dual reference, to mind on the one side and to object on the other, is a basal feature of the content.

In this dual relationship is to be found the ground for the theoretical necessity of the complexity of the content. On the assumption that the content is simple, we are driven to hold that it cannot logically perform its function in the meaning-situation. For, in order that it may perform this function, it must be at once "in" mind and "of" object; and it cannot without contradiction stand in this dual relationship, if its simplicity is to remain inviolate. As simple, it is logically incompetent to do what empirically it actually does; its simplicity must therefore be denied, and its complexity be admitted.

The reference of content to mind has not infrequently been supposed to be its basal relation, and on this supposition have been constructed sundry types of subjectivism and phenomenalism. This supposition is, of course, true to experience, but only provided it is not read so as to exclude the other reference. Undoubtedly, content is a mere abstraction when taken apart from its reference to mind; taken concretely, it is embedded in mind and has meaning only as thus embedded. But, taken apart from its objective reference, it is equally an abstraction, for this reference is equally fundamental to it. It is both references at once; and it is neither apart from the other.

The objective reference of the content is of peculiar importance when one comes to read the metaphysical implications of the meaning-situation, and failure to recognize this fact is at the bottom of relativistic theories of knowledge which would read the content exclusively in terms of its mental reference. Such theories of knowledge are logically possible only provided the objective reference of the content is annulled; but to annul this reference is both arbitrary and vicious.

So far as the meaning-situation itself is concerned, the objective reference of the content is ultimate. Analysis cannot go back of and beneath it. If analysis seem to do so (as, for instance, in the cases of Berkeley or Hume, on the one side, and Thomas Reid on the other), this is only because the distinction between content and object, or between object and content, is supposed to be negated. But such a supposition is baseless; the distinction cannot be negated, if the meaning-situation itself is to stand. And, as we have already urged, the distinction is in the end accepted by those who wish *ab initio* to deny it. If we insist on raising the question, Why the objective reference of the content? our only answer must be, *Ignoramus*. But there appears to be no reason why the question should be raised. The reference is simply an ultimate characteristic of every content which functions in a meaning-situation, a requisite of its office. If to stop here in our analytical procedure is to remain content with a mystery, I at least can see no alternative. On the other side, however, I see no justification for making a mystery out of a fact—unless, of course, all ultimates for analysis are to be called mysterious.

But, if it be impossible to "explain" the objective reference by tracing it to some source beyond, it is not impossible to describe it by noting its characteristics. It is a relation between mind and object such that, on the one side, mind apprehends the object and, on the other side, the object controls. Each of these statements is, I think, amenable to further descriptive elaboration; but there is no space here available for this. I can only urge that the relation cannot be accurately read if abstracted from the mental reference of the content, and that consequently the "object of knowledge" and the "object *per se*" are systematically joined. The object is what the mind intends, but the mind's intention is subject to the directive discipline which the object exerts. Just here, it may be noted parenthetically, is the fact which lies at the bottom of Royce's famous distinction between the "internal" and the "external" meaning of ideas, though the statement of the fact seems to involve an emphasis quite different from that which Royce himself placed upon it: the "external" meaning controls, not the "internal."

But this cannot be entered upon further, and I will conclude the analysis with a summary statement of its results. In the meaning-situation, mind and object are distinct systems; existentially, the content is a part of mind and not a part of object; functionally, the content is dual in reference, on the one side mental and on the other side objective; as functional, the content is not atomically simple but is itself a system characterized by an inner elasticity; as mental in its reference, the content is logically linked with a biographical history and is in some important sense relative thereto; as objective in its reference, the content implicates the object and is subject to its control. The meaning-situation, thus, is a system which is a relationship between two systems through the mediatory function of a third system; this third system is not a "third thing," however, but, existentially, is a part of the system of mind and, functionally, is common to mind and object by virtue of its dual reference. And this dual reference is not amenable to further analytical statement, though it is amenable to further descriptive statement; and such a statement must emphasize the systematic nature of the meaning-situation.

The system which is the meaning-situation may be called a dyadic relationship between mind and object, if the content is viewed in its functional capacity. But if the content is thought of as eventual only, then the relationship constituting the meaning-situation may be designated triadic. In any event, however, the content which bears the meaning in the situation is the functional content, and the problem of the meaning of meaning focuses there. The eventual content, viewed merely as eventual, is without meaning. It is significant only when it is merged into the functional content, only, that is, when its reference to mind and to object is added to its eventuality: the meaning attaches, not to the percipient event or mental state as such, but to it when taken in its ultimate dual reference within the system.

IV

If the preceding analysis of the meaning-situation is in principle sound, it has important bearing on the issue at debate among those traditionally called realists, idealists, and pragmatists, so far at least as this issue centers in the cognitive situation. If the analysis is not sound, then what is needed is a truer analysis devoted to the same end. For the attainment of this end is an indispensable prolegomenon to any clear-cut consideration of this issue, since any attitude one takes with reference to the issue logically involves some disposition of the matters towards which such an analysis is directed.

VI

THE PHILOSOPHY OF SPIRIT: IDEALISM AND THE PHILOSOPHY OF VALUE

Wilbur M. Urban

Yale University

THE PHILOSOPHY OF SPIRIT: IDEALISM AND THE PHILOSOPHY OF VALUE

Wilbur M. Urban

I

Any philosophy written in the tradition of historic idealism is, of course, in its totality a philosophy of spirit. On the other hand, the philosophy of spirit, in its narrower sense, is but a part of this totality. Over against it one must set in contrast the philosophy of nature. *Natur und Geist*, nature and spirit—no philosophy that refuses to make this distinction can be called idealism. The object of this paper is to consider the philosophy of mind or spirit in this narrower sense, to examine some of the problems and tendencies in our more recent thought about mind in so far as they bear upon the larger questions of idealism.

Those familiar with Hegel's classical *Philosophie des Geistes* will at once be aware both of the scope and nature of such an enterprise. His great work begins with the natural soul as conditioned by body; passes on to subjective consciousness; rises then to objective spirit, with its social realization of the good in law and morality; and culminates in absolute spirit in which philosophy appears as synthesis of art and religion. The range of topics includes then all those phases of mind or spirit which appear in psychology, or the science of mind *eo nomine*, but also all those which appear in what are now called the cultural sciences. The nature of the enterprise, as indeed of any enterprise that may be called philosophical, is to bring speculative unity (in Hegel's phrase, unity of idea or principle) into this wide range of facts. In prosecuting his own search for unity, Hegel followed the classical lines laid down by Aristotle, of whose "books on the Soul" he said that they were "still by far the most admirable, perhaps even the sole work of philosophical value on this topic." He believed himself to be simply "re-interpreting the lesson of the Aristotelean books." In prosecuting the same search for unity to-day—and that search is, I believe, one of the major preoccupations of present-day philosophy—we find ourselves again re-interpreting in modern ways the lessons of the classical philosophy of mind. One of the things I hope to show in this paper is that through the dust which obscures the present battle about mind, we may see emerging certain agreements which are in the direction of the strong lines marked out in this classical philosophy of spirit. More particularly, that the philosophy of value is of major importance in this development, and that it is leading us ultimately to an idealistic philosophy of mind.[1]

II

THE IDEALISTIC MINIMUM

First, however, let me make clear what I mean by the statement that any idealistic philosophy is, in its totality, a philosophy of spirit. The point of departure of idealism, as has been well said by one of the contributors to this volume,[2] is "the reality, the existence, the spontaneity, the hegemony of the soul." It gives a privileged position to mind.

This must, of necessity, always remain the premise, expressed or unexpressed, of any idealism; but the misunderstanding to which this simpler and more natural form of expression has been exposed has led modern idealists to formulate the essentials of idealism in terms both more congenial and more relevant to present-day issues. A good deal has been written recently on the question of what constitutes

---

[1] Many still shy when the name of Hegel is mentioned, but we should get over our fright and recognize that Hegel at least found the structural form in which a philosophy of mind can be best stated, and that this form is, in its essentials, not only detachable from Hegel's special terminology, but constitutes the background of our thought about mind to-day, even of those who most strenuously deny any relation to Hegel.

[2] C. M. Bakewell, *The Continuity of the Idealist Tradition.*

the *minimum* of idealism. I shall therefore attempt to state
this *minimum* from three angles.

In the first place, idealists may be said to be agreed that
the world or universe has a meaning. Any philosophy, they
are disposed to think, must assume this. It is not so much
the assumption of a separate type of philosophy as the essence of all philosophy, an assumption, whether admitted
or not, of the philosophical enterprise itself. To them, however, meaning is inseparable from the notion of system. The
world, therefore, is viewed as a "logical" or spiritual totality
—not mechanical in structure, but organic in the sense that
the part expresses within itself something of the meaning
of the whole.

It follows—and here we find a second aspect of the idealistic *minimum* constantly insisted upon—that meanings are
more than bare facts of the "natural order," and cannot be
understood as merely products of the causal order of nature.
Causality itself presupposes a larger structure of meaning, is
a mode of organization by which certain relations within
experience become intelligible. This general position finds
an important specific application in connection with the
meanings of knowledge. Idealists quite generally deny that
knowledge in its character of truth and revelation of reality,
is an empirically describable and observable relation between empirically describable and observable existents, and
therefore subject to naturalistic causal explanation. This
dialectical element of idealism is also inexpugnable and part
of the irreducible idealistic *minimum*.

What is true of "meaning" is *a fortiori* true of "value."
In general, idealists are disposed to think that meanings
themselves presuppose values (the primacy of values); but
the *necessary* characteristic is the belief that values are not
an *addendum* to reality, nor merely emergent within an order
of physical forces. They are not derivative but ultimate;
they are not our contribution to reality, but have a cosmic
significance.

Finally, since "meanings" and "values" are abstractions
unless they are somehow known or appreciated, the existence

of objective meaning and value in the world implies some kind of "mental life" as the core of reality. This also is part of the idealistic *minimum*. The idealist can afford, in the first instance at least, to be quite vague and liberal in his use of this expression "some kind of mental life." From the standpoint of basal issues he may also allow considerable latitude among idealists in their characterization of it. The significant point is his insistence upon the truth that, in the last resort, we cannot detach meanings and values from mind without becoming unintelligible.

III

The Background of a Philosophy of Spirit

The aim of a philosophy of mind or spirit, as conceived by Hegel, was to introduce unity of idea or principle into the theory of mind. The term *Geist* as used by him, had, however, as has been frequently pointed out, this ambiguity, that it covers both of the English equivalents, "mind" and "spirit." For a range of subjects such as he contemplated, the term mind is wretchedly inadequate and commonplace, and a better rendering, perhaps, is spirit—all the more nowadays when the notion of mind has so often been reduced to a mere pittance of its former self. Certainly, while the notion of spirit includes and presupposes that of mind, the notion of mind does not necessarily include and presuppose that of spirit. In any case a task such as that proposed by Hegel, and taken up in the present paper, to be successfully prosecuted, requires that it shall begin with some preliminary notion of the meaning of these terms. It requires, in the second place, some preliminary notion of the structure of reality in which mind or spirit find their place.

In other words, the problems of a philosophy of mind cannot be defined, much less solved, except against the background of some recognized concept of the structure and levels of reality—some accepted system of categories. Fortunately for our purposes such a conception exists and forms the presupposition of the major part of present-day philosophical thought and discussion. Four such levels are, in general, assumed and acknowledged: namely matter, life, mind, and spirit (sometimes characterized as value). Elsewhere I have written of these broad divisions in reality in some detail.[1] The term "matter" is quite generally taken to cover the substance, or modes of action and reaction, which are studied in the sciences of physics and chemistry. It is clear that these sciences do not attempt or, if they attempt, quite obviously fail—to make intelligible the self-movement that is one of the characteristics of life, or the comprehension of things in space and time which is one of the characteristics of mind. But this is not all. The living organism has in its constitution an integral character, a subtlety of coördination and a spontaneity of adaptation, that no knowledge of chemistry or physics would enable the spectator to anticipate. Matter itself becomes fully intelligible—reveals its full possibilities, *what it really is*, only when life supervenes upon it, when it, so to speak, expresses itself in life.

Similarly life is quite generally taken to cover the substance or modes of behavior studied in zoölogy and biology. But life also reveals what it really is only when mind supervenes upon it. No study of zoölogy or biology would enable us to predict the occurrence among living things of a Plato or a Shakespeare, a Beethoven or a Newton. Their employment of faculties, doubtless first used for survival, in the interest of ends that have nothing to do with survival, is intrinsically unintelligible where life is taken in its exclusively biological sense. Even in this limited sense, life is understandable only when we accept its immediate and indubitable meaning as a center of values, values realized in the processes of growth and survival. It becomes really intelligible only when values become explicit in mind and consciousness.

[1] *The Intelligible World*, Chapter XIII, Section IV.

IV

The Notion or Category of Spirit

But now we come to the most significant point in this traditional structure of reality: the levels of mind and spirit. Mind too, as mere intellect, becomes intelligible to us, shows us what it can do, only when it is guided by mind as spirit. Intellect, except as interpreted by this fourth level or category, only too easily appears merely as instrument or means to life and appears oriented towards space and matter. Yet the mere existence of knowledge or science, to say nothing of art and morals—their absolute values and their absolute claims on life itself—suffices to refute this conception of mind. The acknowledgment of these claims and the values to which they correspond, is the very condition of a large part of mind and of its activity being intelligible at all.

We have no difficulty, then, in making clear what is to be understood by spirit as the fourth level of a developing reality. The word spirit in our vocabulary stands for an acknowledgment of values, of their existence and of "something in ourselves, not sense, that perceives and values them." Otherwise stated, just as mind or consciousness itself emerges on certain levels of development, so consciousness of meaning and purposiveness, of value, emerges as a quality of enhanced consciousness. When once higher levels of life emerge, so does the knowledge and acknowledgment that they are higher levels, and ultimately that they are stages of a process that involves the emergence of levels that are higher yet. This consciousness of values is the characteristic of higher levels of mind, and it is this that we have in mind when we use the term spirit.

What I have been maintaining here is that "spirit" is an ultimate and irreducible category, whether the term spirit is used or not, and is part of the background of our thought. Spirit can no more be reduced to the intellect than mind to life or life to matter. This principle of anti-reductionism is recognized quite generally in the case of the three levels, but not quite so readily in the case of the fourth. Yet the same principle which makes matter not wholly intelligible until life supervenes upon it, or life until it finds expression in intelligence, requires that intelligence or mind shall not be understandable except as interpreted by spirit. It is for this reason that the notion is not only indigenous to philosophic or metaphysical thought wherever found, but one which resists all efforts to exclude it from philosophical discourse.

The significance of this structural background of thought lies in the fact, as I have pointed out, that it can be, *and indeed must be,* accepted quite independently of any specific metaphysical prejudices or presuppositions. Without recognition of these divisions and levels no intelligible communication of our meanings is possible and no intelligible account of reality can be given. From this larger point of view, moreover, it is a matter of indifference what we call them, fundamental categories (with the idealist) or empirical qualities (with the realist). The significant point is that each of these levels has sufficient identity in itself, sufficient distinction from the others, to make it *integral* from the standpoint of communication. Intelligibility depends upon their retention, and therefore also that intelligible discourse which we call science and philosophy.

For a philosophy of mind, therefore, we must distinguish mind from the lower levels of nature, and spirit, with its sense for and acknowledgment of values, from mind as mere intellect in the service of life.

V

THE PHILOSOPHY OF MIND AND THE THEORY OF VALUE

I think we may then take it for granted without further argument that the philosophy of mind or spirit revolves about and centers in the theory of value. In a very real sense our philosophy of mind is determined by our theory of value. Spirit is unintelligible except as the acknowledgment of values, and perhaps mind, even in the sense of the psychologist, is not understandable except through the values upon which it is intentionally directed. But of this more later.

This is generally recognized in present-day thought and it is for this reason, among others, that the value notion has become central. The other reasons are of a more metaphysical character. The standing problem of modern philosophy, John Dewey tells us, is the relation of science to our values, and in this he is undoubtedly right. From our present standpoint, however, this standing problem may be stated in another way, namely, what is the relation of spirit, as postulated by the *Geisteswissenschaften* which deal with meanings and values, to the concept of nature as postulated by the natural sciences—in short the place of mind and spirit in nature.

Value is a word of many meanings and its ambiguities have been prolific in misunderstandings. One way to avoid these ambiguities is to take the simplest and most natural definition and to maintain that against all comers. Such a definition is found in the notion of value as any object that satisfies any desire, or that corresponds to any interest. Value would then be a relational quality, the two terms of the relation being consciousness and its object, and the value essentially the subject matter of psychology.

Despite this natural and apparently common sense view, there has been a persistent, and in the end I think successful, tendency to extend the notion of value both below and above the level of consciousness.

The movement to extend values below consciousness is represented in recent philosophy chiefly by certain "realists," notably John Laird. The reasons given are of both a factual and a logical nature. There seems to them no good reason why the notion should be limited to the level of conscious interest and appreciation. Below this level are values of "natural election," relationships which are, so to speak, as significant for the things related as any relation of interest on the level of consciousness. These natural elections or affinities form the conditions or context for the values of appreciation; on what grounds do we deny to them the nature of value? In living nature the parts are not indifferent to each other. In fact we cannot understand living nature if we assume this indifference. It is only, as certain biologists and philosophers assert, only as we conceive the organism as a center of values that it can be understood at all. How far this principle of non-indifference shall be extended is, of course, debatable, but that it extends far below consciousness is factually demonstrable. The extreme of this view is found, of course, in the metaphysics of Professor Whitehead, who makes conceptual value a character of his elements, and who says that if you are to get value into your universe at all you must have it at the beginning.

The argument for the extension of the notion of value beyond and above the level of interest and appreciation is still more significant from our point of view. It is briefly that the "appreciative" point of view cannot stand without somewhere presupposing objective and over-individual values. The arguments here are likewise both factual and logical, and are maintained by both realists and idealists. Factually, men simply do not identify values exclusively with objects of interest and appreciation, and the transcendent reference in the value judgment cannot be explained away by any reference to limitations and defects in language. The logical reasons are, if anything, even stronger. Whenever we examine the attempts that are constantly made "to make feeling potentially objective," we find that they do not succeed, and that any objectivity of values requires the truth of value judgments of an over-individual and over-social nature. Moreover it is equally certain that it is impossible to get any standards or scale of value out of a merely subjective principle of preference. In fine, the appreciative view cannot stand without presupposing somewhere objective timology or axiology. Any theory that attempts to do so, finds itself arguing in a circle.

VI

The Significance of the Ladder of Values

This is obviously not the place to go into these arguments in detail. Assuming this movement to exist—in the direction of extending the notion of value both below and above the level of interest and appreciation—it is for us to ask, what is its meaning for a philosophy of mind? To me there seems to be but one answer. The significance of this emerging "ladder of values" lies in the fact that it gives, or at least suggests, the idea or principle of unity which is necessary to any philosophical conception of spirit. It is, to use the words of Professor Laird, the "thread of Theseus" that may conceivably guide us through the levels of mind. Against our will, as it were, there begin to emerge those same general categories of soul, subjective mind, objective mind, and perhaps even mind absolute, of which Hegel wrote.

The necessity of reading value down into subconscious levels can scarcely be unaccompanied by the necessity of some notion of soul not unlike the classical conceptions. We can scarcely talk intelligibly about *values* of election without some notion of mind, even if we have to "trench upon the mystical" to do it. Nor can we extend the notion of values beyond the level of appreciation and interest without entailing some notion of objective mind, even if here again we have to trench upon the mystical to do so. The important point, however, is that we are doing just these things, even, as it were, against our will. Many *are* doing it even in psychology, as we shall presently see. Certainly it is inevitable in any philosophy of mind which uses as its principle of unity the theory of value. It would be going beyond the facts to say, either that the theory of value, with its ladder, has become the key to a modern philosophy of mind, or that it has yet been able to introduce unity into the phenomena of mind, but it seems to be moving in this direction.

It will be well to compare this principle of unity with that employed by Hegel in his philosophy of mind. For him the principle of unity was the *Idea* and the "realization of the Idea." To understand Hegel's conception Idea must first be equated with our modern notions of meaning and value.

The thread of Theseus for Hegel, which led him from one level of mind to another, was increase in meaning and value. Hegel uses neither of these terms in their modern technical sense, for the very good reason that their presence is so all-pervasive that there was no need of explicitly distinguishing and defining them.[1] Professor Brightman says quite rightly that "his Absolute, then, is value; and morality, beauty and religion are the life of the Absolute Spirit."

The principle of unity of interpretation employed by Hegel consisted in the identification of the principle of totality with the principle of value, through the concept of individuality. It is true that it is only in later developments, such as Bosanquet's, that this identification has become completely explicit, but it was always implied in Hegel's thinking. On this theory, the attempt was made to include the hierarchical principle of scale or subordination within the concept of system by equating degrees of value with degrees of wholeness or individuality, and equating the latter with degrees of reality. For Hegel value is objective; value and reality, if not completely identical, are inseparably related.

VII

PHILOSOPHY OF MIND AND PSYCHOLOGY

It is then, I am suggesting, through the idea of value that a philosophy of mind is developing which may conceivably again introduce unity of principle and idea into the theory of mind. In this notion of value, which the demands of

[1] So far as I know the specific term, "value," is used only once in the *Philosophy of Mind*. Hegel is speaking of *contract* as a from of objective mind. Contract is a form of communication, as he says an "ideal utterance." "In this way there is put into the thing or performance a distinction between its immediate specific quality and its substantial being or *value*, meaning by value the quantitative terms into which the qualitative feature has been translated. One piece of property is thus made comparable with another, and may be made equivalent to a thing which is (in quality) wholly heterogeneous." (Wallace, *Hegel's Philosophy of Mind*, p. 109.) This identification, by Hegel, of value with substantial being is significant. In principle, Hegel never separated the reality of a thing from its value. Reality is, for him, existence plus meaning and value.

fact and logic have compelled us to extend both below and above the conscious values of appreciation, we may have a principle which will enable us to interpret mind in all its forms. But it is first necessary to consider the disunity of a most flagrant kind that now reigns in our conceptions and theories of mind.

The oft-quoted witticism, that psychology first lost its soul, and then its mind, and finally lost consciousness, is a vivid picture of a progressive dissolution which has finally brought on what is everywhere recognized as a "crisis in psychology." The loss of its basal concepts—those notions without which no philosophy of mind has hitherto been written, has involved not only a growing uncertainty as to what the object of its study is, but also a growing divergence in its aims and methods.

This crisis appears at two important points: (1) within the science itself; and (2) in its relations to the *Geisteswissenschaften* or cultural sciences with which it has been traditionally related.

The crisis within psychology itself arises from a deep-seated divergence, a fundamental contradiction as to aims, content and method of the science. For most of us this disunity presents itself in its sharpest form in the contrast of Behaviorism and *Gestalt* psychology; and while the contrast appears at many points it is sharpest, perhaps, on the question of meaning.

Meaning, as many psychologists have said, is all-pervasive in mind, and it is quite generally recognized that it must receive adequate attention or a psychology is *ipso facto* inadequate. Elementaristic theories of whatever kind cannot cope with meanings; and strict Behaviorism, being atomistic in principle, has under Watson's influence, excluded the problem as non-psychological. Only a "purposive" behaviorism,—if there be such a thing—can formulate a theory of meaning. *Gestalt* psychology, on the other hand, recognizes meanings as the very criterion of mind, and in insisting that meaning is bound up with totalities or wholes, also holds that the method of the study of mind must be determined by that fact. In further insisting upon the principle of non-correspondence between stimulus and meaning, it maintains that there can be no understanding of mind by any method that seeks to build up meaning out of the summation of sense elements, conditioned reflexes, or what not.

The increasing influence of the notions connected with the *Gestalt* psychology cannot, I think, be denied. Whatever this fact may mean for technical psychology, for a philosophy of mind, it can mean only one thing, namely the re-instatement in a modern form of that which has been the essentially idealistic conception of mind from Kant on. When the implications of this criterion of mind are thought out, it seems difficult to keep away from a notion of synthetic activity as constituting these wholes.

In the light of this larger perspective—of a philosophy of mind—it is also most interesting to observe that the strictures passed by *Gestalt* psychology upon "atomic" psychologies, whether of the sensationalistic or behavioristic types, have a striking likeness to the criticisms made by Hegel on the sensationalists, the atomistic psychologists of his own day. Of them he said:

"Their ruling principle is that the sensible is taken (and with justice) as the *prius* or initial basis, but that the later phases that follow this starting point present themselves as emerging in a solely affirmative manner, and the negative aspect of mental activity, by which this material is transmuted into mind and destroyed as sensible, is misconceived and overlooked. As the theory of Condillac states it, the sensible is not merely the empirical first, but is left as though it were the true and essential foundation." Allowing for differences of terminology and context, it would be difficult to find any really important point in which the two forms of criticism differ.

But the crisis in our present-day psychology goes deeper than this. It affects, as I said, its relations with the *Geisteswissenschaften* or cultural sciences with which it has been traditionally related.

Ever since the days of the famous dispute of Wilhelm

Dilthey with Ebbinghaus over the nature of psychology, there has persisted a problem (and a dilemma) in the study of mind which has refused to be silenced and which in the last years has broken out more fiercely than ever. Dilthey attacked the "explanatory psychology" of Ebbinghaus, which, as he held, was modeled after the ideal of atomistic physics, and insisted that such a method of studying mind could give no understanding of it and was quite useless as a basis for the *Geisteswissenschaften*. "Die Natur erklären wir, das Seelenleben verstehen wir." Since that time there has been developing a *verstehende Psychologie*, as it is called, which claims for itself totally different aims and methods.

Of outstanding importance in this movement is Spranger and the important school deriving from him. For this cultural psychology, as for the *Gestalt* psychology, meaning is also of prime importance. Psychologically we must start from totalities characterized by meaning relations. A relationship is called meaningful, however, when all its constituent parts and processes become intelligible with respect to a total performance of *value* import. Mind is held to be more than a teleological structure which is regulated by tendencies of self-preservation and adaptation. We must start from the personality as a whole, as it stands in intimate contact with an historically developed cultural environment. The personal can be understood only through the over-personal; subjective mind only through mind objective. Of even greater significance is the notion of what this *understanding* consists in, and of what the method of any such psychology must be. It is quite frankly recognized that the structure of personalities is given only in terms of the predominating evaluative tendencies. The starting point of understanding, the environment in terms of which the person is to be understood, must be recognized, then, as a world of objective values upon which mind, in the psychological sense, is intentionally directed. The concept of value becomes specifically the idea or principle that shall introduce unity into the phenomena of mind.

I have cited Spranger's psychology merely as bringing out

most clearly the true inwardness of a much wider and more far-reaching movement—the general movement, namely, towards a clear-cut distinction between natural sciences and cultural sciences, and the tendency to think of the latter as "value sciences." It is easy to understand why, during the last two decades, dissatisfaction with "explanatory" psychology has constantly increased. It became evident that any psychology starting with elements, whether sensations or reflexes, could not attain to an understanding of the higher processes of mind. It became even more evident that any such psychology was incapable of developing into a philosophy of mind which could in any way introduce unity into the material of the *Geisteswissenschaften*. The modern mind is faced therefore with a dilemma. Either it will hold to the conception of psychology as a science which actually gives us the truth of mind, and in order to secure that truth and understanding, move in the direction of a cultural psychology. Or, holding to the conception of psychology as a natural science, it will deny its function as the exclusive source of such knowledge and turn to other cultural and non-psychological sciences in forming its notion of mind. In either case it means that this aspect of the present crisis in psychology is really an expression of the demand for a more satisfactory philosophy of mind.

VIII

The Emerging Conception of Mind

It is, of course, impossible in the present state of confusion to say just what is and what is not our reigning notion of mind. We may say, however, that there seems to be a general movement in the direction of a consensus of judgment as to what we may call the *criterion* of mind.

I think Driesch is right in saying that "the notion of mind to-day has underlying it the conception of individuality as a category." As a distinguished American psychologist has told me, no psychologist really denies *integration* as the criterion of mind. Moreover, it may be said that the emerging problem of all psychologies is the problem of personality and the question of the methods of knowing and understanding it.

With almost equal certainty it may be said that a further criterion of mind, if indeed it is not really an aspect of the first, is the character of *intentionality*. "The most universal characteristic of mind as such is intention or meaning." The mind is recognized as being different from every other aspect of nature in that it is thus intentionally directed upon something. If use may be made of a familiar concept in philosophy, the criterion of mind may be said to be its transcendence. This self-transcendence is first seen in the intentional direction of mind on the possible and the future. This form of intentionality, as is increasingly seen, cannot however, be understood until the notions of purpose and ultimately of value, are brought in. I should venture to say— although I have no desire to press my point beyond what is justified by the facts, that we are driven more and more to see that no notion of mind can be formed without this idea of direction upon values. Values are not so much understandable through mind, as mind through values.

In the foregoing I have tried to show that in our thinking about mind certain strong lines are beginning to appear which, when made sharp and distinct, are clearly in the direction of restoring the structural features of a philosophy of mind of the classical type of Aristotle and Hegel. It may be well to emphasize some of these lines. The first of these is what I may describe, in the terms of Professor Hocking, as a growing sense of the depth and breadth of mind.

The shallow conceptions of mind that reigned in the latter part of the nineteenth century were due to the wholly arbitrary and artificial limitation that nothing was to be included in the concept which could not be handled by the methods of the natural, in the last analysis physical sciences. It was inevitable that certain things had to go. First of all, of course, the *soul*, in the Aristotelean and Hegelian sense, for it involved the notion of the unconscious. The notion of objective mind or *spirit* had to follow, for this also involved notions of personality and of over-individual mind that the

arbitrarily chosen method could not touch. It is the return
of these concepts, a return forced by a growing familiarity
with the phenomena of mind—that has created the crisis in
psychology.

Psychology lost its soul and of necessity became shallow—
so shallow, indeed, that it became useless for any really
dynamic understanding of human behavior. Other ways of
studying mind through its concrete activities and products
rather than through the abstractions and simplifications
which permit it to be connected with biological reaction,
have forced upon us again the recognitition of the older notions of unconscious and social mind.

Our growing familiarity with psychic phenomena has
served but to impress upon us the reality of unconscious mind
and with it of unconscious purpose. Human behavior, in
all its aspects, emotional, volitional and cognitive, has
shown itself to be so complex, and in a sense so amazing,
that we simply cannot understand it in terms of merely
conscious phenomena. Whatever modifications and limitations Freudian psychology may undergo—and they are
doubtless many; whatever dialectical difficulties in the notion of the unconscious mind—and they are perhaps as
great as ever—it is hardly likely that men will ever be able
again to get along without this notion. But even more
than psychology in the narrower sense, it is the cultural
sciences that are bringing back the conception again. The
study of the products of mind through cultural history and
the sciences of the spirit seems to make the notion inevitable.
Troeltsch, for instance, tells us that the historian must postulate unconscious mind. But this mind is "but the thousand-
fold proved fact of history and sociology, that our acts,
feelings and efforts carry within them many more presuppossi-
tions than we think, and a much greater and quite other
meaning for the whole than we ourselves are conscious of."
The concepts of unconscious mind and unconscious purpose
which the historian and sociologist must use have in the
first instance at least, he tells us, little to do with the difficult
notion of psychology. It is not unconsciousness so much

that we have in mind, as the transcendence of content beyond the actually conscious, and the going back to unknown depths of the spirit. "The psychology that would learn these things," he concludes, "must itself go to school to history and the cultural sciences and not the reverse."

This increasing sense of the depth of mind—not only as selfhood but of mind as displayed in its historical and cultural products, has been accompanied also by an increasing sense of its breadth or extent. Growing familiarity with the products of mind has led to a revival of the notions of social and objective mind. The drift towards these conceptions in psychology and sociology is unmistakable, and the interesting thing about the movement is that it is motivated largely by exigencies of a purely empirical order. It is increasingly realized that the individual and his behavior can be understood and can function efficiently only to the extent that his mental activities are linked up with the psychology of society. Even psycho-analytic science and practice are leading to the conviction that " the Freudian psychology of the individualistic type is inadequate to handle completely those disorders of the personality the essential meaning of which is their unconsciousness." A notion of the common or organic conscious is necessary.[1] Still less is anything like a social psychology possible without some similar notion of objective, over-individual mind. It is true that in reviving this notion, many of its exponents, like McDougall, protest against identifying it with any such ideas as those of Hegel, and insist that it is purely empirical and scientific in character. In view of its undoubted similarity to the older notion, both in idea and use, the student of the philosophy of mind, can gladly permit the upholders of this view to take this pleasing unction to their souls, and secretly smile at the persistence of the Hegel *phobia*. The important thing for a philosophy of mind is the return of classical conceptions without which mind in all its depth and breadth cannot be understood.

[1] Trignat Borrow, *The Social Basis of Consciousness*, International Library of Psychology, Philosophy and Scientific Method.

IX

THE PHILOSOPHY OF SPIRIT AND MIND ABSOLUTE

The deepening and broadening of our conception of mind, as depicted in the preceding paragraphs, inevitably reinstates those structural lines which characterized the traditional philosophy of mind. It is of secondary importance whether we use the terms soul, subjective mind, objective mind, or not. The concepts or categories are there and are operative in our present-day thinking about mind. It remains to see whether the notion of "mind absolute" is in like manner reappearing in the thought idiom of the present.

The "silly old absolutes" of the idealists, of which H. G. Wells spoke with such contempt, are coming back again, and it is the philosophy of value that is bringing them back. In this matter of values, Professor Muirhead [1] tells us there has been, among English philosophers at least, "a broadening of view, a widening of outlook, shared by idealist and realist alike. It has come to be recognized that, as there are transindividual values, so there may be and are trans-social values. Whatever be the origin of values, or more concretely, of the sense of duty, of devotion to truth or love of beauty, these objects, once apprehended, mean not only an *addendum* to existence, but a source of insight into the nature of the world of which they are a product or expression. They thus acquire a *status* and value of their own by which our conceptions of being are extended and enriched." What Professor Muirhead finds characteristic of present British philosophy is *a fortiori* true of German thought, of which it may be said that this is the basal insight, cutting across all divisions of realism and idealism.

Now no one familiar with the spirit of the traditional philosophy of spirit can fail to recognize that in this acknowledgment of trans-social values we have precisely what Hegel had in mind in his concept of mind absolute. The issue then, as I see it, is not the question of the being of over-social absolute values in the sense defined. Idealists and

[1] Introduction to *Contemporary British Philosophy*, Vol. II.

realists alike recognize the difficulty of understanding the values of appreciation without these timological values as Laird calls them, or the axiological values as they are more frequently and perhaps better named. The question is rather whether values of this sort bring with them necessarily the notion of spirit.

The timological point of view, Professor Laird admits, requires not only an absolute point of view, but also in some sense an absolute mind. In Professor Laird's words, "this point of view has to do, in old-fashioned words, with what is excellent from God's point of view." (*The Idea of Value*, p. 321.) One is not sure just what this is meant to imply. It is all very well to say that the absolute values are *there*, but we find it difficult to say just *how* they are there without some such conception of God's mind. It seems difficult to transcend the relativity of the elective and appreciative values without some doctrine of transcendent mind which is not far removed from that of objective idealism.

X

MIND AND NATURE

In this fashion we are brought back to the starting point of this paper. Any philosophy, we said, written in the tradition of historic idealism is in its totality a philosophy of spirit. It gives a privileged position to mind or spirit in its interpretation of the world. If the world is to be viewed as a totality at all—and classical idealism has always believed that there are reasons for so viewing it—that totality must be conceived as organic rather than as a mechanical aggregate, as mental rather than as merely vital, and as concretely spiritual rather than as a system of abstract ideas or essences.

The classical way of stating this has always been—from Aristotle to Hegel—in principle the same. Life is the entelechy of matter, mind of life and spirit of mind. Or, as stated by Hegel, life is the "truth" of matter, mind the "truth" of life, and of mind, in its subjective sense, the "truth" is mind objective and absolute. A philosophy of mind then, in the narrower sense above defined, has as its problem the "place of mind in nature" or more broadly stated, the place of mind in reality. I am inclined to think that our present thought on the problem is bringing us to conceptions not unlike those that I have called classical.

There can be no question, I think, that negatively at least, the emerging conceptions of the place of mind in nature are approaching what was earlier described as the idealistic *minimum*. The point of departure most congenial to the modern mind in this matter is its thinking about meaning and value. There are few thinkers, of any philosophical sect whatsoever, who would not be decidedly wary of reducing meaning and value, which belong to the level of mind and spirit, to any lower levels of being. The wide acceptance of the negative aspect of the doctrine of Emergent Evolution registers this wariness. In interpreting the significance of this theory, Professor R. B. Perry has wisely said that "by employing this notion it has been thought possible to reconcile the essentially *realistic* insistence on the priority, from a genetic and explanatory point of view, of processes of the elementary type such as those of physics and chemistry, with the essentially *idealistic* insistence on the geniune uniqueness and, in a sense, privileged character of the cultural processes of a higher and more complex type." In saying this much, one has said a great deal indeed—something which has all along been one at least of the major contentions of an idealistic philosophy of mind. The next step—and one not so far off—is to say that in the process of *understanding* we can move very much more easily from meaning and value to mind, and from mind to life and matter than in the reverse direction. In face of the alternative—whether the lower levels are the "truth" of the higher, or the higher the "truth" of the lower—the choice, although one we are perhaps loath to make, is nevertheless ultimately forced upon us, and when the option is thus forced, the answer cannot be long in doubt.

So much for the negative side of our present-day conception of the place of mind in nature. Let us turn to the more positive side. Here the important thing is our changing conception of nature.

When used in contrast to mind, nature is the name we give to those levels of reality designated as matter and life. There can be little doubt that our conceptions here have been changing in significant ways, significant in the sense of altering in notable fashion the manner in which we envisage the place of mind. The general situation may be summed up in this way. It is becoming increasingly difficult to pass from matter to life and mind. It is becoming increasingly easy to pass from mind to life and matter.

So far as the relation of life to matter is concerned certain definite tendencies may be discerned which may perhaps be summed up in a statement of the biologist, G. H. Parker, quoted with approval by Professor Julian S. Huxley. He suggests that "had some accident permitted us to make the fundamental biological discoveries of the later nineteenth century before the fundamental discoveries of physico-chemical science, the term matter would have had a different connotation, for it would have connoted mental properties in addition to the matter of present-day physicists." One could scarcely have a more clear-cut expression of the principle that life is the truth of matter, that we do not understand matter in all its depth and breadth until life supervenes upon it. But this is not all. In physical science the concept of nature, and with it the concept of matter, is undergoing a far-reaching change at the hands of the physicists themselves.

This may be defined as a change towards an organic and ultimately, perhaps, a "mental" conception of matter itself. What has been aptly called the growing elusiveness of modern matter is an oft-told tale which need not be repeated here. It is enough to remark that the effects have been of so striking a character that our present outlook would have been a scandal to the tight little island of nineteenth century scientific mentality. We have lost completely the awe of the inorganic, and there are not wanting physicists who tell us in their own words, that the truth of the inorganic is found in the organic and mental.

The organic conception of physical nature, proposed for example by Whitehead, rests in the first place upon what he conceives to be the complete breakdown of mechanism in physics. But it involves something much more fundamental than this, namely a veritable revolution in the conceptual foundations of science. In place of the substantial material entities persisting through time and moving in space, he would substitute as the ultimate components of reality a very different kind of entities and these he would call events. In the language of science it is the displacement of the notion of static stuff by that of fluent energy, but in the language of philosophy it is a great deal more than this. To hold, as he does, that "biology can not be considered a chapter in physics, but physics may be considered a chapter in generalized biology," and that "if you have established the general categories of life, you find that you have already by implication established the categories of your physics," involves a real revolution in our conceptions of the place of life in nature. Moreover, when one adds that in his development of the category of organism mental terms become more and more prominent in his descriptions, it becomes obvious that he finds it not only easier to pass from life to matter than the reverse, but from mind to life than from life to mind.

Professor Whitehead *seems* to remain "realistic" in the sense that he makes the organic character ultimate, although in view of later developments and pronouncements this is at least doubtful. There are other physical thinkers, however, for whom to stop at the organic category is not possible. A recent statement of Sir James Jeans may perhaps be taken as typical: "I incline to the idealistic theory that consciousness is fundamental and that the material universe is derivative from consciousness, not consciousness from the material universe. My inclination towards idealism is the outcome largely of modern scientific theories— for instance the principle of indeterminancy. . . . In the modern scientific view, the universe seems to be nearer to a great thought than to a great machine. It may well be, it seems to me, that each individual consciousness is a brain cell in a universal mind." By this may well be placed a statement of Schroedinger: "Consciousness can not be accounted for in physical terms, for consciousness is absolutely fundamental."

XI

THE COSMIC STATUS OF VALUES

It goes without saying that such quotations are not meant to be of the nature of argument, but merely a suggestion of a tendency. That tendency, I repeat, is in the direction of a change in our conception of nature such as involves an equally fundamental change in our conception of its relation to mind and of mind's place in it. That change is expressed negatively in the proposition, implied in Emergent Evolution, that the "truth" of mind and spirit (value) cannot be found in life and matter. It is expressed positively in the idea that the truth of matter must be found in the organic, and finally in the notion of mind without which it seems impossible ultimately to make the organic intelligible.

In speaking again of Emergent Evolution, we may refer finally to what may be described as a revision of our notions regarding the intelligibility of the evolution process. Many thoughtful men have been pointing out a certain paradoxical element in the notion of evolution as it is ordinarily conceived. If it is interpreted merely in terms of survival through adaptation to environment, we are forced to recognize that such adaptation, or at least a greater measure of it than exists among men, was achieved long ago among beings whom we are accustomed to regard as inferior to man. Considered from the physical point of view, man is ridiculously unfitted for his environment and may even be said to be more destructive of himself and of his environment than are the lower animals. Why, then, if the motive force and driving power behind evolution is the need to secure adaptation to the environment, did evolution not stop at the lower forms so completely adapted? Why did it go on at all to produce man?

The situation becomes infinitely more puzzling and impressive when we take into account the "mind" and "spirit" of man, his intelligence and his sense of values. The same nature that made the sense organs of living creatures merely selective organs that transmit only biologically important stimuli and which, like the organs of movement, serve necessary life functions, this same nature has made possible the acquiring of knowledge in a wholly different sense of the word. The same nature that made instincts and *mores* merely to serve life functions has again made possible the acquiring of a moral and aesthetic sense often independent of this purpose and often in opposition to it.

We seem to be faced here with a curious dilemma. Either the turning of life and nature to ideal ends, at least in man, is an accident, a superfluous luxury; or else it contains in some way the key to a truer knowledge and understanding of the evolutionary process. It is impossible to resist the conclusion that evolution is the expression of some force which is not content with achieving merely survival and adaptation for its creatures, but is even ready to complicate itself ever more dangerously in the endeavor to evolve ever higher forms of life which have their own intrinsic ends. More and more thoughtful men are no longer trying to resist that conclusion even in the interests of preconceived theory. Mr. Shaw's Don Juan cries to the "perverse devil," "Life was driving at brains." More and more it becomes clear that that which life was driving at is not describable merely as "brains," but rather as spirit, in other words at those values, and consciousness and acknowledgment of values, which we mean when we use this ancient and honorable word.

From the foregoing it becomes then quite clear that the philosophy of spirit in the broader sense is bound up with the question of the cosmic status of values. Professor Kemp Smith seems to be justified in finding the cardinal principle of idealism—not in so naïve and primitive a notion as that the world is my idea, but rather in the notion that my values constitute a key to the nature of the world—that values have cosmic significance. Against the background of modern thought, as we have sketched it, this seems to be the *minimum* of metaphysical idealism.

Of these values most modern thinkers are quite ready to say that they are *there* in some sense. With the exception of a few whose notions of being and existence still move within the circle of the ideas of scientific positivism, there are none for whom values are merely subjective states. They may be thought of as entities or relations, as existences or essences, but some sort of objectivity or being they have. It is not, I repeat, a question of whether they *are there;* it is rather a question of *how* they are there, what sort of being they have. Many men are trying to find an intelligible answer to that question to-day—to find a form of sound words in which the relation of value to being can be adequately expressed. The idealist can afford to welcome these attempts, for he feels sure that in the last resort some notion of mind absolute will inevitably emerge.

CONCLUSION

The purpose of this paper has been to show that through the clouds of dust that obscure the battle about mind and its place in nature we may see emerging certain agreements which are in the direction of the strong lines which marked out what I have called the classical or idealistic philosophy of mind or spirit. This purpose has, I think, been in some degree fulfilled. One cannot fail, I think, to be impressed with the return to that "one definite and fundamental scheme" which seems to underlie any philosophy of mind. A very recent instance illustrating this situation may well serve to bring this paper to an end.

In his Preface to *Process and Reality* Professor Whitehead remarks: "Indeed, if this cosmology be deemed successful, it becomes natural at this point to ask whether the type of thought involved be not a transformation of some main doctrines of Absolute Idealism onto a realistic basis." It does become natural to ask this question, but it is also inevitable that we ask another one—has the transformation been successfully accomplished?

VII

THE PRINCIPLE OF INDIVIDUALITY AND VALUE

Joseph Alexander Leighton

Ohio State University

THE PRINCIPLE OF INDIVIDUALITY AND VALUE

Joseph Alexander Leighton

In the interpretation of the meaning of things as a whole, the fundamental antithesis, the great divide, is not between idealism and realism nor even between mentalism or spiritualism and materialism. It is between "*abstract universalism*" and "*concrete individualism.*" Is individuality, concreteness, the organized wholeness of qualitative diversity, the accidental and ephemeral consequence of the blind junction of universals, such as space-time or energy; or is reality perennially concrete and individuated? Is individuality derivative or primordial?

The drift of mathematico-physical science is towards the reduction of individuality to an ephemeral product of the junctions of quantitative universals. On the other hand, in the immediate experience of living and doing, the concrete individual is the center of reference. Our experienced relations to other living beings, and even to inanimate events, appear as an individuating process.

In considering the relations between the Platonic Forms or Essences and the actual real, Aristotle sensed the centrality of this question. He said that, while science deals in universals, the real is individual. Hence the universal has real significance only as the formative principle of the particular. Herein Aristotle was right. The scholastic philosophers showed a true instinct for the heart of philosophy in the controversy between the realists and the nominalists. If extreme realism be the true view, then the individual is an illusion. Their concern was, of course, primarily for the soul of man—for personality. In Spinoza the finite modes have various degrees of individuality; on the other hand all individuals are but determinate parts of the one substance. Leibniz, the modern Aristotle, sees the problem clearly. He makes the real to be individual and self-active, a dynamic organizing form and goes a step farther than Aristotle in finding the true nature of the monad to be appetition. (I find no meaning in the assertion that a physical monad has appetition.)

The artificiality of the preëstablished harmony is due to Leibniz starting with the assumption that every monad must be a self-existent substance, indestructible and unmodifiable by any other finite agency. Hegel embodies the same principle of individuality in his insistence on the concreteness, determinateness of the real. In Bradley it appears as the doctrine that the finite centers of experience are timeless differentiations of the Absolute and "souls" are the temporal expressions of finite centers. McTaggart has a similar doctrine, with the Absolute as the All-Inclusive Harmonious Experience left out. (In this McTaggart is more logical than Bradley.) In Whitehead's *Philosophy of Organism* it appears again as the principle of concrescence. And of course the various expressions of Personalistic Pluralism embody the same insight with varying emphases. Royce tried to hold the balance evenly between a pluralism, for which the individual is the center of value, and the Absolute as All-Inclusive Unity. I do not think he succeeded in this. In his later work, *The Problem of Christianity*, pluralism has the upper hand.

I hold that the individual is real and the universal *as such* is an abstraction from the concrete qualities-in-relation of individuals. But what does one mean by "individual"? The highest empirical form of individuality is that of a community of persons. The lowest form may be the electron-proton or it may be something more minute. What is the primordial in organization or structure we do not know. It would be better perhaps to call the lowest forms *individua* rather than *individuals*, and to reserve the latter term for empirically known organisms. "Monad" would serve, were it not for the association clinging to it of "windowlessness" and of "awareness" or "feeling." "Organism" is objectionable, on the ground that we do not know that the lowest individua have the organismic qualities of self-reparation and self-reproduction with variations. They must be self-maintaining. Perhaps they have all the qualities of empirical organisms. But to say so goes beyond the evidence. On similar grounds I must dissent from Doctor Whitehead's attribution of "prehension" as "feeling" to all individua. "Feeling" loses all definite meaning, if it be taken to include one electron "taking account of another" without sentient awareness. I regard it as an undue concession to the abstractive method of reducing the qualitied to the qualityless, the concrete individual to the abstract universal, to say that all individua must be fundamentally of the same quality; and therefore that all must "feel."

The minimal meaning of an individuum is that it is a dynamic pattern, an activity with structure, an organization; it is a concrete unity; its parts are not parts apart from the individuum. In a broad sense it is a living whole, but not a self-existent whole. It lives and moves and has its being only as a member in an organic system. Electrons are individua (possibly primordial); they are members of atoms; atoms are individual societies; actual physical substances are more complex societies; cells are individual societies; organisms are more complex societies of cells; human persons are unique kinds of organisms living only as members of actual and ideal *communities* of the living, the human, the spiritual; in final sweep, living as members of the cosmic order (I would reserve the term "community" for societies of persons). I consider it a going beyond the evidence and an unnecessary extension of the principle of continuity to maintain that all apparently different types of individua must be reduced to one type—either downward to the electronic type or upward to the personal type. There is a multiplicity of qualitatively unique types of dynamic forms or energy patterns. The universe is constituted by a dynamic, qualitative diversity of individual forms; not merely an enormous multiplication with only intensive varieties of the one fundamental type of qualitied structure. The electrons which make up iron probably remain insensate even when they enter the blood and their course is modified by the unique dynamic form of blood and this, in turn, by the unique dynamic pattern of thinking individua. This is the principle of *qualitative multiplicism*. Reality includes a multiplicity of qualitatively different levels of individuality. I mean by "individuum" what Mr. Boodin means by activity system or pattern. His cosmology and mine seem quite the same.

Much criticism has been passed on the doctrine of *degrees of reality*. It is said that whatever is, is, so long as it is; and therefore everything that is is equally real. But are not *continuance* and inclusiveness measures of degrees of reality? The more comprehensive and richly organized and dynamic an individuality, the greater the extent and persistence of that individual whole. The degree of individuality coincides then with the degree of reality. An atom of oxygen has more reality than one of its electrons. A national state or a church has *more* reality (not better) than any single citizen or member. It is much more comprehensive and enduring.

What is the meaning of the higher individuality, of the *individual* in the full sense? An individual is a complex organized unity, a dynamic system or structure in which qualitative diversity or variety of functions constitutes a self-maintaining, self-active whole. Individuality means that the specifications or differences that make up the whole are not externally juxtaposed. The principle of the whole operates in all its special organs or functional processes, and no one of these has any being apart from the unity. An organism is an individual; perhaps an electron is a true individual. It appears at least to have some of the characteristics—patterned dynamic structure and self-maintenance. A human person is self-conscious, and therefore is a richer individual than a mere organism. A community of persons is a richer individuality than a single person. Indeed it is only as a member of a community that an individual realizes his individuality. On the other hand, it must not be forgotten that, while spiritual structures or wholes, such as a living culture, a nation, a religion and in lesser degree a great art movement or the scientific spirit, include and transcend personal individuals; *these structures come alive only in and through persons, and there is something in the creative urge of personality that transcends the community.* The person is the true *living focus* of the cultural life, as well as of the subcultural basis of culture.

So far there is no ground for divergence among idealists. I assume that all idealists would agree that *individuality* or *personality* is the richest concretion or incarnation, in finite life, of the Principle or Spirit of the Whole. No one of us would quarrel with Bradley's and Bosanquet's thesis that the nature of individuality is to be a whole, a living system, a world; and this means to be a living center in which unity and diversity, comprehensiveness and harmony are balanced. We should also agree that self-realization takes place through continuous self-transcendence; that it is only in so far forth as the individual center continually goes outside itself and lives actively as a member of greater wholes that it lives at all. Ideally, individuality means a world self-complete so far as may be. Its essence consists, as Bosanquet puts it, not in the not-being-something-else but in the *being-oneself*. (See especially, Bosanquet, *The Principle of Individuality and Value*, pp. 69 ff.) Again, as he says, the individual is one with the spiritual, but not with the spiritual as excluding the mechanical. In individuality, the mechanical, the externally juxtaposed system of parts side by side and determined by external relations, is taken up and transformed as a moment in spirit or mind. Individuality will show itself as inwardness and spirituality, not by emptiness and abstraction, not even by blank intensity of incommunicable feeling; but, in a word, by the characteristics of a "world." The individual is the concrete universal. Universals, laws, relations are "abstract," "unreal" except as the common features and interrelationships of the diversity-in-organic-unity of individuals.[1]

[1] Bosanquet, *The Principle of Individuality and Value*, p. 77.

There are then all sorts of degrees of individuality in the finite forms of life. And the richer, fuller, higher individu*lity has more reality, by reason of having greater inclusiveness or comprehensiveness and harmony or logical stability or organization.

The principle of individuality then is the principle of value. All intrinsic value is in individuality. Just as the tendency to hypostasize abstractions appears in the form of setting up some nearly featureless or quite qualityless universal; such as Matter, Force, Space-time, Energy, Neutral Entities, or Essences; as the Substance of Reality from which individuals are derived; so it appears again in the tendency to set up abstract "Values" as having a reality superior to individuals.   Truth, Moral Values, Aesthetic Values are hypostasized.   A "Value" *as such* has no more genuine reality than a "law" or a "relation." Values are only generic names for types of satisfaction of interests by individuals. If my thought finds satisfaction, if my mind is realized, in understanding the relations of the members of galactic systems or of atoms to one another and in formulating physical laws, that activity has much value; but the value lies in the fact of the satisfaction of a fundamental interest of a self.   It is the false worship of abstractions to set up values as real or objective apart from selves.   Values are real only in and for selves that feel them. There are really no such entities or subsistents as *truth* or *beauty* or *goodness* and the like.   There are concrete truths, things felt to be beautiful, satisfying goods for selves. *Individuality is both the locus and the measure of value.* For only in and for sentience which involves a highly organized individuality is there any value; in so far as subconscious individua contribute to the satisfaction of conscious individua (persons) they may be said to have instrumental value, but not value in and for themselves. Perhaps an oyster has intrinsic value for itself. I do not know, but I do not believe it. Therefore I eat oysters without any qualms (except as to their freshness).

What, then, becomes of the objectivity of values—of

truth, goodness, and beauty? These values have the objectivity inherent in the fact that only certain types of activity and experience yield enduringly and massively satisfying values. In the first place, the values of knowing and enjoying the physical and historical orders (truth and aesthetic values) or the values of living as a member of a social order (social-ethical values) are dependent upon the right relations of the individual valuer as member of the actual given orders. He must have eyes to see, a mind to think, a heart to feel and will, in harmony of response to the given, in order to realize the values. It would require a whole theory of truth, an aesthetics and an ethics to expound fully this position. What I wish to insist upon here is that objectivity or reality of values is not anything apart from selves; but consists in the harmonious relations experienced between the active experiencing self and the given conditions of value, which are involved in membership in the world of individuals.

The more individuality, the more value; because the more individuality the richer, the more comprehensive and harmonious the activities and experiences of selves. The objectivity of values, of the criteria of truth, goodness, and beauty, consists in the fact that there is a *community of structure and of function* amid all the individual diversities of minds. The axioms and postulates of thinking are of this character. Mind has a structure and its environing world has a structure. Mind realizes itself through expansion into harmony with the cosmic structure. Amidst all the varieties and diversities of conduct, due to differences of culture and variations of individuality, there has been, I hold, a gradual discovery of certain fundamental conditions of the good life. This is the realization of the ethical community of structure.

In the most inclusive sense, all values are forms of the *Good*. Truth, beauty, and goodness are not isolated forms of value. This principle is recognized in our saying that it is good to know the truth, that certain truths are beautiful, that beauty is good, that there is no massively and permanently satisfying beauty in a work of art that does not express in individual form significant and enduring features of human experience. Beauty without truth is dust and ashes, dead-sea fruit. Truth not felt and served is worthless and powerless. If we take the "Good" as the fulfillment of personality in the totality of its fundamental capacities, then knowledge and intellectual integrity, sympathy with man and nature, love guided by intellectual light quickened and concreted in imagination, are facets of the Good. (I am not attempting a definition, but only a pointing out of the main aspects of the Good.)

If reality consists of a hierarchy of individua, what of totality or unity? Individuals, from the meanest and poorest to the richest, most comprehensive and harmonious, are members one of another, members of a world. Electrons are individua in dynamic relations. The electron's sphere of action is the universe. Organisms are more enduring and inclusive dynamic patterns in dynamic relations in which the lower individua function. Persons are the fullest individuals that we know, and persons are such only as members of the community of organisms, the higher communities of persons and, ultimately, of the cosmic community.

As Bosanquet puts it: the differentia is in the most comprehensive organized harmony.[1] "The sense of unity and reconciliation with the world is a far larger factor in our awareness of selfhood, and one which increases concomitantly with it, than is the sense of collision with the not-self." [2] "We experience one self most completely when we are least aware of its finite selfness." [3] "The positive awareness of an area or quality of self-maintenance is the real foundation of selfhood." [3] "When you have admitted the unity of the person with himself, it is impossible to stop short of his unity with others, with the world, and with the universe; and the perfection by which he is to be valued is his place in the perfection of these greater wholes." [4]

So far I take it that idealists are in agreement. Thus

[1] *Principle of Individuality and Value*, p. 168.
[2] *Ibid.*, p. 248.
[3] *Ibid.*, p. 250.
[4] *Ibid.*, p. 344.

far I acknowledge my adherence to the doctrine so ably expounded by Bradley and Bosanquet. But now we come to a difficulty and a parting of the ways. In his rejection of mere uniqueness, being not like any other self, self-inclosed privacy, as characteristics of the individual, and in his insistence on membership in the greater whole through self-transcendence, Bosanquet goes too far.

Since value is such only in and for conscious beings—persons; and, since individuality, however imperfect, has value just in so far as it has individuality; it follows that, while selves realize their spiritual vocations only by continuous self-transcendence, if value is to be conserved, this self-transcendence cannot mean self-negation or obliteration. Bradley and Bosanquet overwork the idea of *system, totality, logical stability, comprehensiveness, and harmony;* as inclusive Unity, which absorbs and transmutes into its static and stainless-perfection all the variety, color, and movement of finite lives.

Mind *is* the active form of totality. Mind *does* develop through continual self-transcendence. Individuality is the ideal form of totalizing self-actitivy. It is that toward which the whole creation seems to move. A philosophical interpretation of the evolutionary process can only be adequate, for which the chief stages in evolution are the emergences of higher types of individuality. So far so good. But, when Bosanquet concludes that since, where we are strong we come together, our being distinct "we's" is of little or no account, I cannot follow. In discussing Immortality, he starts from Green's thesis that nothing is of value except in and for persons, that *no impersonal mode of being satisfies the principle of value.* But Bosanquet turns this around into the problem of the assurance of our fundamental interests being eternally real in the Absolute, rather than in the permanence of formal personality. Since all interests are to find fulfillment in the ultimate Being, it is of little or no account what becomes of the persons, in and for whom alone (so far as we know) these interests come alive.

This is to me a lame conclusion. Since values are real only in and for persons; then, if values are to be conserved, personalities must, somehow or other, be conserved. Bradley has the same attitude. The "centers of experience" are "timeless differentiations of the Absolute." But "selves" or "persons" are merely temporal expressions of finite centers. Persons may be immortal, but this is not likely. Anyhow it is quite unimportant. Yet, although we are all transmuted, beyond recognition by ourselves or others, in the timeless Absolute; nevertheless our main wants are satisfied therein. Our wants shall be satisfied, but probably we shall not want anything, since probably we shall no longer be persons.

This seems to me little short of nonsense. I understand a materialistic philosophy, like that of Russell in the *Free Man's Worship* or Santayana's, beautifully dressed up in poetic garlands. I understand an Idealism which holds that, since all values, including *all truths* (no less the truths of mathematics and physics than of ethics and aesthetics), are in and for persons, persons therefore must be real and enduring; and the most adequate interpretation of the universe must be that the Ultimate or Supreme Reality is a personality-creating principle and therefore at least richer in nature than any finite person. But an idealism which holds that individuality and value and reality are identical and yet assumes an air of lofty indifference towards the unique distinctness and enduring self-activity of individual persons is to me a contradiction in terms.

I believe that this contradiction is due to riding the idea of system, totality, comprehensiveness and harmony, to death. Individuality is stretched to mean literal inclusiveness of other individuals. Comprehensiveness and harmony are taken to imply that all finite individuals must literally be included, and therefore swallowed up, in one all-devouring Individual—the Absolute. And so the only true and really real Individual is the "Concrete-Universal," *the absolute all-containing and all-digesting System.* I see that there is a real meaning in the idea of the concrete universal. It is the idea of a living organic system, an all-inclusive Cosmic Order. But, if the individuality from which we start, namely *personality*, is so merged and transmuted in the Absolute, that it becomes a mere unknown adjective, the Concrete Universal, the Living Organic System of the Whole is no longer concrete in any genuine sense; for the only clue or standard of concreteness of truth and value has itself been transmuted beyond recognition. It seems to me, one must either affirm that finite selves are genuine self-active, self-worthy members of the whole; or one must cross the great divide and admit that all the variegated individuality and plurality of concrete existents is the inexplicably engendered and transitory mirage of abstract universal forces.

When recognition has been given of the much more adequate development of the notion of mind as the active form of totality, and thus the best key to the nature of the whole, the position of Bradley and Bosanquet with regard to the place of the finite self in the cosmos seems to me essentially that of Spinoza. Viewed *under the form of eternity*, and by the *scientia intuitiva* which gives the vision of absolute totality, the *idea* of the finite self has a certain eternity; that is, in so far as there is in the Absolute an idea of the finite self as a transitory mode of the Absolute. But then every sort and degree of finite mode has this sort of eternity, since every one has some reflection in the eternal and self-complete mind of the Absolute and it is this reflection that is the real reality of the finite self.

I quite understand the motivation of this position. On the one hand, the finite self is always imperfectly a whole, always a changing, growing, or disintegrating, complex; subject to all sorts of strains and vicissitudes; the sport, more or less, of finite circumstance. On the other hand, it is desired to anchor the values of selfhood securely in an eternally poised, wholly stable and self-coherent Whole. The finite self is to find its values by recognizing its own insignificance and ephemerality and living in the light of the Eternal Order.

It is worth while to note the ultimate similarity between the Idealism of Bradley and Bosanquet and the Indian philosophy of Samkara. I do not say that they are identical but I do say that, in the final position of the finite self, Absolute Idealism is very close to that of Samkara. Professor Radhakrishnan says that the philosophy of Samkara does not hold that *Maya*, the realm of multiplicity and individuality and change, is sheer illusion. It is the inexplicable expression of Brahman, the Universal Atman. But the true destiny of the individual soul, the jiva atman, is to realize its *identity* with the Brahman Atman. If the writings of southern Buddhism represent its primitive form, then Buddhism means the same attitude with a more positivistic or phenomenalistic basis. The source of all suffering is the clinging to the illusion of individuality, and the way of redemption is the release from this cardinal illusion and the consequent evanescence of individuality—Nirvana. What remains, beyond sheer nothingness, I do not understand. I take my stand with the western empirical and humanistic affirmation of the central significance of individuality. Give that up and the world becomes a disappearing wraith!

If, on the other hand, by identity of various selves—from man to God—is meant only a fundamental sameness of spiritual organization, incarnated in various degrees, that is not an essentially different insight from the basic faith of the classical Christian—"Beloved now are we the Sons of God." But if *identity* means *existential oneness* then the individuality of the finite self is lost. Greek philosophy in Plato and less clearly in Aristotle, and the Christian view of life, have this in common—affirmation of the significance of individuality. Certainly, the Gospel of Jesus and its interpretation by Paul and John are based on the primary faith in the reality and value of the individual person. The Christian life-view faces the facts of error and sin, even of unmerited suffering. In its doctrine of vicarious suffering as an instrument of redemption, which is incarnated in its picture of the Saviour, it makes the most

heroic venture that the spirit of man has yet made in the
face of the tragic issues of life. Accepting the reality of evil
and of unmerited suffering, it affirms these to be means to
the fulfillment of spiritual personality. It does not say
that the way out is the suppression and final extinction of
personality, but rather the ethical development of personality in solidarity with the community. Here I think Royce's
interpretation of Christianity is profoundly true, although
I cannot share his confident speculation as to the relation
of the Temporal and the Eternal nor accept the theory of
"The World and the Individual" that imperfect finite
selves are literally parts of the Absolutely Perfect Timeless
Self. No real self is merely part of another self.

I admit that to believe that in personality is the best
key to the meaning of the universe is to make a venture of
faith, to make a bet against odds. If I hold it, in the face
of all the burden and the weary weight of this unintelligible
world, and through the gloomy days made for our searching,
it is because the *only logical alternative* is *Materialism* and
despair of everything—of science no less than beauty and
goodness. Emergent evolutionisms *et hoc genus omne* are
evasions of the ultimate issue in cosmic philosophy. They
owe their plausibility to an equivocation—the richer qualitied, the more individuated existent is not the mechanical
by-product of the less, but nevertheless it is blindly produced therefrom!

There are three logically consistent cosmic philosophies—
materialism, dualism, and an *idealism of individuality,* or
personality. Either: (1) All the wealth of psychic life—all
feelings, ideas, ideals, values, choices, volitions—are the
episodic by-products of blind, insentient energy omnipo-
tently rolling along; or (2) there is an unsettled cosmic conflict between the integrating and the disintegrating, the individuating and the dissipating forces; or (3) all appearances
to the contrary notwithstanding, the goal toward which
the whole creation moves is personality: if so, then clearly
the richest individuality, the spiritual personality, is the
key to the meaning of the whole. The structure or plan of the

whole cosmos must be essentially more akin to the nature of personality than to the nature of anything else in our empirical order. It is a personality-engendering plan or structure.

The final paradox of our being is that, while spiritual Individuality or Personality *seems* the highest form of existence, the outcome of the evolutionary process, and certainly *is* the center and ground of all values, the course of the cosmic process seems to show an indifference to the fate of personality. Is the richest, the most integrated form of existence ultimately nothing but dust and ashes on the cosmic scrap heap? Is all life nothing but a stupendous Aeschylean tragedy? We cannot know. But, if increase of individuality and value is the burden of the evolutionary process, we may believe with good grounds that, all appearances to the contrary notwithstanding, it will not be reduced to nothingness. An idealism which finds in personality the key to reality and value I hold to be the only consistent form of idealism. I do not find it an accident that Hegel, who is cryptic and evasive about the place of finite personality, as about the personality of the Absolute (I do not think his Absolute can be called "personal" or self-conscious spirit), showed a lack of appreciation of the social and ethical conditions of personal individuality. I have in mind his glorification of the objective mind and his practical apotheosis of social organization in the form of the state. Bradley and Bosanquet were Englishmen and had more practical appreciation of individuality, but I think Bosanquet's political philosophy suffers, though not to the same degree, from the same overemphasis on social organization and the "real social will." Make any form of social organization, whether State, Church or Soviet, God-upon-Earth and a blow is struck at the sacred spring of creativity in the individual. A consistent personal idealist must esteem individual self-determination above every other social value. This does not mean *laissez faire* in the economic sphere. For our economic order is now so collectivistic in fact that it must be controlled to insure a living and spiritual opportunity for all the individual members.

The whole trouble arises from assuming that, since the whole is the Perfect All-Inclusive Individuality, the Absolute, all other individuals are merely *parts* of it ("adjectives," Bosanquet said in a symposium). Since, after all, we get our conception of individuality and value from the world of finite selves, I maintain that we must keep to them, not abandon them for a timeless all-inclusive Absolute which yet is called a conscious experience (surely an inconceivable monster). A self is real and realizes and conserves value not as a mere *part*, but as a *self-active, intrinsically valuable member* of a world, within which it is a world. I am myself and realize values as a living organism, as a member of a human family, a moral and spiritual cultural tradition, a nation, a human being, a son of the Earth and of the Cosmos.

Idealism commits suicide on the altar of an abstraction, if the finite individual is regarded as merely a *part* of an Absolute Experience or Absolute Self. How can one self be literally part of another self? How can one self's private experience be merged in the total experience of a larger all-inclusive self? The Absolute Utterly Harmonious Experience must swallow and digest all finite experiences, good, bad and indifferent, sane and insane, true and false. So I am unable to accept an idealism for which finite personality (the only one we intimately know) is transitory. How can our main wants be met, if persons are merely transient expressions of eternal finite centers and are transmuted beyond recognition in the Absolute?

Bosanquet says the important point is this—are values realized and conserved, not what becomes of finite persons? But what becomes of values, if finite persons are obliterated or transmuted into that in which they are no longer recognizable selves?

I do not say that empirical values are illusory, if the finite locus of values have no permanence. We can still extract the immediate values of the flying moments. But that is all. If the finite locus of values be transitory, *the Universe, in its totality, has no value.*

It is contended that the Supreme Reality cannot have

"personality"—if the latter term be taken strictly. Bradley puts the matter with his usual vigor and clearness. For him a person is finite or meaningless. The Absolute is the all-inclusive, self-existent whole and, therefore, cannot be a person. "If by calling it personal you mean that it is nothing but experience, that it contains all the highest that we possibly can know and feel, and is a unity in which the details are utterly pervaded and embraced—then in this conclusion I am with you. But your employment of the term personal I very much regret, . . . because it is misleading and directly serves the cause of dishonesty. For most of those, who insist on what they call the 'personality of God,' are intellectually dishonest. They desire one conclusion, and, to reach it, they argue for another." [1] They desire a self amongst, and over against, other selves and they argue for an Absolute. The Absolute cannot be absolute and a self. It is personal in the sense that it includes personality; but, being above all these distinctions of the finite, it is better to call it superpersonal.

Certainly, Bradley is right in holding that an *all-inclusive Absolute* cannot be a self or person. I find no meaning at all in a self which includes and digests all other selves in its devouring maw. If the Supreme Reality be a Self, it may be the ground of whatever degree of world-order and value there is. But it must be finite, if "finite" means to be a self in relation to a world of selves and things, even though it be the ground of the society of selves. I do not know how to harmonize the concepts of one World Ground and of a Perfect Self. I do not understand how a Perfect and Supreme Person can be the Ground, as well as the Goal, of all that is.

On the other hand, I think Bradley and Bosanquet (and all who think like them) are in an even worse quandary. They are intellectually muddled. For the central question is— *what is the Ground and Seat of Values*, the principle of Individuality and Value having been identified. Then the real issue is this—are we entitled, even forced, to say that, *if Individuality and Value have cosmic status, the Supreme*

[1] *Appearance and Reality*, p. 532.

Reality must possess selfhood or Personality and this must be its highest character? I answer, unequivocally Yes! If the Supreme Reality is self-conscious, self-active, thinking and willing, it is personal. If it has not these powers in full actuality, it is not only not personal, it is even *subpersonal*. It might, in such case, be a mass of dumb feeling, but it would be lower in value-quality and power than the humblest self. Strictly speaking, there cannot be a conscious unity of Experience that is superpersonal. If the Absolute Experience is conscious, it is personal and is not *The Absolute*. If it is not conscious, it is unconscious and beneath personality. The notion of an Absolute or Perfect Experience, in which all Value and Individuality are conserved, but which is not a self-conscious self-active being, is a *contradictio in adjecto*.

The Bradleyan absolute or any similar absolute cannot know in any sense in which we know. All its knowing would be self-intuition, but what is self-intuition if there be no Other? The Absolute cannot do anything, for there is nothing to be done. All change—progressive, retrogressive or even circular—is mere "appearance" swallowed up and transmuted into the static timeless being of an Absolute which, though it contain histories without number, has no history. Certainly such an Absolute could not be a God; for it has neither the practical, ethical nor even the theoretical functions of a Godhead. By what right it could be said even to feel passes my comprehension. How could the all-inclusive statical Unity have any feelings?

If the Absolute cannot be God, certainly a God cannot be the Absolute. A being who is to serve as the Ground of real Individuality and Values cannot be the unvarying and indiscerptible Unity of all that is. If there are to be genuine individualities with values, there must be plurality, some looseness of conjunction, real change.

If Individuality and Value are conserved in the cosmic process, the Conservator has personality and that is the highest we can say about it. To talk about personality and value as having cosmic status, and then to say that their

Ground is not in personality; but in impersonal personality-producing forces, seems to me utter intellectual and axiological confusion. Either the cosmic force that produces personality is personal, or personality is an unaccountable but none the less ephemeral by-product of brute unconscious forces.

A timeless self is a psychological monster, says Bradley. I agree. But a timeless Experience, which includes and transmutes all temporal experiences and experients into an eternal harmony; and in which there is no longer any world of distinct selves of which this Experience is the experience; and no selfhood which has the experience and is distinguished from, in being related to, the objects of its experience; such a being is at once a psychological and a metaphysical monster.

Finite individuality must have its ground in a Supreme Individual, if individuality be inexplicable in terms of abstract Universals. But this Supreme Ground of Individuality, this Super-Personality, must be a *member* of the world of which all finite selves are members, as well as the ground of the spiritual community. I reject the notion that finite persons are mere parts of an all-inclusive Mind or Experience on three grounds. (1) I cannot conceive *how* this could be so in terms of experience. (2) It conflicts with the conception of individuality as implying the free *membership* of self-active beings in a community. (3) It undermines the entire notion of value. If value is real only in and for selves, it disappears if selves disappear.

Personal Idealism does not logically imply *mentalism*. *Personality is the supreme principle of value and the best key to the meaning of reality.* But I cannot see that all that exists is mind. It seems to me that the simpler forms of dynamic structure are not minds. They are dynamic patterns which may be taken up into and made subservient to the higher conscious dynamic organizing principles which we call "minds."

The differences between mental and non-mental individua are most significant. Mind supervenes upon an enor-

mously complex physico-vital organization; mind has a
range of sensitiveness or discriminatory response, of selective-
ness, of organization of experience (through memory records
and creative synthesis), of creative synthesis by which it
spans time and space from the infinitesimal to the infinite;
in short, of varying and supple adaptation, self-maintenance
and self-creation, which make the difference between mental
and non-mental individua the most significant of all differences in our world.

It *may be* that all dynamic structures or patterns are
minds of sorts. It may be that the electron is a low grade
soul, with which we are unable to hold communication,
because of the differences in tempo between its psychic
rhythms and our own. It may be that its self-maintenance
is due to appetition. Absolute proof or disproof is impossible
here. But, in view of the poverty of the electron's behavior,
it seems to me very implausible to maintain panpsychism.

Such a thesis is motivated by making continuity or qualitative identity one's paramount category. The logic of the
argument runs thus: psychical life cannot be derived from
a combination of factors in which it was not present. But
all existence must be continuous, of identical quality. But
this is a purely *a priori* argument. Empirically, the lower
forms do not behave like minds. Empirically, they do not
communicate in any intelligible fashion with us. And yet
there appears to be interaction, interdependence.

Well, what is gained by the assumption of identity of
quality? What light is shed on the problems of personality
and value and of the place of man in the universe by assuming that rocks and seas, galactic systems and atoms are really
assemblages of souls? None whatever, that I can see. Personally, I should feel very uncomfortable if I seriously held
that what I walk on, breathe, eat and drink is psychic life.
Is it not more consonant with fact to say that "mind" is a
unique form of organization and control which is capable
of self-development beyond that possessed by any lower form
of individuum, and let it go at that? Values lie wholly for us
men in the uses we are able to put our environments and

our selfhoods to. The realizable values of mind are what they are, regardless of the question *how* the minded and the mindless dynamic structures interact.

Why should we sacrifice everything to abstract continuity or identity? To reduce everything to "mind" is to reduce mind to vacuity, to a quantum of mere energy. I hold rather to *multiplicism*, as more consonant with the evidential data. There is a *hierarchy* of dynamic forms or patterns. Mind is the richest and most significant of these forms. In our empirical world, that is in our spatio-temporal section of the universe, mind supervenes upon an arrangement of simpler or less structured and less qualitied forms. I would not say, without qualification, that mind "emerges," for that seems to imply that mind, a higher individuality, appears miraculously in a universe which once upon a time was mindless.

The higher individuality, the "minded" form, cannot be accounted for in terms of poorer forms. If it be assumed that it can be so accounted for, we must go on and say that, not only mind but life and even qualitied inorganic structures, are the blind products of the interaction of spatio-temporal conjunctions of atomic quanta of bare energy. This hypothesis is inadequate to account for our complex richly qualitied world of individualities. For: (1) It is highly improbable that the complexity of persistent dynamic structures, cumulatively enriching themselves in the process of evolution, can have arisen in an environment in which anything might happen, an environment wholly random in its behavior. Adaptation implies an order to which the adaptor adapts itself. (2) Qualitatively rich and organized structure is not explicable in terms of the qualityless, the featured in terms of the featureless. An infinitude of randomly occurring quanta, atomic "events" or "point-instants" cannot take on structures, habits, self-maintenance, self-expansion, self-reproduction with variation, in the absence of any persistent order or arrangement. Pure Tychism will never account for any structured whole getting started, persisting and growing.

It is significant, in this connection, that Samuel Alexander has to invoke the *Nisus* to provide for the progressing qualitied enrichment, from level to level, of his space-time, and that Dr. Whitehead has to invoke God as the Principle of "concrescence" or Individuation. Let it once be admitted that the blindly contingent happenings of mass-particles will not account for Individuality, then one is logically committed to the principle that the highest type of Individuality is rooted and grounded in the Order of the Whole. Individuality is primordial. Absolute genesis of individual wholes from random fermentations of atomic space-time particles is ruled out. (3) If the emergence and enhancement of finite individuality be, as I hold, the most outstanding feature of the world process, the meaning of evolution, is it not in the highest degree improbable that in the universe as a whole this process should reverse itself and individuality be reduced to nothingness? (4) The world-process has been obviously a creative process, including a succession of levels of novelties. If the principle of entropy or energy-degradation be an all-including or cosmic principle, then, since its presupposition is that there is a definite amount of energy in the universe, the state of heat-death in which a world operating according to the second law of thermodynamics must eventuate, should have eventuated endless ages since. It is impossible that the principle of entropy should rule in a creative or novelty-producing cosmos. In short, a cosmos in which individuals emerge and grow is not a mechanical system in any precise sense of the term. In Eddington's terms, continual increase of the random element and decrease of organization, in the universe as a whole, involves a dead universe.

Matter I conceive to be a limiting concept. As such or as a thing-in-itself it does not exist. Empirically, matter is the principle of routine, of habit, a tendency towards sameness and fixity, a groove into which the habits of energy life and mind *tend* to run. It has no principle of activity of creativity. Its rules are the *identical laws* of Eddington— the laws of Conservation of Mass, Momentum, Energy. When matter changes from one state to another, it is subject to the principle of quantitative equivalence. What is gained on one side of the equation is lost on the other. Equality of action and reaction, purely quantitative give and take, non-creative, non-initiating motion, absence of self-activity are basic characteristics of matter.

On the other hand, the patterned dynamic structures of atoms, whether minute solar systems or waves, the quantum theory and the principle of indeterminacy all point towards the idea that the strictly material aspects of the physical order are simply the results of our statistical, crude, in-the-lump way of describing the behaviors of minute dynamic individua; and that everywhere in nature what is real is a dynamic organization, an energy-pattern.

Life and mind gain, develop, by giving away, by activity, by going beyond their existential states. Mind or spirit is self-active and the more self-active the more living and spiritual. Spirit does not lose itself by self-expression; but rather so finds itself. It is not impoverished but rather enriched by giving. The more it spends the more it has. The more it goes outside itself the more it is at home with itself. The more it risks the more it wins. The laws of spirit are: compenetrability, self-realization through self-transcendence, self-activity, through living in and for other selves, the richest individuality through the fullest commonalty.

I do not mean that matter is thus explained away or shown to be a by-product of mind. All attempts at such a solution are mere verbalisms. Matter or Blind Energy must be accepted as a primary datum. Mere animal and vegetable life are also primary data. There is a *multiplicity* of forms of existence that interact—not a simple duality of matter and mind. Such notions as "mind-stuff," or universal "organism," to bridge the differences, seem to me to conduce merely to confusion of thought. What is a "mind-stuff " that is not exactly "mind," nor a "stuff" at all?

It is quite possible that the richer forms of finite individuality are the highest or most complex expressions, thus far, of an immense but finite current of life that surges against and oozes and trickles through obstacles that are not hurdles set up by itself. There are many features of the life-situation for which such a conception as Bergson's is the most plausible interpretation.

Livingness cannot be derived from non-livingness. Either life is an original constituent of a universe, qualitatively dual or multiple in its constitution, or all matter is alive. The career of life is best accounted for by the hypothesis that there is some sort of non-living factor which is a partial hindrance to life. In this hypothesis Life is the creative principle, which has, up to now, achieved its highest and most paradoxical creation in spiritual selfhood or personality. Life is finite and hindered, but it is increasing in individuality and power and it *may*, in some far-off divine event, dominate the cosmos.

I say this view is very plausible. The greatest difficulty with it is that a reflectively-minded life seems, in comparison with a lower organism, at least just as much *sui generis* as does an organism in comparison with an inorganic thing. (Indeed, I would say *even more* so.) If the urge of mere general livingness is inadequate to account for the emergence of personality, the latter must either be grounded in a creative principle of its own order or be eternal. Either personality is just the richest emergent form of the organic urge or it has a super-organic ground.

Individuals emerge but their emergence is the expression of the enduring plan or structure of the whole cosmos. The weight of evidence indicates that the history of our geocosmic epoch is one of the emergence of a succession of levels of increasing individuality-in-association. By a tidal tug from another sun rushing past, a sun was torn to pieces. A spiral nebula was formed, new knots formed upon this gave rise to our sun and earth and other planets. Our planet was, like the other planets, composed of very complex highly radio-active atoms. Through the breaking down of these, molten compounds and hot vapors were formed. Earthquakes, volcanic storms, meteoric hail gave rise to molten lava and hot rain. The earth's crust solidified; hot water and steam were very abundant on it. Unicellular organisms emerged, then multicelled organisms in immense variety and succession from hydra to dinosaurs, and finally to the primates and man.

We must accept the historic sequences determined by the earth sciences as the most adequate, available description of the emergence of successive levels of individuality; culminating, so far as our empirical evidence goes, in personality-in-community. To call this geocosmic process an "emergent evolution" is to recognize the qualitative uniqueness of each emergent level, in relation to lower levels; it is to admit the inadequacy of a mechanical explanation. The qualitatively novel level emerges and adds new significance and richer reality to the process. For, as Spinoza put it, the more attributes anything has, the higher its degree of reality; and, I would add, the more persistent and pervasive the pattern of its dynamic organization.

If new levels of individuality are inexplicable in terms of a sheer mechanical process (the random rearrangement of fixed particles having simple locations in time and space) then their emergences imply a *perennial cosmic dynamic structure* or *plan*, which is their enduring ground. Then the emergence of individuality-in-association is the self-expression (the revelation, if you like) of a *Cosmic Principle of Creative Order* which can only be described as the Eternal Ground of Individuality-in-Association. Since Personality-in-Community is the richest form of Individuality-in-Association, the Cosmic Ground is conceived, with least inadequacy, as the Superpersonal and perennial spring of Personality.

Freundlos war der Grosse Welten-Meister.
Darum schuf Er Geister.

This is a poetic license. The Great World Master can never have been friendless. The aeons of time and the vast reaches of space must have always been pervaded and permeated by individuality-producing Energy; therefore, by Individuality-in-Community raised to the nth power.

I do not say that this Creative Spring of Selfhood, eternally includes and wholly subdues all that is. There remains an apparent surd.

Moreover, it must be admitted that all attempts to form any definite conception of the World Ground as Overself or Superpersonality must end in failure. We needs must interpret the ultimate in terms of the highest and fullest life that we know. But the greatest of us men are at best but very imperfect and dependent personalities. We are finite, not merely in requiring the Others for our lives and living in and through them; we are very finite in power and range and possibility of achievement. And even the richest cultural community which transcends the individual lives of its individual members and spans the generations, is fragmentary and full of vicissitudes. Even the life of the greatest nation or church rises and falls, subject to the changes and chances of this mortal life. As Plato said, the Maker of all things is very difficult to know and hard to communicate in so far as known.

Nevertheless, we can at least say this—insofar as there is a meaning discernible in the life of this cosmic epoch, that meaning lies in the cumulative fulfillment of individuality-in-association, of which the highest form is personality-in-community. And this enduring meaning must be rooted and grounded in the total cosmic structure which therefore reveals its significance most fully in the communal life of a society of persons.

What is the place of the abstract uniformities of routine, repetitions of similars, in the scheme of things—the "Laws" of the physical order, the vital order, the mental order? These express the stable environmental systems or conditions for individuality. The repetitions of the physical are the expressions of the interrelations of individua. Their regularities are those of the natures of the component individua and are the environmental substructures for the emergence of higher individua. Vital order has its own social habits or "institutions." These are environmental conditions of mental individuality. Persons have their own habits or institutions. These routines change much more than those of vital individua—these in turn more than those of physical individua; because the richer, the more self-active the individuum, the less is it a creature of the environmental substructure, and to the greater degree it is self-creative.

There is then no order of iron law or set of iron laws, outside or above the individuality of the real and imposed upon it; not even in the physical sphere. All universals or laws are immanent in the relationships of individuals—physical laws in the electronic relationships, vital laws in the organic relationships, spiritual laws in the mental community.

Insofar as all these orders or structures constitute an ultimate system, insofar as there is a universe, there must be a preëstablished harmony—an *Order of orders;* therefore a Principle or Ground of Order. But this Supreme Ordering Principle cannot be something in which finite individuality is swallowed up. It can be nothing other than the Supreme Individual, which, as the creative source of all lesser individuals, is the ground of their interrelations, as well as of their inner potencies. Potencies and relationships are nothing apart from one another. I do not say there *must* be a Supreme Individual, the Ground of all finite individuality. I say, *if* there be an Absolute Ground of individuality; as the ground of a developing community of developing finite individuals, it can neither absorb all these individuals, which would be a nullification of its own world-creating and sustaining activity, nor can it impose on the finite individuals *ab extra* an order of laws that is other than the relationships of a community of individuals that issue from the joint natures of the individuals composing it.

In brief, if there be one World-Ground, its nature is expressed precisely in the variety and active movement of finite individuals. The term "universe" means only the actual community of the diversity of an immense multiplicity of finite individuals. It is either an eternally existing community of individuals or it has a ground, an ultimate Individual. The interrelationships of the various orders of individuality (electronic, physical, vital, and spiritual) and their apparent genesis in time point towards one creative and sustaining ground. The conflict and confusion between the orders and within each order (struggle for existence, egoism *vs.* altruism, etc.), make the hypothesis of one ground dubious. There are many considerations that make for a radical pluralism. But I think the truth probably lies between an absolutism such as Bradley's, which also has a strongly pluralistic tinge (his "finite centers" are timeless differentiations of the Absolute), and a radical pluralism.

On the ground that the various orders of individua are interdependent and thus point towards one supreme order and also on the ground that the continuity of meaning and value implies a world goal as now real, a terminus *ad quem* as well as a terminus *a quo*, I elect the mediating position. The real is individual. There is a supreme Individuality, a World-Ground of the orders and self-activities of finite individua. This World-Ground includes the World-Goal— the multifarious and harmonious values and ends of finite individuals.

I do not say that, from factual evidence alone, an idealism of personality and value is the world-view that alone has plausibility, much less compulsiveness. I admit that there are perplexing problems for one who embraces this world-view. And it can no more be explained *why* and *how*, in a world in which value-creating-and-enjoying personality is supreme, the obstructive and oftentimes seemingly destructive blind material forces operate as they do; than it can be explained *why* or *how*, in a world in which blind and insensate event-particles rule and are alone substantial, a realm of culture-creating personalities should arise and appear successful.

Cosmic pluralism is the world-view that best meets all the issues. The members of the world do hang together; but in a loose-jointed way, which permits some free play among them. There is a cosmos only in the sense that its members are in intercommunication; they interact and inter-suffer. All manner of interchanges take place between them; they are dynamic organizations or activity-forms; and not only quantitatively plural, but qualitatively various.

The only world-view in which values and meanings can have a permanently real status is one for which minds, personalities, and their values are supreme. After all, what preferred meaning has materialism, energism, or any other world-view in a riotous chaos of material energies in which all world-views, all ideas, valuations, ends, ideals, and volitions are equally illusory product's of the fortuitous concourse of bare event particles?

The personalist can account for the materialist. He is one whose thought is dominated by mathematico-physical concepts, and by the empirical correlation between the physical and the mental. He takes a set of useful, and so far true, *abstractions* to be the *whole truth* about reality. The materialist cannot explain why and how reason, valuation, and volition should seem to be creative agencies in the world; as they plainly are in the cultural world of human kind. He cannot even account for his own theorizing and theory. He cannot account for anything significant in human culture. For culture, in all its forms, is a creation of mind. It is not dictated by the dance of electron-protons nor by the empirical *milieu*. In the applied arts, manners, morals, social organizations, sciences, fine arts, philosophies, and religions of humanity there have arisen, *in the same physical environment in which the other animals produce no cultures*, all the varied, stately, and changing cultures by which man is man. The existence and career of human cultures in their totality is to me the most convincing evidence that mind is the supreme creative principle. Man is ever creating and re-creating, by the activity of mind, values, purposes, ideals; and forms of social culture, in which he may put these values, purposes, and ideals into good effect. All the institutions and forms of human culture are utterances of self-active spirit, of the creative life of mind.

In certain forms of Personal Idealism the finite self is treated as a tiny Absolute, a kind of self-existent or self-complete spiritual entity. This is just as erroneous a notion as that which regards the self as only a mechanically assembled complex. The finite self is an imperfect developing product of the Cosmic Order. It is the richest concentration of the macrocosmic forces. But it is a dependent member, not a self-existent entity. Its centrality and value lie simply in the fact that it is the richest finite expression of the Cosmic Whole, and that its supreme activating form—individuated reason or spirit—cannot be accounted for in lower terms and, therefore, is the most significant expression of the spirit of the Whole, of the Cosmic Structure. I will put it this way—since the universe gives rise to persons, these must be a revelation of the Nature of the universe. This, of course, is true, but in everlessening degree, of subpersonal individua. And certainly reason or spirit is never anything but individuated. Consciousness, Spirit or Reason *in general* is an empty abstraction. If the Creator be nothing more than a cosmic mathematician, he is no creator.

Finite selfhood is a complex, a composite of many factors. It has many degrees of inclusiveness and integration. The fullest selfhood is a time-spanning and space-binding power. It is freighted with knowledge and insight in regard to nature and humanity, integrated into a living whole. The poorest selfhood is that of an inharmonious complex of impulsions and habits, or partial complexes, that cannot achieve unity and so remains divided or even alienated from itself; arrested in its growth and protecting what it has by a make-believe world of illusion.

Personality or selfhood is always growing and developing. Its basis is a complex organization, a dynamic equilibrium of electromagnetic energies in which emerges the creative organizing form of vitality (if indeed vitality be not present all along). On the basis of this vital organization there emerges reflective mentality—selective and recognitive memory, analytic and synthetic thinking, creative imagination and rational valuation and self-directive choice. The organization is always a moving equilibrium in a *milieu;* never self-complete. The moving end is integration of self by integration with its physical, social, and cosmic *milieus.*

The higher, more inclusive, more creative integrating pattern is not the mere by-product of that in which it emerges. Nor, on the other hand, is it an eternally self-complete monad. It is a supervenient dynamic structure granted, as Lotze put it, by the cosmic *milieu*, to a specific pattern of material and vital organization.

The dynamic pattern, the form of individuality is not something apart from the stuff and the process in which it is expressed. Classical philosophy did tend to separate the forms from the matter and make the forms in themselves transcendent. Just as Energy and Matter are one, so organizing form and process of realization are one. There is no stuff that exists apart from its organization. There is no vital principle other than the immanent dynamic organization of the body. There is no soul or mind other than the immanent dynamic and reflective selective and elective principle of conscious and rational organization.

The older materialism and certain forms of rationalism emphasize structure at the expense of function. Instrumentalism and analogous forms of biocentric philosophy emphasize function at the expense of structure. Function appears as an indefinitely plastic capacity to make something out of nothing. Dualism really rests on the duality of structure and function.

Structure and function are two aspects of the same thing—patterned and organizing activity. Structure is meaningless, except as a definite dynamic pattern of activity or function. Function is nothing except as patterned activity. Patterned processes, varieties of individualities mean structured activities.

This principle must be as true of the whole universe as it is of its various members. If there be an Originating and Sustaining Ground of Individuality, the ultimate Individual, he must be continuously immanent in the cosmic order. He can have no structure which does not function. The only sense in which an Ultimate Individual Whole could be said to transcend the cosmic order is that his organization or structure, which is his immanent nature, in its inner unity must transcend the functioning structures of any, or of the mere sum, of finite individuals. His substance transcends the finite multiplicity only in the sense of being the substantial ground of all finite multiplicity.

It is not the function of a philosophic cosmology to explain the details of phylogenesis nor of ontogenesis. The natural sciences, as evolutionary, can trace and describe a succession of steps. But the emergence of Emergent Evolution, in these latter days, is significant testimony to the inadequacy of any sheer mechanicalism, as the ultimate principle of genesis.

What we find is a hierarchy of individuated forms or structures in manifold interplay. The universe is a richly complex living whole of multiform types of individuality. Mind or Spirit is the most inclusive and self-active form of totality, of organizing individuality; therefore it is the most adequate principle for the interpretation of the meaning of the Whole. In the universe, Life and Mind must always have been present. The universe is too rich to be dissolved into any of the lower categories. The Whole, in its highest and most significant sense, is a community of minds.

Personality cannot be derived from less than itself. "Emergence" does not ultimately account for anything significant. The fullest significance of the universe lies in that it is a *personality-in-community creating process.* The creative ground of the universe must be personal, and how much more we cannot know. But that more must transcend, without annulling, finite personality.

A pantheism which talks of an impersonal Absolute, of which all persons are literally parts, is the most inconsequent kind of attempt to conceive the whole and at the same time provide for the conservation of values.

There are three final metaphysical possibilities: (1) Such an eternalistic pluralism as McTaggart's. This seems to me to suffer shipwreck on the data of creative evolution. If it is the true interpretation, then all the apparent coming-into-being of finite individuated structures is illusory. There can be no genuine emergent evolution nor any genuine significance in the development of the single individual, if all finite individuals eternally exist as such. The history of the world as well as my own history are, in such case, tales without meaning or end. (2) A finitistic theism which recognizes a supreme self as the ground and goal of the lives of finite selves, but not of all that is. This leaves an ultimate rift in the universe between the ground of individuality and value and the tendency that thwarts individuality and value. (3) A theism which makes Deity the Eternal Individual, Creative and Sustaining Ground of all individuality; but recognizes that in his own nature as given there are hindrances to the full realization of individuality. This view has to swallow the problem of evil with as good a grace as possible. The total real is a world of individuals of various kinds and degrees, interacting.

Individuals clash and suffer apparent defeat or extinction in this world. The great enigma is this—individuality is the significantly real and valuable, and yet it seems to suffer shipwreck. Life is struggle, tragedy. The individual seems to be "cast, as aimless, to the void."

A fundamental postulate of idealism is that Nature is organic to spiritual ends.[1] But the trouble is that, evidentially, Nature appears far from being always organic to spiritual ends. Indeed, in the latest theory of the career of the physical cosmos, stars and systems arise through the breaking down of very complex atoms whose constituents vibrate at very high frequency, matter is radiating into space and the world is headed towards heat-death—apparently a process of *de-individuation*. I am not saying this is true for the entire cosmos. Indeed it cannot be; else how could there now be individuals?

What are we to make of the apparent fact that selves are ruined and hence values are lost? The world seems to make for individuality in increasing measure, as we run through the scale of finite being from the atom and the crystal to man and beyond; on the other hand, individuality seems the hapless prey of finite contingent forces. A youth of great promise is snuffed out or goes awry in mental alienation,

---

[1] See Bosanquet, *The Principle of Individuality and Value*, p. 140.

thousands of human beings suffer unmerited destruction or endure unmerited agonies!

There are here two alternatives: (1) Either there is in the universe an unspiritual impersonal surd outside the personality-creating-ground; and against the brute contingent forces the Eternal Ground of Individuality, as well as his offspring and companions, must contend; or (2) there is in the Supreme Self something we do not understand. A "given," as Mr. Brightman puts it, which constitutes the limitation to his and our creative development of individuality. But God must be perfect; otherwise the concept of God is without meaning or use. I conceive of Him as the perfection of personality; therefore finite in that He does not include all that is. The theory that evil is due to the ethical self-limitation of God in order that persons may be self-determining, if presented as a full solution, is mere verbiage. It has a limited area of application. We may say that, just as a human parent must allow a certain range to the child in order that it may grow to maturity by trial and error, so it is in regard to the Supreme Self and man. But this theory fails to account for the pure brute contingencies that seem to ruin human lives. It does not even explain man's inhumanity to man, insofar as this arises from brutish stupidity or sheer mental disorder. It might account for certain forms of intelligent diabolry, but not for the idiot and the dangerously insane. Some evil is a means to good—stimulus and incitement to individual and social effort. Some is due to remediable thoughtlessness. But a large remainder is an impenetrable mass of mystery. To say that the Creator creates wills whose vocation is to be free, is no solution. To create a will is, in principle, to will what that will wills.

If one says, with the Buddhist, that clinging to individual existence is the root of all evil, the answer is that the uprooting of evil is then the extinction of the seat of all values.

In any hypothesis that meets the issue, tragedy and enormous apparent waste are not eliminated. Reality is an arduous process. But it is creativity, issuing in novelties, richer and richer wholes. And the very notion of a creative whole, of novelty, is taken from individuality. Therefore the ground of the Universal Creative Process must be the Eternal Individual or the Over-self.

I come back then to the point that, since the universe, in the increasing manifestations of its nature, shows ascent through increase of significant organized wholes or the continuously creative process of emergent individuals, and since mind is the most inclusive form of totality or individuality, the ground of the whole process is most adequately pictured as mind. But whether the Principle of Individuality is the ground of the entire universe I do not know. A cosmic dualism is a plausible theory. I have no esoteric insight. I can only indulge a reasonable hope, based on the apparent tendency toward Individuality or Personality.

To sum up this discussion: If the world has a meaning, if it sustains real values, the most coherent philosophical doctrine is personal idealism. The principles of individuality and value are one—this implies that spiritual selfhood is a qualitatively unique self-active kind of reality. Simpler forms of individuality interact with it. Mind-body is a dual, yes, a multiple, interactive system, in which the mental self is the ruling principle. The universe is, of course, in some sense one; but it is not one absolute all-including mind or experience. The absolute of absolute idealism must be rejected. It no more provides place for the unique value-reality of selves than does materialism. To say that there is only one ultimately real Individual is, in effect, to de-realize individuality. Since personality is the principle of value, and persons are self-active members of a community, reality in its highest terms must be a community of inter-related selves. The histories of selves have dramatic significance. Reality as an eternal motionless One is valueless, because value-destroying; value-destroying because selfhood-annihilating.

There are two consistent ultimate philosophies: Materialism, which makes individuality and value illusory and unaccountable by-products of the blind fortuitous concourse of atoms; and Personal Idealism, which takes its stand on the reasonable faith that, since the meanings and values of existence reside in individuality, everything in the universe must in the end be subservient to the fulfillment and perduration of personality-in-community. I elect personal idealism; as a hypothesis based on the evident individuation of the empirically real and a postulate based on the faith that the cosmos must have Meaning and must honor Value.

Note. The above essay is a condensed restatement of the metaphysics of my *Man and the Cosmos* with a more pluralistic emphasis. I first formulated this position in 1893–94 in my doctoral dissertation, which was published in 1902, under the title "Typical Modern Conceptions of God." I was led to it by reflection upon the *place of human life* in the cosmos, after a somewhat extensive study of biological evolution and of chemistry. In formulating my theory of individuality, I was much influenced by Plato, Aristotle, Leibniz, and T. H. Green; later I was influenced chiefly by Kant, Hegel, and Bradley, although I never could accept the latter's view of Time and his Absolute. I profited by Royce's *The Conception of God* and *The World and the Individual,* but the latter appeared too late in my development to influence me much. His *Problem of Christianity* is to me his greatest book. I was also influenced a good deal by William James and Bergson.

VIII

THE FINITE SELF

EDGAR SHEFFIELD BRIGHTMAN

Boston University

THE FINITE SELF

Edgar Sheffield Brightman

The problem with which we are now to deal is that of the nature of the finite self. This phrasing is perhaps misleading, for it might suggest some implied infinite Absolute Self as a counterpart to the finite self. But such a suggestion is by no means intended here. The expression is used partly because of its historical place in idealistic discussions and partly to emphasize the finiteness of the selves that we are and associate with. The question of whether there is either an infinite Self or a finite, but supreme, Cosmic Self will be left out of consideration in our treatment of the finite self.

In the light of the general aim of this volume, the intent of the present chapter is to develop an idealistic view of the finite self. In undertaking to fulfill this purpose, we shall seek to analyze and criticize the chief traits of finite self-experience as they have been apprehended by historical idealism. By way of an experiment in testing the validity of the idealistic view, we shall go on to consider some of the main features of the account of the self given by a thinker who is no metaphysical idealist, namely, Franz Brentano. At the end we shall draw such inferences as the facts considered seem to suggest.

I

A preliminary inquiry may render the advance of our investigation more profitable. If we ask what contributions idealists have made toward the discovery of fundamental traits of the finite self, we confront an embarrassment of riches. Not only is there an amazing abundance of material, but also there are amazing contradictions in it. It cannot be said that there is a single consistent doctrine of the self shared by all idealists. However, there are four propositions which conspicuous idealists have held, although relatively few have held consistently and with equal emphasis to all four. The propositions are: (1) The self is a system (organic); (2) The self is a self-existent unity (monadic); (3) The self is conscious experience (mentalistic); and (4) The self is active (activistic).

To say that the self is organic means that every phase and experience of the self is so interconnected with every other in the self as a whole that no single experience can be understood until it is interpreted in the light of its membership in the whole self. The organic idealist would say that it is, of course, possible to describe the phenomena of vision apart from the character and personality of John Jones who sees. Such description is essential to psychology as an abstract causal science. But the idealist would add that complete knowledge of the laws of the phenomena of vision falls far short of giving us an understanding of what any visual experience means to John Jones. When Mr. Jones sees a Chinese character, he is filled with mingled perplexity and amusement. When he sees an English word written by a friend, the whole current of his life is changed. Each of his experiences is affected by the whole of his experience, so that no part is exactly and in all respects what it would be in any other whole. This organic view is characteristic of Hegel, although his interest is more in societies than in finite individuals. It appears in Royce's teleological theory of the self in his Gifford Lectures and more recently in G. W. Cunningham's lectures on the self at the University of Texas. It is, indeed, the most widely agreed on trait of the self among idealists in general. It obviously conforms to the cardinal principle of idealism, namely, that of organic logic. We shall, however, resist the temptation to consider the implications of this logic with reference to the relations of the self to the universe as a whole.

The second trait of the self which we mentioned was the monadic; the self is a self-existent unity. One who describes the self in terms of this proposition has observed that a self is radically different from what we commonly (although, in the last analysis, falsely, as the idealist would say) take to be the character of a physical thing. A thing seems to be made up of separable parts which enjoy an independent existence both before and after their conjunction in what we call a thing. An apple has an aesthetic and organic unity; yet every particle of matter in it existed before it entered into the apple and will continue to exist in some form long after the apple has decayed. But the parts of a self (a mind, I mean, as distinguished from its body) exist only in the unity of the experience of the self to which they belong. A sensation has no continuous existence analogous to that of an atom. It exists only when and as sensed by a self. The organic wholeness previously mentioned can become an actual function only in the concrete unity of the self. Moreover, each self is a unity as distinguished from other selves. It is this trait in particular which justifies us in using the world monadic. It may be that Andrew Seth was one-sided when, in *Hegelianism and Personality*, he made the famous statement that the self is "perfectly impervious . . . , impervious in a fashion of which the impenetrability of matter is a faint analogue." [1] However much supplementation these words may need in order to be a nicely balanced account of the whole truth, they embody admirably one genuine fact about the self. No inspection, observation, or inference can give to the observer such access to a self as that self has to itself in its own immediate consciousness. Each self, then, is a unique unity, a unit that exists only for itself and shares its immediate existence with no other self, although experience shows that it knows and communicates with many other selves. As every student of the history of philosophy is aware, this view received its classical formulation in Leibniz, and a significant re-interpretation by Lotze and, in America, by Bowne. Among others, H. Wildon Carr advocates this insight of idealism. The monadic unity of the self has been most thoroughly attacked by Hume and by John Stuart Mill,

[1] Page 227.

yet each of these men expressed frank misgivings about the success of his attack. The attack in both cases was due to imperfect idealism: an excess of mentalism, combined with a deficiency of organic logic.

Already in discussing the monadic factor we have to some extent anticipated the third trait of the self, namely, that it is conscious experience. This we called the mentalistic trait. Powerful currents of thought at the present time tend to depreciate the fact of consciousness; physiological behavior tends to usurp the place of mind. These currents, as interpreted by organic logic, have not been without influence on some idealists. Nevertheless, the predominant intent of idealism is to magnify the importance of actual conscious awareness. The idealist who does this starts with what he regards as the undeniable fact that consciousness exists and that all statements about what is not the present consciousness of the speaker must find their validation ultimately in some future conscious experience of his. The idealist also believes that consciousness exists only as a self, so that to be conscious means to be a self, and conversely, selfhood consists in conscious experience. Descartes and Berkeley were among the first to call emphatic attention to this aspect of the self. The self is *res cogitans*. With Locke and with Kant there survived relics of the scholastic theory of a substantial soul which is other than the phenomena of consciousness; but in both of these men, especially in Kant, fundamental interest was centered on the analysis of consciousness. In the arch-idealist Hegel, this interest was so highly developed that Professor Theodor Haering has characterized him as the great empiricist of consciousness. Among recent idealists, the late Professor Mary W. Calkins, whose passing is universally lamented in American philosophy, was a conspicuous proponent of mentalism, in the sense defined. We may relate this view to current discussion of the nature of what is given in perception by asserting bluntly of the datum (which has evaporated into the ghostly unreality of essences at the hands of the realists) that this datum is the self.

A fourth trait of the self emphasized by idealists is, as we have said, its activity. Idealists have very generally opposed the view that the mind is a *tabula rasa* and have been critical of all theories which have asserted or tended to assert the passivity of the self in knowledge. The activity of the mind in knowing has been a major theme of idealistic thought, perhaps most conspicuously in Kant and those influenced by him; although interpreters of Kant have varied in their view of the meaning and importance of this activity. But the activistic trait is, according to many idealists, not manifested in knowing alone; they hold that it is the very nature of the self as a whole to be active. For Berkeley the spirit was throughout active. For Leibniz activity was the very essence of the monad. The voluntaristic idealism of Schopenhauer embodied the same insight. Lotze and Bowne and others continued the tradition.

As we said at the start, not all idealists would agree that all the traits mentioned are essential to the self. There is, however, an almost universal acceptance of what we called the organic factor. That factor is perhaps least evident in Berkeley's empirical idealism, yet there are traces of it even there. There is less unanimity about the other traits. Absolutists even incline to believe that there are contradictions between the organic and the monadic views; they hold that the point of view of the whole precludes the ultimate separateness of the monads. It must be granted that complete separateness is impossible. But absolutists and pluralistic idealists differ regarding the nature and degree of the separateness and of the relations among the finite selves. This problem lies beyond our investigation, as does the mind-body problem.

II

More substance may be imparted to the foregoing outline view of the self as seen by idealists if we consider the idealistic account in its distinction from other accounts.

If we ask how an idealistic view of the self is distinguished from other views, it lies close at hand to say that the idealistic view is complete, concrete, whole, while other views are partial and abstract. As Hegel says, "The knowledge of the Spirit is the most concrete, and therefore the highest and hardest."[1] Yet it is doubtful whether this statement would wholly satisfy anyone but an idealist. To be satisfied by it is already to be an idealist! In fact, it might be argued that completeness and wholeness are the common property or at least the common aim of all philosophical thought, so that the suggested criterion fails to distinguish idealistic from other philosophical views of the self.

Postponing for the moment any attempt to differentiate the idealistic from other philosophies of the finite self, we deem it necessary to dwell somewhat on the differences between a psychological and an idealistic view of the self. Both views, obviously, deal with the same self, operate with the same facts, are activities of the same mind. There can, therefore, be no absolute separation between them. It must be confessed that some philosophers (notably logicians and epistemologists) have given the impression that they have enjoyed access to a realm of mind of which the psychologist could know nothing. Their opposition to psychology has savored of incantation. Such excess of abstraction, however useful it may be for some special purpose, can only confuse the essential issues. There can be nothing in the mind that is not psychological fact, although the psychological fact must for many purposes be studied by other methods and with other problems than those of psychology.

It needs, then, to be made clear that the methods of psychology and the methods of philosophical idealism are distinct, although their subject matter, the mind, is identical. The psychologist is primarily concerned with the observation and causal explanation of the experiences of finite selves. Hence his chief interest is in fruitful methods of experimentation and in the data which can be gathered by those methods. The idealistic philosopher, on the other hand, while relying on the psychologist for experimental procedures and their results, differs from the psychologist in having an even greater interest in the presuppositions and implications

[1] Hegel, *Encyclopädie*, § 377.

of experimental method than in the method itself. Moreover, he is concerned to interpret the results of psychological science in at least two ways: First, by relating them to a system of ideal values, that is, by a normative study of the results of psychology. The fact that the norms themselves, as conscious experiences, are subject matter for psychology in no degree lessens the difference which we are mentioning; for the difference in method of studying the same subject matter remains, and differences in method are fundamental. Secondly, the idealistic philosopher aims to relate the whole point of view and field of psychological science to other points of view, such as those of the physical sciences, and also to our non-scientific experience. In so doing idealism stands far closer to actual life than does the point of view of the scientific technician. Science is, for cultivated people other than scientific specialists, a relatively small part of civilized living, and that part chiefly instrumental. Music, art, social organization, recreation, literature, and religion bulk larger than science in the life of most human beings. Idealism, regarding this phenomenon as significant and justifiable, seeks to interpret it.

A mind that finds no problem in the relations between philosophy and science in general, or between philosophy and psychology in particular, must be either singularly placid or singularly provincial. Who can rest content, for example, with the humanly explicable, yet logically indefensible, hostility of experimental psychologists to philosophy, evidence of which fairly peppers the pages of E. G. Boring's *A History of Experimental Psychology?* [1] Indeed, the impression which Boring's book leaves is that, for the experimentalist, interest in his method has run away with every other intellectual interest, so that comprehensiveness of view and even the facts of immediate experience are subordinated to the demands of method. If the act "is a datum that does not lend itself to experimentation" [2] the experi-

---

[1] Edwin G. Boring, *A History of Experimental Psychology* (New York, Century, 1920). Hereafter referred to as Boring, *HEP* (1929). For the hostility of experimentalists to philosophy see pp. 21, 412, 424, 452, 521, 539, 589, 638, 659, 660, etc.

[2] Boring, *HEP* (1929), 442.

mentalist loses interest in it. Important as method is, exclusive interest in any one method is nothing short of intellectual provincialism. Methodological dogmatism is not intrinsically superior to other types of dogmatism. Boring himself sees clearly that reasoning is not secondary to observation [1] and thus holds out an olive branch to philosophy. All this makes clear, I think, that the major problem regarding psychology is not that of psychology *vs.* idealism, but rather that of psychology *vs.* any philosophical criticism at all. The anti-philosophical psychologist has dug a pit into which he will fall.

In addition to the difficulties arising from these general considerations, idealism has to face special difficulties in defining its position relative to certain empirical psychological facts. Idealism deals with wholes, with unitary structures, with coherent meanings. But mind as experience is notoriously disunified, subject to normal and abnormal interruptions, lacking in coherence and meaning. The fragmentariness of consciousness is to many a decisive argument against an idealistic view of mind.

Here, indeed, idealism must despair unless it can find footing in actual psychological experience. If it cannot be shown that ideals of logical meaning actually function, explicitly or implicitly, in all consciousness, and that time-transcendence is an actual property of every mind, binding its seemingly scattered fragments into a unique whole, then idealism fails for lack of a foundation. Hence, while an idealistic interpretation is not the same as a psychological description, it must be emphasized that every idealistic interpretation rests on a psychological foundation. Otherwise what is there for idealism to interpret?

An idealistic account of the self is, furthermore, to be distinguished from the accounts given by non-idealistic philosophers. As we said above, all philosophers agree in their attempt to see the self as a whole. Idealists, materialists, analytic realists, and most pragmatists agree on the view that the world is homogeneous, *i.e.*, that there is no radical

[1] *Ibid.*, 14.

and insuperable distinction between "mind" and "matter." Yet there is a marked difference between the idealistic and the realistic ways of conceiving the wholeness of the self. The essence of this difference may be stated concisely by saying that the realist explains the whole mind in terms of its parts and their relations, whereas the idealist explains all parts and their relations in terms of the whole mind. This formula serves also to distinguish idealism from empiricism and rationalism. Empiricism tends toward an exclusive interest in terms (and when it includes relations, tends to view them as if they were kinds of particular terms). Rationalism tends toward an exclusive interest in relations (and when it views terms, tends to view them as if they were complexes of universal relations). Idealism seeks to understand terms and relations through their membership in a concretely whole self which is a universalizing particular.

It cannot, however, be denied that the idealistic view contains distinctions within itself. We may best state these distinctions by referring back to the traits of the finite self to which idealists have called special attention. Substantially all idealists agree, as we have already said, that the self is organic. But there are at least two issues on which idealists differ among themselves. The first is that of monadism vs. absolutism. The monadist regards the separateness and privacy of each individual self as an ultimate trait of the world; he therefore inclines to some type of quantitative pluralism, yet recognizes some sort of interrelation among the plural monads. The absolutist holds that the many finite selves are members of one Absolute Self, and so are not ultimately separate or private; he therefore inclines to what James Ward has called singularism, yet seeks to provide for the many selves within the one. It seems to the present writer that this issue is indissolubly connected with that between epistemological dualism and monism. Idealistic epistemological monism—the doctrine that the object is immediately present as idea—leads straight to the Absolute Self; but if epistemological dualism is true (and I believe that

A. O. Lovejoy's Carus Lectures [1] have conclusively proved it to be true), then the absolutistic view is practically excluded and the monadic becomes possible. The second issue among idealists is that of mentalism *vs.* logism (as it may be called). The mentalist finds the essence of mind to consist in and to be inseparable from conscious awareness. The logist is less interested in consciousness than in logical wholeness, and he speaks more of system and of transcendental, extra-psychological egos than of mind as consciously experienced. Logism has sometimes generated a fine contempt of empirical fact and of individual selves.

My own bias in favor of monadism and mentalism is perhaps too evident from my statement of the issues. But the reader who is warned of this bias will be able to evaluate it more successfully and will be prepared to consider some reasons for preferring one member of each pair of alternatives which will appear in the course of the chapter to the other.

III

An idealist should be even more alert to the defects of idealism than any external critic could be. It may help us to understand the finite self from the idealistic standpoint if we consider some of the respects in which the idealistic vision has failed of realization. That vision may be stated simply: The self is a genuinely organic unified whole. In all its variety and change, it is one. A writer so remote from idealism as E. G. Boring makes the somewhat sweeping statement that "the unity of the soul has been an echo from Aristotle to Descartes, from Descartes to William James, and is today the central dogma of *Gestalt* psychology." [2]

It must be admitted that, while idealists of almost every type have asserted the unity of the self, they have failed to frame a theory of that unity which consistently lives up to initial expectations. The dualism which runs through Plato's whole philosophy infects also his view of the soul, despite his

[1] Arthur O. Lovejoy, *The Revolt against Dualism* (Chicago, Open Court Publishing Co., 1930).
[2] Boring, *HEP* (1929), 156.

conviction of its unity. Aristotle set the νοῦς ποιητικός apart
from the rest of the mental life, so that it alone was immortal,
but doubtfully personal and doubtfully related to sense and
to individuality. Berkeley placed passive and inert ideas
in active spirits, without welding, or apparently feeling the
need of welding, these refractory elements into a living whole.
Kant came nearer to the goal than did Plato, Aristotle, or
Berkeley; but for all his transcendental unity of apperception, he falls short of genuine unity in at least three points:
the manifold of sense with which the categories have to deal
seems to have in itself a Humean discreteness; the speculative and the practical reason are not sufficiently unified by
the assertion of the primacy (and immortality) of the practical (as contrasted with Aristotle's primacy and immortality
of the speculative); and the unity of consciousness is reduced
to an *als ob* status which is far from satisfactory.[1] Hegel
was too much concerned with the social and the absolute
to pay sufficient attention to the problem of the finite individual. Schopenhauer's preoccupation with the will blinds
him to the empirical details of consciousness and the unity
of the whole self. Fichte's preoccupation with the epistemological subject-in-general causes the treatment of the finite
self at his hands to suffer; logism crowds out monadism and
mentalism.

In short, the very nature of reason, which is the principle
of unity, has been fated to prevent the attainment of unity.
Reason proclaims its utter superiority to sense, its universality and so its independence of the empirical self, and its
own complex structure as both speculative and practical.
These three interests of reason have stood in the way of its
interest in the unity of the finite self, and therefore idealism
has, to a degree, frustrated itself.

Yet the conception of organic wholeness, which is the
cardinal principle of idealism, contains the cure for these
ills, if it be applied rigorously to the problem of the self. The
finite self is a genuine whole, an experienced unity, in which
reason and sense are inseparable aspects of one indivisible

[1] K d r V, A 672 [Sup. 54].

mind. That mind may be studied from many points of view; but it is one and the same mind whether empirical or transcendental questions are asked about it. Even so clear an idealistic thinker as H. J. Paton breaks down the living unity of the self when he continues the traditional confusion by distinguishing the subject-self from the object-self, or the empirical self from the transcendental self.[1] If idealists were to speak of empirical aspects or problems and of transcendental aspects or problems, constantly making clear that both types of aspect and problem refer to one and the same identical finite self, then thought would become less ambiguous, idealism would be more consistent, and much confusing, half-intended hypostatization would be avoided.

But if this program were carried out, what a revision of terminology would ensue! Instead of "consciousness in general" we should have "principles common to all finite selves." Instead of the "pure ego," that strange being which has engendered far more nonsense than sense and which stands in a very vague but very superior relation to the empirical ego, we should speak of "certain rational functions of the finite self, considered apart from sense experience." It would become unambiguously clear that the "pure ego" and the "empirical ego" are experiences of the same finite self, namely each and every normal finite self in the known world. Moreover, the careful idealist would avoid speaking of an "epistemological subject," for he would not wish to give the impression that this subject is a different being from the psychological subject. Rather, he would make clear that the subject in all its functions is one and the same self, considered from the standpoint of different scientific problems. In short, he would recognize that Experience exists only in experience; that real consciousness exists only as real selves. Thus idealism would come to have a more adequately empirical cast. While retaining its organic logic, it would become explicitly monadic, and thus might tend toward an organic pluralism.

[1] H. J. Paton, "Self-Identity," in *Mind*, 38 (1929), 312–329, especially 316–317.

IV

Thus far we have been looking into the problem of the self from a particular idealistic standpoint. As was indicated at the outset, we are now going to submit the idealistic view to the test of considering it in relation to Franz Brentano's theory of the self. He is a peculiarly appropriate thinker to bring on at this point. On the one hand he is an Aristotelian, who is out of sympathy with modern idealism, notably with that of Kant and Hegel. On the other hand, he has avowed a certain relation to idealism. " My standpoint in psychology is the empirical; experience alone is my teacher. Yet I share with others the conviction that a certain ideal view is well to be reconciled with such a standpoint." [1]

Brentano is but little known in America, partly because he was not an experimentalist in psychology and partly because the bulk of his work is still in process of posthumous publication. A word about his personality would therefore be appropriate. His life was marked by three great crises in each of which he exhibited a high degree of practical idealism. In 1873, at the age of 35, he resigned his professorship and his priesthood in the Roman Catholic Church. He had been appointed to his chair as a priest and had written against the doctrine of papal infallibility. His double resignation was a result of his unwillingness to conform to the decree of the Vatican Council in support of that doctrine. In 1880, having fallen in love with a Roman Catholic woman whom he desired to marry, he found himself confronted by an Austrian law prohibiting the marriage of a Catholic with a former priest. He then resigned his new professorship, withdrew entirely from the church, and

[1] The quotations in the text will be derived from the following volumes; the translations are made by myself.

Franz Brentano, *Psychologie vom empirischen Standpunkt* (herausgegeben von Oskar Kraus).

Erster Band (Leipzig, Felix Meiner, 1924). Hereafter referred to as *PES*, I (1924).

Zweiter Band, *Von der Klassifikation der psychesihen Phänomene* (Leipzig, Felix Meiner, 1925). *PES*, II (1925).

Dritter Band, erster Teil, *Vom sinnlichen und noetischen Bewusstsein* (Leipzig, Felix Meiner, 1928). *PES*, III, 1 (1928).

The specific quotation referred to by this note is from *PES*, I (1924), 1.

left Austria, in order to marry the woman of his choice. At the outbreak of the World War, having the convictions of a pacifist, he moved to a neutral country, Switzerland, where he died in 1917, in voluntary exile. He displayed in his intellectual life the same sturdy consistency that he manifested in his practical conduct.

Brentano is worthy of our attention on account of his influence. Since the great post-Kantian era, Lotze, Brentano, and Dilthey are perhaps the chief names in modern philosophy. To say Lotze is to call to mind Bosanquet, Royce, Bowne, Ladd, and many others. Dilthey's name calls up the whole *geisteswissenschaftliche Schule* and the renewal of interest in Hegel. But Brentano has had an even more impressive following, at least in German and Austrian philosophy. Under his instruction came Meinong, Ehrenfels, Kraus, Kastil, Külpe, Heidegger, Husserl, and others. Oddly enough, Husserl, the most prominent thinker of contemporary Germany, was regarded by Brentano as one of his least promising pupils. Brentano's influence bids fair to be further extended by a translation of his works into English which is now in preparation.

We shall confine our attention to his theory of the self, which is best known to English readers through the misleading over-simplification in Bertrand Russell's *The Analysis of Mind*. Disregarding Russell's treatment, let us proceed to look into his account of the self.

By way of introduction, one or two general traits of his theory should be noted. His empiricism means that he thinks concretely, in terms of actual experience. He has a predilection for the actual, a feeling for the real, which many professional realists seem to have lost. Hence he has no sympathy with realistic attempts, whether by his followers or others, to construe the mind in terms of ghostly essences or substanceless subsistents. The mind is *Sein, Reales, Wirkliches;* the self is "der ein Reales Vorstellende." [1] In his latest phase, Brentano entirely denies the existence of unreal objects of consciousness, *irrealia*, and,

[1] *PES*, I (1924), lxvi.

in thus criticizing Meinong and Husserl, by anticipation criticizes much of American neo-realism.

Moreover, his view aims to bring out the unique properties of mind. He is no reductive thinker, seeking to prove consciousness to be a form of something else. Hence he opposed those who, like Maudsley, aimed to base psychology on physiology and to show that consciousness was not essential to mind.[1] He distinguished psychology sharply from physiology, and also from the sciences which can use mathematical methods.[2]

All of this is, in a general way, in harmony with certain forms of idealism. There are, however, definitely anti-idealistic currents in Brentano's thought. He makes a sharp, dualistic distinction between psychical and physical phenomena, using the distinction, it is true, to vindicate the non-spatial character of consciousness.[3] But the idealist would find such a Cartesian view of the relation of mental and physical phenomena artificial and unintelligible.

In another direction, Brentano's psychology stands in opposition to idealism. He holds, namely, to the belief that what he calls "descriptive psychology" not merely reveals the facts and causal laws of consciousness, but also leads to the discovery of *a priori* intuitions. Now Kantian idealism rests, of course, on the recognition of the *a priori*. But the Kantian *a priori* must in some sense be "deduced," while the *a priori* of Brentano is an intuition, which is "evident," because it is an ultimate presupposition of all proof, itself incapable of being proved.[4] Yet, while this seems to be close to a logical atomism of first principles, it is not sure that Brentano's real intent is very remote from that of organic idealistic logic; for, in discussing the intuitive "evidence" of inner perception, he says, "Whoever might wish to attack this ultimate foundation of knowledge would find no other on which to erect a structure of knowledge." "A structure of knowledge" (*Gebäude des Wissens*) seems to imply the idealistic principle of the whole,

[1] *PES*, I, 7, 79, 81–82.   [3] *Ibid.*, 124.
[2] *Ibid.*, 100–102.   [4] *Ibid.*, III (1928), 1–2.

and to admit left-handedly that unprovable intuitions must be proved by their relations to the whole of which they are essential members.

A further trait of Brentano's psychology which is at least not typically idealistic is its marked interest in classification. The idealist is more concerned to grasp the unity of the self than its constituent elements; he regards the search for such elements as based on an abstract method of analysis which is useful in many respects, yet not fruitful in leading to a concrete understanding of the self. But Brentano makes the search for "fundamental psychic elements" one of the first and universally important tasks of psychology [1] and devotes to it the entire second volume of his *Psychologie*.[2] Yet here also his treatment is very much less atomistic than his language would imply. His analysis leads neither to "neutral entities" nor to sensations as professional sensationalists view them, but rather to "representation, judgment, and feeling (including love and hate and will)," which he regards as a division far superior to the thought-feeling-will analysis which has dominated thought since Kant. The details of his discussion here need not detain us. There are, however, certain important points to note. Every moment of consciousness includes all three. Moreover, the three are interdependent. Judgment presupposes representation, and feeling both of the others. The outcome of this analysis is more nearly an emphasis on mind as system than it is on the elements as independent. Brentano goes on to carry out an idealistic speculation on the basis of his analysis when he develops certain aspects of his theory of value. "The highest perfection of the representing activity lies in the contemplation of the beautiful. . . . The highest perfection of the judging activity lies in the knowledge of truth. . . . The highest perfection of the loving activity, finally, lies . . . in the practice of virtue or of the love of the good for its own sake. . . . The ideal of ideals consists in the unity of everything true, good and beautiful." [3] There is but a step from

this to metaphysical theism, a step which he defends in
full detail in his great work, *Vom Dasein Gottes.* The resemblance to the idealistic thought of Lotze's *Microcosmos*
is evident.

V

We have seen that Brentano does not consider himself an
idealist and yet that some of his utterances intended as anti-
idealistic are in substance less so than at first appears. Now
we turn to a closer consideration of some of the main points
in Brentano's theory of the self, looking for their relation
to an idealistic view.

Perhaps the most fundamental proposition of Brentano's
psychology is his thesis that consciousness is given fact.
"What we perceive with immediate evidence is something
psychically active, that Descartes designates in the widest
sense as 'thinking.'" [1] This given in all perceiving is not
merely an object, although all consciousness refers to an
object, but is a self. In a sense, he tells us, "every observation is aimed at ourselves. He who analyzes a complex
sound apperceives really constituents of himself as a hearing being. He finds that in being one who hears a complex
sound, he is at the same time one who hears this or that tone.
There is no sound at all." [2] Here is not only an idealistic,
but specifically a personalistic or self psychology. It is
peculiarly interesting to find him combining, as most idealists do, the subjective nature and immediacy of consciousness with its objective meaning and reference.

While his interest in this objectivity leads him to attack
the Kantian theory of phenomena, it is noteworthy that
his substitute for that theory consists in a more-than-
Kantian emphasis on the reality of the individual self as
bearer of phenomena, perhaps an unconscious return to
the first edition of the *Critique.* "The so-called phenomenal
existence of anything," says Brentano, "amounts to nothing else than that there exists a real being who represents
it, intuits it, and so refers to it psychically. With the dis-

appearance of the knowledge of something really existent, that so-called phenomenal existence necessarily disappears." [1]

The self (to use my own language rather than Brentano's) not only is a datum, but also is the only datum. "Beyond ourselves as psychically active beings we have no immediately evident knowledge of any fact." [2] "Inner perception is really the only perception in the true meaning of the word." [3] This is not intended in any way to deny the validity of external perception. It is Brentano's explicit view that a double object is present in all sensation—an outer as well as an inner—but that the outer is never given in isolation from the inner. [4]

This emphasis on the self as given in all consciousness stands in a somewhat curious relation to his Aristotelian-scholastic heritage of a substantial soul. In his earlier phase he holds to the great importance of such a substantial soul, because the truth of the belief in immortality seems to be at stake. [5] Yet in his later view he holds that this psychical substance is perceived and is not a transcendent assumption. [6] In other words, he abandons the Lockean for the Berkeleian view of substance—a greater change than is commonly recognized by those who contend that Berkeley retained spiritual substances, for Berkeley transformed the meaning of the category of substance from that of an X-substratum to that of active spirit. At any rate, Brentano was wise enough not to allow his theory of substance to interfere with his study of the conscious self.

We have been saying that Brentano holds to a direct and immediate knowledge of self. The status of the self in his thought may be brought out more clearly by amplifying his distinction between direct (*modo recto*) and indirect (*modo obliquo*) knowledge. *Modo recto* we know only ourselves, as perceiving, loving, etc. Everything beyond ourselves

[1] *PES*, III, 5.
[2] *Ibid.*, I (1924), 4.
[3] *Ibid.*, 128. See article "Innerer Sinn" in Eisler's *Kantlexikon*.
[4] *Ibid.*, III, 1 (1928), 37.
[5] *Ibid.*, I (1924), 15, 16, 21, etc.
[6] *Ibid.*, notes on 257, 258.

which we have as object we know *modo obliquo*.[1] Brentano
correctly points out that there is a tendency in Kant to
hold that all knowledge is *modo obliquo*. This tendency is
a weakness of organic logic which monadism aims to correct. A delicate point is involved in Brentano's view that
consciousness is a *Beziehung*, but not a *Relation*.[2] This I
paraphrase by saying that consciousness is a relating person, not a relation among impersonal terms. All knowledge
modo obliquo is thus an act of a relating person.[3] Hence
Brentano is plainly sympathetic with mentalistic and activistic views of the self.

To say that knowledge is an act of a person leads our
thought to the best-known aspect of Brentano's psychology,
a doctrine logically affiliated with one type of idealism,
namely, his theory of the act. This doctrine is simply the
proposition that "consciousness," "psychic phenomenon,"
and "psychic act" are synonyms.[4] All consciousness is
activity. This view of Leibniz and of Lotze has had a
marked influence on psychology through Brentano. The
analysis of this doctrine in detail would lead us too far afield
for our present purpose. Suffice it to say that it is central
for Brentano.

Not only is consciousness directly perceived as act, but
for Brentano consciousness is always a unity. All psychic
phenomena are "part phenomena of a unified phenomenon
in which they are contained."[5] The psychic datum is not
a Collective, but a Real Unity.[6] This unity is involved in
and demonstrated by all knowledge of comparisons and of
relations and of simultaneity.[7] He brings out a point vital
to the idealistic view of mind when he asserts that the unity
of consciousness implies neither simplicity nor indivisibility.[8]
In this connection he shows that a real unity may be complex, so that one may speak of its various aspects as "divi-
sives," which exist only as members of the unity.

This emphasis on the unity of consciousness brings him

[1] *PES*, III, 1 (1928), 37–44
[2] *Ibid.*, XLV.
[3] *Ibid.*, 42.
[4] *Ibid.*, I (1924), 142.
[5] *Ibid.*, 136.
[6] *Ibid.*, 222.
[7] *Ibid.*, 226–228.
[8] *Ibid.*, 243. Cf. Aristotle, *Metaph.* A, 7.

much nearer to the organic principle of idealism than do some other currents of his thinking. For instance, it leads him, as we have already seen, to overcome in a measure the apparent atomism of his classification of conscious phenomena. He speaks of the three basic classes as intimately interwoven with each other. There is no psychic act in which all three are not represented. Judgment presupposes representation and love presupposes judgment.[1] Yet this interrelationship, it must be admitted, falls considerably short of the idealistic conception of the self as an organic whole. Brentano sees the self to be a complex unity. He does not see so clearly the truly systematic character of that unity.

The theory of judgment stands in close relation to the theory of the self. Since the self is, for Brentano, a unity, one would expect him to view the judgment as a unitary act of a unitary self. That is, one would expect him to be more sympathetic with an organic than with an atomistic logic. We have, it is true, found a certain tendency to atomism in his theory of intuition and there have been few indications that he grasped explicitly the logic implied by his view of the unity of consciousness. Yet his theory of judgment shows "a nisus toward totality" which is significant. Like idealistic logicians, for example, he is critical of the traditional view that a judgment consists merely of a combination of concepts. This traditional view he ascribes to an accident of linguistic form rather than to the nature of thought. A judgment, in its true meaning, is the conscious act of acknowledgment (*Anerkennen*) or rejection (*Verwerfen*) of something (*etwas*).[2] This is not unrelated to Bradley's view of judgment as description of reality. The theory of the *Urteilsakt* as *Glaubakt* (act of belief) or *Anerkennen* is also related to W. M. Urban's use of the term "acknowledgment" in *The Intelligible World*,[3] although Urban seems not to mention the relation. We may paraphrase Brentano's view by saying that the judgment is an act of

[1] *PES*, II (1925), 125–128.
[2] *Ibid.*, I (1924), 125, 200–201, 255n.
[3] Wilbur M. Urban, *The Intelligible World* (New York, Macmillan, 1929).

the unitary self-consciousness in which it acknowledges or rejects something.

This view of judgment must be taken in connection with the theory of knowledge in order to make the status of the self fully clear. Earlier in this chapter we pointed out certain issues on which idealists differ, namely, monadism *vs.* absolutism and mentalism *vs.* logism. It is evident that monadism and mentalism ascribe a greater significance to the empirical finite self than do absolutism and logism, which often tend to lose the self in the larger whole to which it belongs. It is arguable that the finite self may not be "lost" in all forms of absolutism; yet, as we have pointed out, the status of the self is much more secure under epistemological dualism than under monism. If monism be true, then ultimately the self is identical with its objects, be those objects mental or non-mental; and a complete description of the objects of self would leave no place for the finite self as a constituent of reality. But if dualism be true, the knowing self is always other than the objects known, and consequently the realm of finite selfhood is secure.

Brentano places himself squarely on the side of epistemological dualism and so on the side of the rights of finite selfhood. To this end he avails himself of the scholastic phrase, "the intentional (or mental) inexistence of an object," by which is meant *reference to* an object. This objective reference, he says, is an exclusive peculiarity of psychic phenomena; the physical realm contains nothing like it.[1] Brentano's refusal to assimilate knowledge to models furnished by the physical sciences is significant for his affinity with idealism.

Brentano distinguishes between what is represented (*das Vorgestellte*) and the act of representing (*das Vorstellen,* which is a *Vorstellung,* a pyschic phenomenon).[2] The so-called secondary qualities, such as color, belong to the act. "I do not know that color is, but that I represent or intuit color."[3] Considerable confusion has arisen from Brentano's unfortunate early tendency, in speaking of *das Vorgestellte,*

[1] *PES,* I (1924), 124-125.
[2] *Ibid.,* 111-112. There is an interesting relation here to Lloyd Morgan's *-ing* and *-ed.*
[3] *Ibid.,* III, 1 (1928), 4.

to use object and content as synonyms. He himself has admitted that it was poor usage.[1] It has led Bertrand Russell and others to suppose that "content" meant an aspect of consciousness to be distinguished both from act and from object. If this had been his view, it would have been hard to reconcile with the unity of consciousness and impossible to reconcile with his theory of mind as act. But content is, for Brentano, no part of consciousness. It is simply the object referred to. The notion of a "content" which while in mind is yet not mental, is, as Professor Mary W. Calkins once remarked, a source of many evils in psychology and philosophy. Brentano's language, but not his thought, may have been partly to blame for these evils. His intent was always to assert that the mind in its acts refers to objects (contents, things). Content is that to which mental acts refer. In other words, Brentano was an epistemological dualist. For our purposes it is not necessary to inquire into the metaphysics which he adopted; for epistemological dualism is metaphysically neutral and is as consistent with an idealistic view of the object as with a dualistic ontology.

VI

We have found in Brentano an excellent illustration of several idealistic principles. His view of the self is primarily mentalistic and activistic, and is in principle monadic. In spite of his emphasis on the unity of consciousness, he falls short of a clear apprehension of the organic nature of the self.

After our study of the self through the eyes of Brentano, a few concluding reflections on an idealistic view of the finite self may be in order. We have said that the self is organic, mental, monadic, and active, and that the organic principle is the governing one, the cardinal principle of idealism. This may now be illustrated by showing how each of the other traits embodies the organic.

To say that the self is mental or essentially conscious is to lay stress on the temporal aspect of the self. Conscious-

[1] *PES*, Brentano's last edition of 1911, 39n. Cf. *PES*, I (1924), 174.

ness is always a process in time, whether its experience has
spatial form and reference or not. Yet the idealist has usually dwelt on the eternal and the time-transcending features
of experience. If the idealist is sufficiently empirical, however, he will perceive that time-transcendence is not a denial
of time, but is both a fact of temporal experience and a logically necessary condition of it. All mental existence is complex and every field of attention is a flowing stream or moving whole, such that in one mental act conscious events are
apprehended which actually succeed each other by the clock.
The field of attention, from this point of view, is often called
"the specious present." Royce called it the time span. This
really means that for time to be experienced at all, the mind
must be able to grasp successive times, not at one time
(which would be logical and psychological nonsense) but
in one mental act. This given fact of time-transcendence is,
as idealists have often pointed out, also logically necessary;
for if successive instants were not present to a mind that
included and transcended them, no experience of time could
arise at all. Experience would be a changing but timeless
present. In other words, the temporal structure of mind as
conscious experience is that of a system or organic whole,
in which the parts (the successive events) derive their
meaning from the whole (the time-transcending act of the
mind).

Regarding the monadic aspect of mind in this chapter
our attention has been directed especially to its unity. It is,
however, to be noted that there are many varieties and degrees of unity. The minimal unity of a self is the unity of
self-identification, *i.e.*, the fact that all experiences of a self
belong to that self and to no other. But such unity is barren.
A self is significant in proportion as it achieves meaningful
unity through rich systems of moral activity or aesthetic
appreciation within the limits of self-identity. To bare experience a kind of unity is given, or, to use a Kantian term
in a somewhat non-Kantian sense, *gegeben*. But unity is also
aufgegeben, as an ideal to be achieved, a task to be performed.
Following Brentano's classification, we may say that higher

unities of representation, of judgment, and of love always lie ahead. But these unities find their realization in and derive their actual unity from the fact that they are the experiences of one monad. Whatever the objective significance of conscious structures may be—and this I am not now concerned to interpret and much less to deny—their subjective significance is undeniably dependent on their presence and psychological interconnections in one mind, although the bare fact of mental unity is admittedly barren of significance. This interrelation between unity and variety and among different forms of unity further illustrates the organic nature of the finite self.

The self, we have said, is also active. Yet common sense and reflective thought alike have difficulty with the concept of activity. Some have even found it more natural to think of the mind as passive in knowledge than to think of it as active. Is not the self at its best when it is receiving truth and mirroring reality without any activity of its own to distort its objectivity? Must not the self feed on its environment and receive far more than it gives? "What am I," asked Augustine, "but what I have received?"

These considerations lead to a revised statement of the activity of the self. It seems that the activity of mind is never pure, wholly self-determining, or self-creating action. Rather it is the selecting or forming of a conscious content that is given.[1] This content is conscious experience and is an inseparable part of the very structure of mental action, yet it is not produced by that action. Brentano cites the intuiting of color as a mental act. The mind must indeed *do* something in order to apprehend color as such; yet redness is surely no product of will or of mental activity. Here, again, the organic nature of mind is illustrated; for the indissoluble union of act and content in one conscious experience which is evidence both of a self to which it belongs and a world to which it refers is another instance of an organic whole.

[1] The use of the word "content" here is sharply to be distinguished both from Brentano's identification of content with object and from the use which Miss Calkins condemned. It is a constituent, but not a product, of mental activity.

This discussion has made evident how incomplete a treatment of the self must be apart from a consideration of the world to which it belongs, yet has also shown that the self has a structure of its own which corresponds to the main insights of idealism.

IX

GOD AND COSMIC STRUCTURE

JOHN ELOF BOODIN

University of California at Los Angeles

GOD AND COSMIC STRUCTURE

John Elof Boodin

It is a momentous venture to attempt to frame an hypothesis of the universe. But if we reflect upon the meaning of life, we are forced to make such an effort. The only way we can escape the responsibility is to be guilty of the great refusal—the refusal to think. If we frame an hypothesis, it should be such as to assign the proper significance to all the facts of human experience—not merely the physical facts but the biological and mental as well; not merely our scientific interests, but our aesthetic, ethical, and religious interests as well. And it should do so in the simplest possible way. It would be futile and impossible to examine all possible solutions. Henri Poincaré proved long ago that if there is one explanation of a class of phenomena, there are an infinite number of explanations. We must follow the example of science and work out from the significant efforts in the past. We must try to discover the hypothesis which is most probable. In general we may say that the theories of the universe fall under two fundamental types. One type starts with the assumption that the world is a shifting heap of elements, which arrange themselves by external relations. This type of theory denies any guiding whole, whether in the small or in the large. The opposite type of theory presupposes that the events in the universe are guided by form or pattern. In a broad sense it assumes that the universe is in some sense organic, *i.e.*, that the activities of the parts have reference to one another and to the whole in such a way as to supplement one another and to promote the continuity and harmony of the whole, though the indeterminacy and inertia of the parts limit the realization of such harmony in our world of change.

We may assume the doctrine of evolution "in the broader

sense of the continuity of the physical universe throughout all time, and the orderliness of the processes of change which go on unceasingly. Every physical unit which we recognize in nature—electrons, atoms, crystals, cells, stars, galaxies— has at some time come into existence and at some time in the future will pass out of existence; and furthermore the manner of their coming and going is quite orderly, and, within certain limits, is even predictable."[1] But we must keep in mind that nature is not just one evolution "from the homogeneous to the heterogeneous with the corresponding dissipation of motion," as Herbert Spencer conceived it and as it has been the custom to conceive it. Even S. Alexander, in his *Space, Time and Deity*, thinks of evolution as one process where everything, including Deity, emerges from an original matrix of Space-Time. Alexander's Deity is earth-born. To conceive of evolution as one history is to think of it as a finite drama, where the curtain is rung up on an original distribution of elements—however they be conceived—and is rung down with the dissipation of the available energy. This leaves the beginning and the end in the dark. Evolution as science conceives it, on the basis of the available facts, is multiple. There are an indefinite number of cosmic histories at various stages of integration. In some way these histories must sustain a give-and-take relation to one another, so that the available energy is kept constant. Running up and running down, expansion and contraction are relative, depending upon the frame of reference. For we do not conceive of the cosmos as running down, though we know that individual parts run down. The cosmos must be conceived, not merely as a dynamic equilibrium, but as a living dynamic equilibrium of such structure or "curvature" that the loss of available energy in one part is compensated for by an equal increase elsewhere, for only a living equilibrium can be self-sustaining. This conception of equilibrium must apply to the organization of energy as well as its intensity. Energy apart from organization is an abstraction. There is not *one* evolution, but an indefinite

[1] Professor W. D. MacMillan, *A Debate on Relativity* (Open Court, 1927), p. 118.

number of local evolutions, with compensations amongst
them. This is implied in our conception of the universe as a
going concern.

The real question then is not, What does evolution in general mean? The cosmos as a whole does not evolve. The question is rather, What does local evolution mean? And the
local evolution of which we are a part, *viz.*, the evolution of
our earth, has naturally a special interest for us. The theory
of "strict emergence" holds that new forms, characteristics,
events, arise from a state of affairs in which these novelties
did not exist; and this happens without any guidance whatsoever, immanent or transcendent. According to the probability of chance, if you shuffle certain elements, any combination can occur in infinite time. To be sure, science does
not allow infinite time for the cycles which it studies. On the
contrary, evolution in any one cycle, including an astronomical cycle, takes place in a finite and calculable time. But the
emergenist points to the fact that the configurations in question, with their novel characteristics, have occurred. On our
earth such configurations as possess the characteristics of
life and mind do exist. All we need to do is to examine what
sort of configurations give rise to such properties as life and
mind. In this respect emergence is merely descriptive.

The theory of emergence need not commit itself to any
special conception of world stuff. It may, like W. K. Clifford,
start with mind-stuff. It may assume with Haeckel that
the simplest matter is endowed with soul. But the emergence
theory now in vogue calls itself "materialistic emergence,"
which means that everything emerges from "configurations
of matter." This theory owes its precision to the fact that
it assumes the nineteenth century conception of matter and
mechanism. Just now it would not be so easy to say what is
meant by matter and configurations of matter. It is certain
at any rate that the billiard ball model of the seventeenth
century is no longer applicable. Professor R. D. Carmichael
has well summed up the present plight of mechanical materialism: "It is absurd to speak of a mechanical explanation
of life and thought when we have found ourselves in such

difficulties that we no longer know what we should mean by a mechanical explanation of phenomena not invol‧ing life."[1] But, as Hegel with great sagacity observed, when philosophers arrive on the scene, the owl of Minerva has taken its flight.

We may say that "materialistic emergence" owes its plausibility to the fact that it is built on an antiquated science. The conception of the world which is implied in the science of to-day gives the lie to the idea that the world as it is can be accounted for on the probability of chance. On the contrary, it makes necessary the conception of *cosmic control* or *cosmic structure*. The quantum of radiant energy is universally measured. The electron carries a constant charge throughout the cosmos. The shifting of an electron from one energy level to another is constant for the various elements. Hence the identity of the spectra of the various elements wherever observed. The organization of matter is the same everywhere. The atoms have the same patterns and fall into the same natural order everywhere when the conditions permit. The only difference (aside from mass) between our earth and the sun, and between our sun and other stars is a difference in temperature, permitting the organizing process to take place. Matter, moreover, has no privileged character. Matter and the patterns and laws of matter emerge in the various local histories. But there is correspondence amongst emergent histories, and such universal correspondence cannot be accounted for on the probability of chance. The postulate of the uniformity of nature may be predicated throughout, from nebulae to the most advanced types of organization, such as human intelligence. Any *ad hoc* hypothesis which violates the law of the uniformity of nature must be treated as suspect. But the uniformity of nature is possible only because of a universal cosmic control. Moreover, if the stages of nature which we are able to observe, are universal, we are justified in holding that this uniformity of nature holds for evolution at all the stages, though we must allow for variations due to local conditions.

[1] *Op. cit.*, p. 148.

Our information in regard to the structure of nature outside our earth is scanty enough. We have established the law
of the uniformity of nature only within the realm of inorganic
nature. We have no direct evidence of the appearance of life
outside our earth, unless it be on Mars. But the implications
of the evidence, which we do possess, are far-reaching. The
universality of the structure of matter, within the limits of
our scientific observation, shows that the cosmic control
which we must postulate operates as mathematical genius
in the sense that we can discover number and measure in
nature. This means that the laws of logic, whatever they
may be, hold for the entire universe. The human intellect
is at home in nature. "Even inorganic matter," to quote
Trystan Edwards, an artist, "is everywhere subject to the
laws of logic which are essentially intellectual." Moreover,
the architecture of nature is such as to give aesthetic satisfaction. The principles of aesthetics, whatever they are,
may be said to be universal. Cosmic control operates not
only as mathematical genius, but as aesthetic genius. A
scientific hypothesis, to be acceptable, must satisfy not only
the demands of convenience, but our aesthetic demands as
well. Art has its claims as well as science and indeed possesses a logic of its own. While the human mind is a local emergence, it finds that its structure is universal, *i.e.*, it applies
not only locally but everywhere. This is no accident. The
emergence of mind locally may be due to temperature conditions, but its relevance is universal. Hence we must conclude that it owes its character to cosmic genius. We are justified, I think, on the basis of present science in ruling out
emergence by accident, *i.e.*, without cosmic guidance, as
impossible. The uniformity of the constituents of matter
and of the structure of matter could not result on the probability of chance.

If we assume *guidance* in the evolutionary process, we
must try to see how this guidance operates. We need not
here consider fiat creation, such as has been attributed by
theologians to the first chapter of Genesis, since such an
hypothesis cannot be regarded by philosophers as a living

option. There are two types of hypothesis of interest to us—
one is that of preformation and the other that of creation,
i.e., emergence under guidance. Strict preformation means
that the structure of a process in its actuality, as Aristotle
would say, *i.e.*, in its complete stage, must be present somehow in the process from the beginning, in order to guide the
development towards the observed outcome. Preformation,
like emergence, takes a local view. It fastens its attention
on the particular history and holds that the form or structure
of the final stage must have been immanent throughout the
history. The philosopher who is usually regarded as the
author of the hypothesis had in mind exclusively embryology.
For Aristotle, species are eternal. Evolution, therefore,
means individual genesis or ontogeny. Even here individual
characteristics emerge in the process. It is the formative
impulse which is present from the beginning. Aristotle is
not a strict preformationist even in embryology. Hans
Driesch has tried recently to revive the Aristotelian conception by holding that we must assume an entelechy as
guiding the genesis of the embryo. Driesch, like Aristotle,
limits the hypothesis to embryology. He is no clearer than
Aristotle as to how the individual entelechy originates,
though of course in some way it has reference to heredity.
Preformation as a special scientific hypothesis must be fought
out in the realm of science. We are interested in the emergence of structure. This means the relation of the emergence
of structure in the individual to evolution generally, not
merely the origin of species and other structural characteristics of life, but the emergence of life from matter and the
emergence of matter itself, as we know it.

Is it possible that the whole evolution of life with its
branching and radiations and its progressive manifestation
of structure is latent in the first life-compounds and not only
in these but also in inorganic matter back to its primitive
constituents? The Stoics were the only consistent preforma-
tionists in ancient times. The seeds or germinal reasons are
supposed to be latent from cycle to cycle, when everything
returns to fire. But they do not show how the seeds could

be latent. Leibniz in modern times developed a thorough-going preformism both in cosmology and embryology. But in cosmology he required a *deus ex machina* to make his theory possible; and in embryology the microscope has refuted the presence of a homunculus or miniature man in the early stages of embryological history. A recent vitalist, Henry Bergson has, unintentionally I think, offered a suggestion of universal preformation: "Life," he says, "does not proceed by the association and addition of elements, but by dissociation and division."[1] Everything is thus present in the original vital impulse. It is like a rocket shot up in the air which, owing to the resistance of matter, splits up into its manifold inherent impulses, thus giving us the display we see. But matter for Bergson is not real. It is the mere downward trend of life. Reality is fundamentally life and consciousness. Bergson, however, has not seemed to see the implication of his theory of dissociation, or he would have seen its inconsistence with his idea of evolution as creative synthesis. The solution is probably to be found in his pantheism. In a later statement he professes "the idea of a God, creator, and free: the generator at once of matter and of life: whose creative efforts as regards life are continued through the evolution of species and the constitution of human personalities."[2] Bergson has not yet shown us how he would account for evolution on this basis. What is the relation of God to the evolutionary process? If God is eternal, what is his relation to evolution? It was easy for Hegel to say that the absolute is present in the beginning, wherever you begin, because reality is fundamentally a system of dialectical implication and hence eternal. But that does not account for evolution.

We may say, I think, that there is not, at present, a theory of strict universal preformation, *i.e.*, a theory attempting to account for real evolution from nebula to man on the basis of a structure latent somehow in the process from the beginning and only waiting to be called forth under specific

[1] *Creative Evolution*, p. 89.
[2] Letter from H. Bergson, in the *Nation* (London, Jan. 4, 1913). Quoted by Sir Francis Younghusband in his beautiful book, *Life in the Stars*.

conditions. Even if we could conceive of such preformation in individual histories we should still have to account for the intersupplementation of such histories into a cosmos. Leibniz, who did conceive of reality as made up of an infinite number of preformed individual histories (every history having its own entelechy or inner principle of development), was obliged to add the hypothesis of a preëstablished harmony to account for the correspondence of these histories. God, like a clock-maker, constructed the monads so that they would run in unison. But such an appeal to God to make good our failure in scientific theory is out of fashion now.

The theory which I have advocated is that of creation through interaction, under cosmic control. The analogy of reality to an organic whole is not new. It was advanced by Plato in a mythological fashion in the *Timaeus*, and in a simpler and more dogmatic way in the tenth book of the *Laws*. It was stated by Aristotle in terms of a teleological hierarchy, which is also an astronomical hierarchy, in which God is the supreme and final cause. Aristotle's cosmological scheme was revived in scholasticism and formed the framework of Dante's *Divine Comedy*, but its astronomy has given place to the Copernican theory; and its rigid hierarchy of forms has melted into Darwin's origin of species. It does not meet the demands of the epoch of evolution. In modern idealism the essential whoseness of reality has indeed been emphasized. But the wholeness contemplated is that of an eternal, inclusive psychological ego. Modern idealism has been afflicted with psychologitis; and in spite of its great contribution to the interpretation of human institutions, it has failed to connect with the main current of modern thought. We cannot banish the galaxies of stars and their space-time relations by retreating within our own subjective world and declaring matter, time, and space to be mere appearances. No day-dreaming can undo the fact that we have emerged in the history of the earth, which in turn is part of the sun, which in turn is a member in one of multitudinous galaxies of stars. If we are to understand the meaning of our existence, we must understand it in terms

of the whole of which we are a part. If the cosmos functions somehow as an organic whole, the guiding field must
be as wide as the galaxies of stars, and it must explain the
interrelation of the multitudinous cosmic histories, in one
of which our life figures.

An organic whole requires both a control—a genius of
the whole—and interacting parts. We may use the human
organism as a type. In the human organism we have a
hierarchical organization of levels of control in which the
lower levels are subject within limits to a dominant control.
Through this control the parts of the organism are regulated
so as to serve one another and the whole. This wholeness of
the organism is made possible by the interaction of the parts
under the guidance of the dominant control. This interaction
is effected through two kinds of "messengers" or energy
patterns—neural patterns and chemical patterns—which
carry determining influences from part to part. That neural
currents communicate patterns of behaviour to the various
parts of the organism has been known for some time. Chemical patterns are carried by the hormones, probably through
the blood, to regulate the growth and stimulate the energies
of the parts consistently with the life of the whole. But a
human being is not merely a physiological organism. It
is an organism endowed with mind. Its actions are in part
meaningful or purposive, not merely mechanical. This
means a whole-control by mind. The development of mind
in turn involves a milieu of social relations—the interstimulation of individuals by means of language and other
signs. The environment of mind is a social organism. Within
this there is an overlapping of generations so that the new
generation may develop its life under the nurture of older
generations. This is admirably provided for in the family.
There is also the contact of various cultural groups with
their varying advance and varying quality of culture.
In human life, therefore, there is a level of spiritual control
as well as various levels of organic control. And this spiritual control is made possible by the communication of
energy patterns—determinate social influences to which the

individual responds. The response, in the case of interaction on any level, depends not merely upon the character of the stimulus which is communicated but also upon the organization and plasticity of the responding individual. The response is a synthesis of the communicated influence and the character of the responding individual. The control in society consists partly of the consolidated structure of custom, but also involves, at a higher level, the evaluation of the social sanctions in the light of reason. The relation of the individual to society is not a closed control, but is open through reason to revision from a broader relation to the genius of universe.

Now let us think of this vast starry world as analogous to a super-organism of some sort, with a dominant control and with the interrelation of parts by means of interaction. We cannot of course carry over the analogy of the organism literally. The universe may function as a whole under a guiding field without being integrated into a single organism. But in some sense the action of the parts must have reference to one another and to the whole in the vast cosmic drama. The interstimulation from part to part, within the cosmic whole, as within the physiological and the social organism, must be by means of energy patterns, carrying determinate influences from part to part. These determining influences have to do with all the levels— material, vital, mental, spiritual. So far as the universe functions as a whole it must be by such intercommunication. Every part must send out characteristic impulses to the other parts in space under the control of the whole; and no influence is really lost, though the motion at the receiving end is determined in part by the state of affairs at that end. Thus while the correspondence between various cosmic histories seems absolute on the level of atoms, the correspondence must become more generic and variant as the degrees of freedom increase. This we find illustrated in the more complex reactions on our earth and especially in human interactions. I am taking for granted that, when energy is communicated from part to part of the cosmos,

it is not just energy in general that is communicated—
this is meaningless—but that characteristic or patterned energies are somehow communicated. The energies we are
able to observe from other parts of the cosmos are specific
types of material energy or of radiant energy. These types
are communicated as energy patterns. Within the earth-field
of communication we know that the communication of energy
is always the communication of patterned energy whether in
material or spiritual communication. This I have already
shown to be the case in the human organism and in society.
So in the cosmos spiritual patterns as well as material patterns contribute to the steering of things in space-time.

We must get over the false notion that unless we are
cognitively conscious of the communicated patterns they
cannot be real. Neural messengers and chemical messengers
do their work whether we know it or not. It is not long that
we have known of neural messengers; and it is only within
a few years that we have known of the existence of chemical
messengers. Within the psychological realm, suggestion
may operate all the more effectively when we are not at-
tending to the stimulus. Moreover, since spiritual influences
are energies, they must produce effects in the steering of
matter even though there is no organization to respond to
them in kind. The patterned impulse of sound has a characteristic effect on matter even though there be no one to
understand its meaning. As it is by hearing good music
that one becomes musical, so it is by responding to stimuli
of a higher level that a lower level eventually becomes
tuned to them. As it is through the influence of air waves
that the organism is brought to construct an ear, by means
of which we may respond by *hearing sound* instead of merely
getting its electrical impact, so one part of the cosmos is
stimulated to advance by the influence of other parts upon
it, though it cannot become conscious of these influences
in kind until the proper organization has been perfected
for the specific response. And even then we may not be
intellectually conscious. For intellectual communication a
common medium of signs is necessary.

All this may sound like poetry. But conceptions need not be less true because they are poetical. I challenge anyone to form a conception of the universe as an organic whole in any other manner than I have stated. Cosmic control there is, and it must operate through the interaction of parts. In the part of the world of which we know most, cosmic genius is mediated by the interaction of parts—in chemical synthesis, in the origin of a new individual, in the cultural development of individuals. I believe that this is the way in which development is mediated in the life histories of stars and of galaxies of stars. And here too, as in the earthly relations, the response is due to the character and initiative of the responding agent as well as to the stimulus.

The possibility of distant parts influencing one another has been made clearer to us through the quantum theory. The radiations sent out by means of matter over the ether are communicated as quanta or constant finite pulses of energy. They act as the same quanta over any distance, when there is no interference. The number of quanta depends upon the wave length, or rather constitutes the wave length. Each individual impulse, when it strikes matter elsewhere, exerts its original force. A particular impulse of soul may occur at a distance of a million light years, and yet exert its energy undiminished when it strikes matter in any stage of organization elsewhere. It has recently been discovered that living tissue sends out radiations and its wave length has been ascertained. This discovery furnishes a new possibility of accounting for the unity of the living organism. But such radiation does not stop with the limits of the living organism. It must be effective through the whole of space, sending its quanta everywhere to act upon matter as the conditions permit. And mind, the highest organization of living energy, must also send out its radiations through the whole of space to effect results in accordance with the readiness of the recipient—steering the energies of nature towards mental organization under the guidance of the genius of the whole. We have no idea of the penetrative character of mental radiations. We do know that the power of a mental impulse in social communication is not affected by the sense medium. If it passes the threshold of sense at all, it effects its characteristic results. Good news or bad news has its characteristic effect, though the sound be weak. We do not know the effect, upon our mood and attitude, of all the spiritual influences which we do not sense. Here lies the real power of the Weltgeist. In the curvature of cosmic space no influence is dissipated. The quality as well as the quantity of energy is conserved. This is what the law of conservation of energy means in the last analysis.

What is the nature of the whole-control? May it not be merely the automatic result of interaction? Of late, great emphasis has been placed upon the function of the ductless glands, especially the pituitary and thyroid glands, in regulating the growth, proportions and tone of the organism. It has been assumed that the secretions of these glands furnish a sufficient explanation. But the growth, proportion, and health of the organism cannot be merely the result of the automatic interstimulation from part to part within the organism. There must be a control by the whole which regulates the production of glands with their secretions and their rôle in the whole. Else how can the glands know how to grow, what amount of secretion to send out and where to send it? We know that the control sometimes fails and then we have abnormalities. In the universe there must be a control which determines the size of the quantum of radiant energy, the charge of the electron, the organization of electrons into atoms, of atoms into molecules, of molecules into crystals. The whole cosmic situation with its dominant pattern is a factor, though ordinarily a neglected factor, in every transaction. There must be the genius of the whole in all creative synthesis. In our attempt to comprehend nature, this genius must be conceived as mathematical and aesthetic genius. The history of science shows that the hypotheses which are most effective pragmatically in the prediction and control of nature are also the most beautiful, as Sommerfeld has pointed out. This genius of the whole can be best understood if we regard nature as permeated by creative spirit. For this control of the whole cannot be regarded as a function of matter, since matter owes its organization to this control.

The hypotheses of cosmic control and of compensatory interactions between the parts do not conflict, but on the contrary imply and supplement one another. We cannot account for the constituent elements of nature or their structure without assuming cosmic control, nor can we account for the behavior of nature without assuming a plurality of individuals. On the level of matter, it is the cosmic field which determines the constancy of the electric charge and also prescribes the levels at which an electron can appear. These levels are statable as integral numbers. But we cannot predict absolutely at what level the electron shall appear, though it must appear at one of the levels prescribed by the field. It is clear that there is both determinacy and indeterminacy in nature—a structural field which indicates the permissible routes of transformation and a certain indeterminacy of individual reaction. This duality of determinacy and indeterminacy holds throughout nature. There is a determinate pattern of relations according to which we must live, if we want to live healthfully and efficiently. But we need not obey this pattern even when we know it. We cannot say that nature is indeterministic microscopically (*i.e.*, on the primary levels of nature) and deterministic macroscopically (*i.e.*, on the complex levels of nature). This misconception has arisen from the fact that macroscopically we deal with nature by the method of statistical averages, as we do in insurance tables. But statistical averages are not norms of nature. They are merely conveniences for dealing with large numbers where we cannot follow the individual transactions.

We may think of the structure of the cosmos as a hierarchy of fields. We are familiar with such a hierarchy in the human organism. There are the fields of the lower centers of the nervous system; there are also the cerebral fields and the psychological fields. The cerebral fields give definiteness and organization to the lower neural fields, as we see in the difference between the precise and quantitative epicritic reactions, when the cerebrum is in control, and the indefinite all-or-none reactions when the cerebrum fails. The cerebrum with its habits in turn is controlled by dominant interests which give direction and purpose to our activity as contrasted with the chaotic reveries when psychological control is weak. In the cosmos we must suppose a far greater range of fields—electromagnetic fields, gravitational fields, chemical fields, organic fields, psychological fields, and, over and above them all, the supreme spiritual field which prescribes the architecture of all the subordinate fields, each with its variant individual factors. The measure and structure which we find in matter is not due to matter alone. Matter by itself would be as chaotic as the old mechanistic theories pictured it. But it is no longer possible to picture the material world as a world of chance. It is a work of genius. We must not, however, make the ridiculous mistake of looking for this genius in the amorphous background of nature, call it ether or what you like. The genius of nature must be sought in the activity which gives measure and organization to nature, not in its raw material. It is somehow akin to the spiritual activity which we know as creative genius in man but vastly nobler. The beauty of matter and the beauty of art are intimations of its activity, but it is beyond them—ever and everywhere present in activity and essence to create and to heal, but surpassing in quality all that is created.

In trying to picture the control and interrelatedness within the whole in the language of modern science, I have stressed perhaps unduly the analogies borrowed from the physical sciences. If the universe is controlled ultimately by a spiritual field, we must not think of interrelatedness within this field as indiscriminate, mechanical communication from part to part in space and time. We must rather think of the interrelation as mutual adaptation and selection. The target selects the appropriate stimulus, but also the stimulating energies select the appropriate target. They do not hit it by chance. If the cosmos is controlled by a spiritual field, such must be the interrelation even in the field of physical radiation. We know that such is the interrelation on the organic and psychological levels open to our investigation. The interactions within the organism and of the organism with the environment are determined by the unitary life of the organism in its self-maintenance. Energy is not communicated at random but in subservience to the genius of the organism as a whole. In the economy of the organism there is selection of relevant energies. There is suppression of the energies which do not fit into the dominance of the whole, and in this suppression the suppressed energies do not count in the integration unless they are transformed into the control of the whole. Else there would be endless confusion.

Where the control becomes psychological this selection becomes even more obvious. The tendencies which are irrelevant or hostile to the dominant field of interest are suppressed unless they can be sublimated into the dominant pattern. This may be serious for the life of the individual, but it may be necessary for the life of society. If we think of the control of the cosmos as a spiritual field, we must think of this pervasive spiritual control as regulating the intercommunication for the maintenance and health of the life of the whole. We must suppose that the tendencies which are irrelevant or hostile to the spirit of the whole are inhibited or rather held by the gravitation of their own desire in selfish isolation. They fail to seek integration within the spiritual field of the whole and thus cut themselves off from the life of the whole, to run their own tragic course of defeat and disintegration. Only what tends to upbuilding and health can have a part in the on-going spiritual drama. Whatever there is of goodness, truth, and beauty in finite striving becomes immanent in the spirit of the whole and goes on towards its own development and the development of life within the whole. Here lies the secret of salvation and immortality within the spiritual economy of the whole, where individual willingness is an essential condition, but there must also be the abounding grace of the spirit of the whole. Within the unity of the spirit of the whole, effectiveness is no longer measured by distance in space and time. What is immanent in the spirit of the whole is immanent to all the parts that are in spiritual rapport. All the patterns of energy are immanent somehow in this spiritual field and have their characteristic effect in due season when the conditions are prepared.

God is the spirit of the whole which, in the words of Clement of Alexandria, "gives spiritual tone to the universe." For moral and religious purposes we need a cosmic Presence which answers our craving for companionship and communion. This the aesthetic conception of Aristotle did not do and, therefore, it must be re-defined to meet the aching need of the human heart. The God we discover as cosmic control, as mathematical and aesthetic genius, is also a God to whom we can pray and whom we can worship. He must be capable of giving love for love and be willing to pity and pardon our failures. No other idea of God will serve. A universe which meets our intellectual demands shall not fail us in meeting our moral and religious demands. We must remember, however, that this organic conception of the universe places a momentous responsibility upon us for the influences we send out. If no atom can be set in motion without affecting the remotest part of the universe, shall not new impulses in the spiritual field have effect through all time and space? Even now, by sending out noble impulses I may help to save a soul somewhere in the Orion—not to mention some one nearer.

However much the meaning of this life in the whole transcends my imagination, I am certain that in my noblest moments of devotion my soul lives in the spiritual field of the whole and participates in all that is immanent in that field—in the field of life and mind on the earth and in all the life and mind in the cosmos. All that work in the spirit are my comrades and co-workers, however distant they may be in space. As the electron is part of the harmonics of the physical field, so my mind is part of the harmonics of the spiritual field; and it is the harmonics of the spiritual field which in the last analysis determine the harmonics of the physical field. So far as my willingness and insight make it possible, my life is interwoven with the web of the whole under the supreme master genius. If Tennyson's Ulysses could say, "I am a part of all that I have met," I can say, I am a part of all the struggling, suffering, victorious life of the cosmos. With my beloved teacher, Josiah Royce, I believe that I am a member of a universal spiritual community and that it is my vocation to participate creatively with the eternal Spirit of truth, goodness and beauty, in companionship with all spirits that create in like manner, to spiritualize this temporal world. And I take courage from the faith that however confused and discordant the life of this world may seem, there is ever present, like a Pilgrim Chorus, the eternal harmony of the Spirit of the Whole; and the music of this in my soul—distant and faint though it often seems—is the inspiration to strive to bring more harmony into a chaotic world.

X

THE THEORY OF MORAL VALUE

Radoslav A. Tsanoff

Rice Institute

THE THEORY OF MORAL VALUE

Radoslav A. Tsanoff

In the study of human nature, of body and mind alike, understanding of the normal has often been furthered by knowledge of the respective pathology. To Spinoza's mind, truth revealed its own nature as well as that of error; but the opposite is as likely: more tragic and more gripping, evil in disclosing itself likewise points to the nature of good. On the same principle and more obviously, by examining the characteristic defects of the traditional varieties of ethical theory, we may more clearly perceive the demands which an adequate ethics must satisfy.

The broad topic of this essay is thus briefly indicated; perhaps another word will make clearer the problem which prompted its writing and determined its aim. In my recently published work on *The Nature of Evil*, the critical examination of pessimism and theodicy in the history of thought leads to the formulation of a *gradational* theory of the nature of evil.[1] The value-character of reality is postulated; nature discloses value in situations of a certain self-involvement or self-commitment, centering interest on what is or what is to be realized or negated, enjoyed or endured, pursued or resisted. Value of whatever sort implies a gradational outlook, a recognition of higher and lower, a positive or negative *rather*, an incipient or determined preference. Whether it concern truth or beauty or justice, value-experience is never merely factual and passive, but conative, prospective, espousing. In this gradational view of things, evil is disclosed as literally degradation: the sur-

---

[1] Occasional sentences and phrases from this book, *The Nature of Evil* (New York, Macmillan, 1931), are cited or adapted to the purposes of this essay without further specific reference. The ethical theory here outlined was discussed in briefer form in the closing pages of "The Beginnings of Modern Ethics," published in the *Rice Institute Pamphlet* for October, 1931.

render of the higher to the lower in the scale of being, effective and ruinous drag. Evil is not a discrete quality of particular things or experiences; it is relative and has no status in isolation; it is essentially directional. A profound saying of St. Augustine's repeatedly comes to mind: "When the will abandons the higher and turns to what is lower, it becomes evil, not because that is evil to which it turns, but because the turning itself is perverse.—Cum enim se voluntas relicto superiore ad inferiora convertit, efficitur mala: non quia malum est, quo se convertit, sed quia perversa est ipsa conversio."

Differences of judgment as to what in any specific case is higher or lower would involve a corresponding difference of judgment as to what in the circumstances is evil and would thus reaffirm the fundamental conception of the nature of evil. But precisely this detailed use of the gradational conception is needed if our philosophy of value is to have, not only a guiding principle, but also concrete content. "Normal" valuation in different fields of experience provides ample warrant and illustration of the gradational principle, and in the concluding chapter of the above-mentioned work, I considered very briefly, from this point of view, disease and other bodily ills, and also perversion and frustration in the field of the higher values: logical, aesthetic, social-economic, political, moral, and mentioned some religious implications of the gradational view.

This theory of the nature of evil has serious implications for systematic ethics: the probing of these is the real object of this essay. Should it make possible a more adequate synthesis of ethical ideas, the gradational view of evil would itself receive thereby added substantiation.

A critical examination of ethical theories discloses two fundamental sources of confusion. The first is the tendency to select some one aspect of experience, concentrate on it as the sole or prime essential of virtue and use it as criterion for the ethical evaluation of the rest. The second source of confusion, characterizing a great deal of spurious ethics, is in the failure to distinguish between the demands of moral evaluation and those of factual description or analysis. The first defect is that of over-simplification and consequent narrowness in the conception and judgment of moral experience. The second defect is that of insufficiency and indeed irrelevance: in the treatment of moral experience, the characteristic moral judgment and attitude are ignored, and consequently we have a sort of anthropology, but not moral philosophy.

A more explicit statement of these two defects will be of advantage here. So, we may reflect, it is a truth that moral experience and culture involve the progressive socializing of the individual, and that moral categories are social categories. But this truth becomes error if we propose to define moral categories as social categories: the nature of virtue is not to be stated simply as social feeling or benevolence. The reduction of good and evil offhand to altruism and selfishness narrows unduly the range of value, and even in this narrow range is largely forced. The expressions self-assertion and self-denial reveal an abstract and artificial view of personality. Properly speaking the term "self" signifies choice and pursuit of aims with which one is identified, devotion to values, and it is clear that through every act the ascendancy of one self marks the decline or eclipse of another. On no act, then, can we say simply that it is an act of self-assertion or an act of self-denial. We may habitually brand selfishness as vicious, but what we really condemn in the vicious man is not his self-assertion: we condemn the sort of self he has chosen to affirm and the sort of self he has chosen to deny. The real problem is thus still on our hands: what self ought to be affirmed and what denied,—the problem of the scale of conduct-values. The issue between egoism and altruism, apparently insoluble at lower levels of conduct, is at the highest levels meaningless: that which we admire in the moral saint cannot be stated either in egoistic or in altruistic terms, for here is utter self-denial together with complete self-affirmation. Contrariwise the definition of moral excellence in terms of assertion of the will-to-power appeals to our normal depreciation of weakness, but while rightly aiming at power, confusedly ignores what it is that constitutes moral power or power of character, which may not be a monopoly of "the blond beast."

Likewise pleasure, happiness, or satisfaction of some sort is a genuine element in the life which we judge to have positive worth. But this element is insufficient to serve as a standard. The moral problem cannot be reduced to hedonistic metrics. Unless ethics were to erect absurdity into a principle by holding that I *ought* to do as I *please*, and ought the more, the more I am pleased, we must recognize not only amounts but likewise grades of pleasure: otherwise we run against the sane judgment of mankind which has always esteemed noble pain above low and dishonorable pleasures. But if pleasures are to be graded, we require a standard other than pleasure for the purpose, and then pure hedonism is disclosed as inadequate. A man's character is revealed in what satisfies or pleases him, but the worth of one's character or of an act cannot be judged by the mere fact that pleasure is experienced. Ethics as well as aesthetics not only measure enjoyment; they also judge taste. Indeed dissatisfaction with a certain sort of life may be the first mark of moral uplift in a man. It was not ill but rather on the way to being well with the prodigal son when his swinish life became disgusting and painful to him. His blessedness began when he realized that his pleasures were wretched. So the real question in ethics cannot be simply: Are men happy or unhappy? It is rather this other question: Is it well that men are thus and thus happy or unhappy? While pleasure and displeasure, satisfaction or dissatisfaction of some sort enter into every moral situation, these require moral evaluation and grading. The moral value of conduct cannot be judged merely in terms of the amount of pleasure it yields.

Again, to mention another example, moral acts have a peculiar dignity in that they express active devotion to a principle. Virtue is loyal to duty; it springs from conviction; it meets the demands of the moral sense; it obeys conscience. No matter how beneficial the results of an act, we say, unless it springs from a person's convictions, it is only a useful act calling for no distinctively moral approbation. But even though an act performed against one's conscience would lack moral value, we cannot define moral acts as conscientious acts, for conscience, like happiness, is only one element in the moral experience; while it cannot be ignored in the formulation of the moral standard, it alone cannot supply it. Unless we take due account of the other elements and factors, conscience itself may prove misleading and defective. Furthermore, while the sense of duty is an important part of many moral experiences, and resistance to it a grave moral hazard, virtue is not simply dutiful self-constraint, for dutifulness is not always a dominant nor even a perceptible factor in moral judgments. Some of the finest examples of moral excellence, we shall all agree, are characterized rather by wholehearted spontaneity of love or generosity, involving no explicit sense of obligation whatever.

Thus repeatedly we see how various ethical theories, while rightly recognizing the importance of certain elements in moral experience, err in regarding these elements as by themselves sufficient to provide a standard of moral worth. The disclosure of narrowness in the criticism of many ethical theories serves to emphasize the complexity of moral experience. Particularly confused is this onesideness, in view of what should be evident, that genuine moral judgment concerns and respects the integrity of human nature and must therefore be opposed on principle to any narrow partisanship in valuation.

The alternative to which fruitful ethical theory proceeds is thus bound to be some variety of perfectionism. The moral value of an act must depend upon the rôle it plays in the perfection of human nature. We need not be misled by the objection that this is a mere tautology: namely, that an act is good if it makes us better. It means considerably more than that; besides the statement itself is decidedly more than tautologous. The perfection of anything is in its characteristic fruition: that it comes to be more fully what it really and distinctively is.

Moral value here shows analogies to logical value. The truth of a theory depends on this,—whether it takes due account of all relevant evidence, with appropriate distribution of emphasis, and whether it can itself be a principle of relevance in the field of experience with which it deals, rendering that field more intelligible and opening new significant vistas of thought and problems. So with a valid ethical theory: the true moral evaluation of a man's act must be one that judges it in terms of what is relevantly and characteristically human. The good act is the act of a man who is not under misapprehension but truly knows what he is about. Aristotle's general definition of the good is to the point: the good in any field of experience is that which adequately performs its characteristic function. The good life thus regarded would be the humanly appropriate and abundant life. Moral judgment involves self-evaluation based on self-understanding and proceeding to discipline, expression, realization and enhancement of personality: the culture and enrichment of character.

How the moral standard and the moral ideal, the direction and objective of human life are to be conceived if we adopt this general point of view, would of course depend on our account and estimate of human nature: our account *and* our estimate of it, essentially and in detail. Thus we are brought to consider the second main defect of ethical theories, that of confusing the description of human conduct with the evaluation of it, the confusion of so-called descriptive ethics, a part of anthropology, with moral philosophy.

The very emancipation of modern ethics from the bonds of theological authoritarianism, as it occasions this error, likewise imposes the critique of it. Modern ethics early realized that it is not enough to declare that we ought to do God's will: before God's commandments can get our moral approval and loyalty, we must be assured that God is *good* and his principles worthy of our devotion. So, far from our being able to establish morals on a theological basis, the very conception of God, before it can be available either for morality or for religion, demands a foundation in our moral consciousness. This is patently clear and induces secular ethics. But what should be equally clear is this: before we can speak of God or of good, we require a view of the world, of nature and of human nature, that can take in these ideas. For all we know they may be mere superstitions, though even if they were, man's capacity to entertain them would call for explanation. It is all-important to consider what grounds, if any, a moral interpretation of human life has in our view of the objective reality of things.

Here is a man engaged in moral activity, or at any rate morally perplexed and engrossed in inquiry. What does this activity or perplexity or inquiry imply regarding his character? What sort of being does his moral conduct show him to be, and how must we think of a world that includes such beings? Modern thought is confronted with these two problems and thus in a sense experiences a twofold enrichment. On the one hand, the study of nature and of human nature leads to a more detailed knowledge and a more critical understanding of conduct and of moral activity, and the science of ethics thus gains in substance what it perhaps loses in sanctity. But on the other hand this very bringing of morality down to earth, from the supernatural to the natural level, as it gives us the setting of the facts of moral conduct, imposes on the modern mind the demand to interpret these facts with the other facts of so-called physical nature in a thoroughly philosophical view of reality. If we say that ethics is a science and that man in his moral activity is to be studied as objectively as astronomer or physiologist studies his respective field, then while on the one hand doing justice to what is distinctive and "natural" in moral activity, we must, on the other hand, consider how it is to be related to the rest of nature. What is the sort of cosmology that can make sense both of physics and of ethics? If justice and veracity are nothing occult or supernatural, but quite as natural as breathing or gravitation, then what is the science and philosophy of nature that can comprehend not only gravitation and breathing, but also veracity and justice?

Hobbes and other materialists may describe man as re-acting thus and thus to various kinds of pressure, contact, and concussion. It makes no difference how complicated the mechanism may be, if it is nothing but a mechanism it may admit of a description, of a reference of effects to ante-cedent conditions, but it is nowise subject to evaluation. Materialistic ethics is thus pure irrelevance.

Though less obviously, yet none the less surely, all merely descriptive or factual ethics is also irrelevant and spurious. Eminent doctrines of naturalistic ethics may mislead in their apportionment of emphasis. We may, for instance, recognize the distinctively personal, human character of moral activ-ity, the truth which Green expressed more largely in his dictum that values are always "relative to value for, of, or in a person:" a statement which is a recognition of a lofty cosmological category and involves a revision of meager naturalism. But the statement that values are personal or human may, by a depreciating shift of emphasis, be taken to mean that they are merely human. In that case how is man's serious devotion to virtue, as distinguished from his sentimental attachment, to be sustained? With more perfect knowledge of reality, as we are enabled to see things in their true cosmic setting, we should presumably come to perceive our own life of moral activity as something to be analyzed or explained, and with a cosmic sense of humor may come to see things as they really are, "beyond good or evil," Eter-nal Actuality. But if ultimate nature is morally neutral, if good or evil, justice or injustice, lack ultimate status, then ethics, properly speaking, is a sublime and solemn misappre-hension. Thus Spinoza's ethics may indeed be one of the noble systems of morality, but how is its nobility to be sup-ported by his metaphysics? Even the Aristotelian functional definition of the good requires a warning qualification lest it mislead us as to the essence of moral value. The "excellence" of everything is indeed in its adequate characteristic func-tioning, but in the case of man this excellence is distinctively

moral in that it expresses the presence in man of what is
more than morally factual.

In personality nature reveals its hierarchical character.
There is higher and lower in the universe, and our moral
consciousness is preëminently a recognition of this gradational character of reality. The moral judgment is not a
judgment merely of like or dislike, of desire or aversion,
though it does include these: it is distinctively a judgment
of approval or disapproval, of preference not only felt but
judged to be defensible. Whether or not the sense of obligation is dominant in a specific moral judgment, the sense of
the superior right or demand of what is judged good over
what is judged evil is always dominant. That something is
better and worthier is the basic certainty; to ascertain what
it is in any past situation is the aim of deliberation; to have
spurned or missed it, the sting of remorse; to be unresponsive
to its appeal, moral dullness. This sense of the gradational
and of the rightful dominance of the higher colors the entire
moral consciousness. Moral conviction is man's active self-
identification with the upward trend in this scale; moral
devotion, the wholehearted direction of the will in the line of
this conviction.

Naturalism need not always be meager and bound to the
factual. A really scientific ethics is one which, in dealing
with moral experience and moral judgment, perceives in
balanced view the characteristic factors of human nature
that enter into it: perceives that the act which we call morally good satisfies in appropriate measure all the demands
which the will is called upon to meet. In this sense moral
activity is man's adequate and complete functioning; scientific ethics is thoroughly naturalistic and for the satisfactory
treatment of its task must be in constant touch with all the
biological and humanistic sciences. But just because it is
thus in a true sense naturalistic, it is bound to perceive what
sort of nature moral experience reveals: bound to recognize
that a moral judgment is not merely about things, but
a judgment of and on things, an evaluation and a verdict
implying approval or condemnation because conceiving of

human nature as ennobled or degraded by the act which it judges. The recognition of this moral-gradational view of nature is the recognition of an ultimate category, as ultimate as intelligence, as life. It is not of the world apart, any more than life or intelligence are, but if we pursue a truly scientific method, we should see it for what it is, and not try irrelevantly to reduce it to something else. Factually viewed, all things are on a par: carbons and chromosomes and consciousness. But evaluation, the moral view of things, consists just in the gradational recognition that some things ought to be rather than others, that they are preferable to others, higher, worthier.

"Rather" is a most important term expressing the very essence of conscience: not the mere description or explanation of this or that, nor the distinction of this from that, nor yet the relating of them, but the gradational contemplation and engagement of them as alternatives: this rather than that. Here we have to do with more than a recorded preference, as with the pease-porridge of Mother Goose: "Some like it hot, some like it cold;" it is the claim for a defensible preference; not merely an expression of liking, but a judgment of and on taste. Hence the imperative temper of conscience as distinguished from science: it does not merely state but dictates; it states differences as alternatives between which it dictates an order of worth: "Rather seek ye the Kingdom of God; and all these things shall be added unto you." Observe that the main point here is not in what is chosen, but in that a choice is imperative and defensible. "Rather," said Democritus, "would I discover the cause of one fact than become king of the Persians." The choice itself may be the kingdom of God or it may be scientific knowledge; what it is will depend on our ethical conclusions. The judgment of the choice as imperative and defensible is the judgment expressing the moral outlook, the moral view of things.

Man's moral recognition of himself as a member in this hierarchy is twofold. First, he recognizes that this membership engages all his faculties and energies, involving in active relation all the factors of his personality and his environment: body and mind, passion and reason, natural and cultural setting, yielding self-expression and self-understanding. All that is true in hedonistic, rationalistic, altruistic ethics may find its place in this recognition: enjoyment in satisfaction of desire and natural aversion to pain or distress, long-range vision and balanced perspective in a reasoned ordering of interests and efforts, socialized consciousness and disinterested, generous participation in the lives of others. All these partial insights, which various ethical theories misleadingly champion as all-sufficient, may be incorporated without partisan narrowness in an inclusive perfectionism. This is an important aspect of our discussion of systematic ethics and will be taken up further presently.

But there is another element in man's twofold self-recognition which we should not ignore. Man also recognizes the unrealized but worthy nature that reveals itself in the moral challenge: what ought to be and only through moral achievement can be. Moral experience is not merely observable behavior of whatever sort; it is likewise and essentially a self-involvement. The distinctively ethical note in the idea of freedom should not here elude us. The traditional issue between the freedom of indifference and rigid determinism may be resolved in a compromise leaning towards necessity, self-determinism; or the fagged champion of spontaneity may be stirred to new zeal by promising rumors of unexpected initiative within the atom itself. But this is all beside the point in strictly ethical thinking. The crux and the kernel of the moral idea of freedom is not disclosed in the question whether an act is "determined" or "spontaneous," nor whether it could or could not have been predicted, nor whether it could have been omitted altogether. These are all questions of the factual description or explanation of events. The complete survey of the causal realm appears to be still in progress: how much, if any, spontaneity or indeterminacy and of what sort it may include within its borders, is presumably still to ascertain. As to unpredictability, Spinoza's warning may not be neglected. An act may be judged "free" merely owing to our ignorance of the operating causes. But an event may be thus unpredictably "free" and still have no moral quality whatever: recent physics is citing instances of this sort and promises more. An act may on the other hand be quite predictable and yet be through and through moral: "Ask, and it shall be given you; seek and ye shall find; knock and it shall be opened unto you:" these are not propositions in mechanics. And as to feeling that "it might have been" otherwise or not at all, we are apt to overlook that the lured or deliberating self, contemplating its deed in prospect or actually doing it, is not the same as the self that ruefully or otherwise reviews it in memory: not the same by just the margin of the deed, if no more.

Is it not evident that the real meaning of the sense of freedom in moral experience eludes us so long as we consider the problem in factual terms: whether spontaneity is an admissible exception to the uniform necessity in nature. The real question here is not whether moral activity is determined or arbitrary: the real question is in what sense and to what purpose it is significantly and responsibly mine: not an event like others, but my act, which would not be except for me and for which therefore I am responsible, in a judgment that joins its worth and mine in the same verdict. Therein is the sting of remorse which the thought of the inevitable does not relieve: "It is impossible but that offenses will come: but woe unto him through whom they come!" The moral view of events is neither retrospective nor anticipatory, but alert to the impending. Our life is morally free not in that it is arbitrary; it is free in that it is not done and disposed of, settled once for all, but in the making and in our making; save for it, things would not be as they are, and may yet be different. And this for us is not a fact to record, but a challenge to meet. On some anvil the iron is hot and the hammer ours alone. The ideas of self-determinism, of personal responsibility, of self-involvement and dutiful obligation: all these elements in the idea of freedom are here reflected on their distinctly moral side. Only as we thus feel that it is "up to us," do we also come to feel that we ought or ought not. In this sense Kant would be right in regarding freedom as a postulate of the moral imperative. There is no possible recognition of duty, of "I ought" unless the matter-of-fact disclaimer "What is that to me?" is precluded: and precluded it can be only by a view of the self and of nature which reveals our course of deliberation and decision as *the* course of nature that may yet be. "There is a tide in the affairs of men"—and through men of the world-sweep itself. The river before us is any river until we come to see it as our Rubicon, and then we realize what is freely and responsibly in our power and alone morally significant: not whether the river will be crossed, but whether we should and shall be crossing it.

This idea is at the basis of the sense of moral obligation, conscience, moral creativeness in conduct and character: the vigilant, heroic, self-enhancing, self-transcending element in all distinctively moral experience. Profound insight is revealed in a sentence of Josiah Royce: "This is my duty, nobody in the universe—no, not God, so far as God is other than myself—can do this duty for me. My duty I must myself do." Only as a man is possessed by this consciousness of being somehow more than a mechanism living or conscious, only as he sees himself as a member of a world of possible values, loyal to unrealized ideals that challenge his achievement and in such achievement finding his own ever truer self, only thus is he morally conscious and morally active in the full sense of the term. But in a measure this characteristically moral nature is disclosed in each one of us daily, and all approval or disapproval, all love of honor, compunction, fair play, devotion, shame or aspiration, duty and piety are evidences of it.

Moral experience thus conceived engages all the energies of man, but engages them in such a way as to integrate his personality, to reveal ever more clearly and more naturally his character: what is within his grasp and his reach, but also what is worth his reach and his grasp: his range of capacities and also the grading of them, his thorough self-understanding and self-estimate: the recognition of what in him is the line of his fruition, realization, enhancement, and what in him is backwash and atavism, discordant and unregenerate: the recognition of himself and of his life as the concourse and interplay of ennobling and of downpulling tendencies, achievement and debacle, an urge and a drag, the gleam of the ideal and the lure of the degenerate. Here are we all, moving not on a level plane but on a slope, an upward but also a downward slope; and every act and every thought of ours is either uplifting or degrading us, and through us uplifting or degrading the world in and of which we are.

The moral problem is not a specialized problem dealing with one fragment or corner of life; it is rather a synthesis of all problems of specialized value which confront men and women. Ethics is both comprehensive and directional: the core and the summation of the philosophy of value. Modern insight demands a livelier sense of this more inclusive morality. Though Christianity quickened our moral sensitiveness, yet it allowed a certain shriveling of the moral frame: we may compare the connotation of the Greek term *arete* with the meaning we are apt to convey by such expressions as "an immoral man" or "a woman's virtue." The Renaissance revolt against Aristotle notwithstanding, do we not observe in modern thought a reaffirmation of the Aristotelian integral view of virtue: of that perfectionism which absorbed the truth of hedonism without yielding to its error? Yet rich in significance as this ethics was, incorporating theoretical and practical life in its ideal of well-balanced characteristic human functioning, it yet missed one important note. Perhaps Christian thought put an exaggerated emphasis on this note, in its notion of sin, yet it expressed on the positive side a central factor in the moral judgment: the exacting, imperative, dutiful aspect of moral value.

It is not enough, in the traditional manner of the ethics manual, to classify moral theories as formalistic and teleological, and the latter into perfectionist and hedonistic, and then leave the choice between them to a better day. To

disclose these three: happiness, perfection, duty as an indissoluble triad must be the goal of systematic modern
ethics: to disclose it and to vindicate it. Neglect one or
another of these and you get a onesided moral theory. Argue the case of hedonism, socialize it most generously in
the formula, the greatest happiness of the greatest number,
and a Carlyle may still style it a pig-philosophy and ask
you sharply: "What *right* hast thou to be happy?" Espouse
the cause of rational perfection, and exalt Platonic, Stoic,
Spinozistic rationality: the common man, and even more
the uncommon, may yet protest: "But why should I control or otherwise order my life in accordance with your or
anyone's formula?" Along with Kant set all these aside
and champion devotion to the moral law, dutifulness pure
and simple, as alone morally good, and the rest of us, deeply
impressed, yet remain undecided. This ethics, we say,
lacks content and substance; we are asked to sail all the
way through under sealed orders; our hand is raised to
take the oath of loyalty, but the oath is not forthcoming;
we ask, what shall we *do* to enter this Kingdom of Ends?

Now it is precisely this synthesis of duty, attainment and
satisfaction, perfectionist and hedonistic, which the gradational theory makes possible. Recognize the impending-
challenging character of value, the active-creative character of personality, the inexhaustible-perfectible character
of nature, and moral worth is revealed as more than a mere
experienced quality of events or than an ambiguous, transcendent "as if." Virtue in a gradational world is expression, realization, satisfaction in the fullest naturalistic sense:
the sap and the savour of man's soul. But in a gradational
world man's distinctive career makes his life more than
passive enjoyment or Topsy-like growing.   Each value
which he contemplates is an alternative, unrealized *not-yet:*
alternative, and so involving rival loyalties and preferences;
unrealized, and so challenging. Man as a moral agent is not
a member of a realm of "as ifs." His moral activity itself,
and the values he pursues and achieves disclose the nature
of the world as a process of malleable perfection. In this

sense we may hold that reality is history: it is not only a sequence of events, no matter how law-conforming, but also a significant course of activities: a drama of achievement and a tragedy of frustration. The morally enlightened consciousness, then, perceives that it is not a mere cog in the machine, nor a mere spectator or passive recipient of whatever sort, but in every distinctively personal experience, perfection or frustration of some sort is impending. So the very nature of value, and the value-attaining process invests moral activity with the imperative of duty. In the drama of human life every man has a rôle, and conscience calls out each man's cue. A morally enlightened mind is a mind emancipated from thoughtlessness, a cosmically alert, responsible mind. Here self-understanding, realization, and satisfaction fuse with duty: man acts his part. "In Labrador," writes Dr. Wilfred Grenfell, "I have been allowed to find that there was a job that would not be done if I did not do it."

So morality dramatically integrates all our capacities: consciousness matures as conscience. It relies on the self-criticism and perfection of intellectual activity and its logical truth-values. We are committed to the pursuit of knowledge and we have an intellectual conscience. We demand freedom of thought, champion tolerance, and resist intellectual tyranny of whatever sort on the principle by which we object to asphyxiation, and also on the principle of *noblesse oblige:* if we are not to think straight and freely in the world, who or what else is to do it? Morality demands the ever more reasonable and just revision of economic and social processes and systems to prevent neglect of the human factor in industry and trade, to respect essential human dignity and diminish the human hazard. It resists the preoccupation with the mere amassing of material possessions; man, we say, ought to be more than a man of means, but we may not ignore the importance of these *means* to further attainment, nor deny the rightful claim of the many to the material conditions of more human activity. We remember Mazzini's great political and economic maxim: "A man is entitled to the freedom which he needs for the performance of his duties." Morality champions a socializing of our character, spiritual growth through living with others, but likewise it sustains the eremite vigil of man's soul, man's pilgrimage to the solitude of his own intimate self. It counsels an ever saner attitude of man to the larger nature which envelopes him and which he tries to grasp and exploit, that it may vicariously be ennobled through his own human imprint on it and not degrade and brutalize and mechanize him. Here is Rodin's Thinker: thought stamped on hard rock and living; yet wherever we turn we may also see the stony look of spirit hardened into inert unresponsiveness. Morality sanely respects our bodily nature, not scorning it in misguided asceticism yet keeping in mind that man is neither steer nor squirrel, that if he is to keep his body fit, it is to be fit for something, a fit instrument from human achievement and self-expression. Furthermore it cherishes the whole field of aesthetic appreciation and creativeness; to it the word virtuoso is more than a term with a curious etymology; it seeks that intelligence in taste which distinguishes culture from vulgarity: the enrichment or the cheapening and corruption of the soul by the experiences which arouse it to aesthetic delight. And highest and deepest of all, morality finds its consummation in man's utter self-yielding in worshipful devotion to what he regards as Supreme Perfection and calls his God: a most ennobling and yet most hazardous devotion, for it confirms the soul in its ultimate direction and being the pole-star of life's voyage, determines its course and its destiny.

All this and more does the moral outlook on life embrace: in all judging life as a process of progressive understanding, mastery, individual and social, expression and perfection of character, or as disintegration, degradation, and defeat of capacities. Morality thus thrives on the mellowing of man's intelligence in all the fields in which he is realizing his values, and always it voices the imperious demand of the larger life and character against upstart caprice or dis-

cordant and debasing passion. In each case it would keep
clear the rational sense of man's total enterprise in appropriate distribution of emphasis: what man is really about
in this world; "what he ought to do and to be, considering
what he is." Logic, aesthetics, social philosophy, philosophy
of religion are all tracing their curves of man's rise up the
scale of values: truth, beauty, social order, saintliness. All
these moral philosophy would see as various paths to the
goal that is its goal: a moving aim of perfectibility, the
achievement of character and the cultivation of a humanized,
civilized environment.

The gradational theory of moral value roughly outlined
here utilizes the results of the more significant ethics of the
past; it seeks knowledge of the thing which is to be known
and not of some other thing; it does not distort moral experience in order to make it fit in the conceptual molds of
factual science, nor sets up morality as somehow transcendent and exalted above the actual lives of men and women,
but on the contrary undertakes to grasp what is distinctive and characteristic in moral experience, and then tries
to make sense of it by suitable interpretation.

XI

THE MEANING OF OBLIGATION

CHARLES W. HENDEL, JR.

McGill University

THE MEANING OF OBLIGATION

Charles W. Hendel, Jr.

In the beginning of the modern age there were dicta on law and politics very strange to us of the present: "The laws cannot govern; only men can govern." "The laws, or rules of reason, oblige merely *in foro interno*, not *in foro externo*." "The laws of themselves cannot oblige, but only the power of a superior." "No man can lay himself under an obligation to law, that is, law as coming from a superior." Today, it is thought, an obligation exists only when the individual himself has assumed it: laws that are self-imposed do verily oblige, and are indeed the only effectual ones; and self-government, or the government of laws, is precisely the right polity. The maxims of our times are thus a defiance of all the pronouncements of political wisdom that once gained the assent of men. All the impossibles of those early days are the very truths on which we base our political order. We are not even aware of the paradox that they would once have seemed to involve. How has this change come about? The answer to this is the story of idealism in modern life and society.

The maxims of any age possess their reasonableness not in themselves but in reference to the whole scheme of life of the time. Their logic depends on the experience of the people who accept it. That experience includes not only the historical events but also what men imagine and think about themselves and the world they live in. And it is more largely the order of things in imagination that gives the meaning to any particular opinions such as these on law, obligation, and government. The first step in an interpretation of men's beliefs, then, is to understand the experience, and particularly their own theory of it.

I

AUTHORITY AND OBLIGATION

"Our present unquiet world." The phrase is from Richard Hooker and tells how things appeared to him and many others in the days after the Reformation. They were witnessing wars among the nations, civil and religious conflicts within them, and in every quarter shocking violations of law and right and the common precepts of Christian charity. In every one's view too there was very present the occasion of all such trouble and unrighteousness, a mortal sin of disobedience, the assertion of "private judgment" in the matter of the religious discipline of the Church. To the more pagan-minded its analogue was the vice of "ambition" which had created such havoc in ancient societies. In either aspect the individualistic motif was deemed a prime cause of the universal warfare and all its consequences and demoralizations. The separatist effects of that spirit were growing apace. The recalcitrancy of sects came to plague even the reformed and established churches, and so it came to pass that those who were thoughtfully concerned for the peace and common life of Europe regarded the individual conscience, from their own experience of its workings, as essentially a *divisive* thing. Conscience was looked at askance, as but a "pretext of disobedience." It was a cause of disunity in every province of human relations. The wise men of that day naturally looked for something better than conscience, something that would evoke a common allegiance, produce a general attitude of obedience to law and rule, and thus compose and unite men once again into a peaceable life in one community, "the Christian republic." An age that was seeing itself thus projected into such a career of error and disorder because of the liberty of conscience was bound to interest itself in *authority*. They were seeking some control over people generally that would be a "superior" to conscience. And the thought of such a thing was not felt to be in the least alien or repugnant,—a superior was acceptable because it promised them an escape from intolerable oppositions in matters of the spirit, and from strife in all the nations of Europe. There was a deep-lying expression of the contemporary ideal in the epic titles *Paradise Lost*, and *Paradise Regained*, and in the story, too, of the Divine Will triumphing over all disobedient men and angels. The great desideratum of thinking men was a righteous rule like that everywhere in the world, a divinely *superior authority*.

The first thoughts were reminiscent of antiquity, for they came in a time of revival of learning when the ideals of Greece and Rome seemed of eternal value and directly applicable to their own situation. Thus Jean Bodin saw new meaning for the Platonic idea of the Republic, as the great community which contained, properly ordered within it, all the different elements of the existing society, the many "families, colleges, corporations, estates." Here was the common and universal ground for the existence of all such particular bodies and it was a very real body itself. To discover this plainly to men might lead them to acknowledge it, the Republic, as something above themselves and having superior claims upon them all. On the other hand, Richard Hooker, moving likewise in the Greek tradition, exalted The Laws as just such a superior and he made out a case for their supremacy by showing that while each order of human association possessed a peculiar law of its own, as law ecclesiastical, civil, political, or even as the law of nations, yet these various systems and polities articulated with each other perfectly so as to regulate the whole order of human relationships. They were nothing short of a consummate Law of Nature, exhibiting such as fitness of detail, as well as a universality, that they must be conceived to have issued from God Himself as their Author. Thus Law seemed a grand enough authority for men. And Grotius, likewise, demonstrated the universality of a system of Natural Right, or "laws of perpetual obligation," which obtained among men everywhere, whether in or out of political societies, or at war or peace, and he wrote about them as one confident that such laws of right had a force to restrain princes and peoples in their strife, if only these rules were well expounded, in the plain language of reason.[1]

Nevertheless all such sublime trust in reason and law and in the ideal of a republic was far too much in the ancient mode, and out of tune with the times. Those writers who had begun thinking of ideal and universal authorities turned increasingly toward some visible and particular powers efficacious in their own modern world, for they could not escape the fact that their day was not ancient but modern. The eternal authorities fitted only a static picture of the past, not their present. The times were those of rapid and marked change; commerce and armies alike were conspiring to bring men and nations into unprecedented relations with each other which called for adjustments and actions suited to the need of every moment. To meet such new conditions there had to be a positive legislation over and above the traditional laws and polities. And the power of making such laws had to be likewise a power applying them and imparting to them the force which they would be lacking from the very fact that they were not habitual to the life of the people and had to be laid down without waiting for their consent. The power to do all this necessary law-giving was *sovereignty*. It required very eminent capacities, an intelligence of the affairs of State and a competence of will to command and carry out policies. The persons so gifted seemed right at hand in the national sovereigns of Europe. They were the *personnages* who could truly be conceived to act for "the common body," either as its protector or as its representative. They had appeared in history as defenders of "the commons" against all the small holders of power whose barbarous and particularistic antagonisms had made them intolerable in country and city, and especially detrimental to commerce. The rising chiefs of State were welcome to peoples who were cherishing

---

[1] J. Bodin, *Les Six Livres de la République* (Paris, 1583), Bk. I, Ch. 1, p. 2; Ch. 2, pp. 10–15; Bk. III, Ch. 7 (Des Corps et Colleges, Estates, et Communautés), p. 476.

R. Hooker, *Of the Laws of Ecclesiastical Polity*, Bk. I, especially X, pp. 188, 191, 193, 201; XV, pp. 219–221; XVI, pp. 224–225, 228, 232. (Everyman Ed.)

H. Grotius, *The Rights of War and Peace*, in Three Books, wherein are explained The Law of Nature and Nations, etc. (English translation, London, 1738), Preliminary Discourse, XXVII.

ambitions of a civilized life, to equal if not to better that of
the ancients, and who needed therefor security and peace.
Besides, the sovereigns enjoyed a certain authority in their
own right, for the nations retained something of their medi-
eval habit of thinking, and fancied themselves rendering
allegiance to their sovereign as to a personal overlord. Their
obedience would be the more effective because he was a
visible, familiar authority. To appreciate the authority of
an invisible republic, or impersonal law, or natural right,
required a difficult exercise of the reason. Men could accept
rule more readily from a person than an abstraction. And
the concrete imagination of poets tended to embellish this
figure of the ruling power. Noble offices kindled the expectation that their incumbents would be noblemen. Those
of ready fancy, reading their Plutarch, transported his
heroes into the high places in their own civil order. The
drama of the time told of Statesmen, Princes, Courtiers, and
imparted to these rôles an additional glamour through the
arts of language, music, and action. Many were the pictures
of the glorious sovereign, as great in his fidelity to his trust
and piety as in his magnificent power. So if there were
dreams of fair women in those days, there were also dreams
of superb men. Even the political writers, who were not
dreaming, were caught by the common persuasion, and when
they argued for the utility of the rule of sovereigns who
could act competently for the whole State and bring some
composure into the life of humanity, they wrote with an
eloquent enthusiasm, and represented those beings as grander
by far than the mere "guardians of the laws" they had ad-
mired in their Plato—they saw their sovereigns as "the
living laws" superior to the letter of laws. So it naturally
happened that their first ideal of the republic and the rule
of law faded out by comparison with so illustrious a sovereignty. However fine it might be to live "where only the
law is dame and mistress of all," it was better still to live
under a more masculine rule, under a Prince. Yet with all
that eulogy, such writers did not think of the sovereignty
as the all-embracing reality of the State—it was only the

eminent and active part of the republic and it dwelt along-side the other parts, able to give the law to them and make adjustments among them but not to destroy them or their liberties or their properties, for all together constituted the community and without the lesser estates, bodies and properties, the sovereignty itself would be of little avail. Indeed the sovereign was even subject to laws above him, though they were not made by any other human authority.[1] Which then was *the* authority—the invisible laws or the visible princes? The early writers could not make up their minds, and could scarcely pose the question, and their predicament was not unlike their predecessors in the Middle Ages who had lost themselves in their notions of both a purely Spiritual Power and a Church Visible.

But, quite apart from that confusion of mind, the modern theorists had some difficulties in regard to the visible sovereignty itself. They differed in their choice of the actual rulers. Hooker, anxious over the threat against the Established Church of England by the Presbyterians, and recalling how the General Councils of the Church had, many times in the past of Christendom, settled such disputes, favored such a "council" in his day. His argument seems at times wholly directed in the interest of the Episcopate, but it was also forward-looking, prophetic of the supremacy of the Parliament of the English people. On the other hand the greater number of writers followed the example of Bodin in France who preferred the rule of "one man," and thus sponsored monarchy.[2]

By offering authority in all too many forms those early writers on politics and society defeated their practical aim. Now the desired superior appeared to be something ideal, like Law or the Republic, and again a concrete person, maybe one man or else a council of men. Their intention was to direct the people's minds to an object of common allegiance

---

[1] Bodin, *op. cit.*, Bk. III, Ch. 5, p. 429; Bk. I, Ch. 8 (De la Souveraineté), pp. 131, 140–142; Ch. 10, p. 221; Bk. VI, Ch. 4, p. 938.
Cf. Grotius, *op. cit.*, Bk. II, Ch. IV, Sect. XII, pp. 182 ff.
[2] Hooker, *Ecclesiastical Polity*, Preface VI, p. 120; Bk. I, X, pp. 200–201; Bk. IV, XIII, p. 418; Bodin, *op. cit.*, Bk. VI, Ch. 4, p. 961.

and thus to foster in them an attitude of obedience to something genuinely superior to themselves and decisive of all issues that might arise amongst them; but they failed in this because they presented so many different, and competing alternatives. For this eventually left the choice of what to do to the judgment of the individual who could still appeal over any one authority against him to some other who might be for him, now to the King, now to the Parliament, now to Natural Law, now to the Church of God,—and so everything would remain much as it had been before. An authority would not be an authority unless it had none other beside it, and were absolutely supreme.

Yet the tendency toward the recognition of an absolute sovereignty was resisted. Those political philosophers were unable to be entirely single-minded in their proposals about authority. They were, despite themselves, men of the modern age, and could not fail to cherish some deep and silent regard for things other than kingly rule, for something, that is, of the conscience and claims of the individual. Their very action in writing books on politics was indicative of this, for they thereby made appeal to the "natural light" of all who could read, and evidently had some expectation that their readers would act rationally and according to their own good. These authors were trying to *induce* their fellow-men to obey, not to trick or force them. This implied that they placed a real value on the inner convictions and will of humanity. So another train of thinking ran alongside that directed to authority and it was of this purport: the obedience and lawful conduct of the people is founded upon their own will as subjects, so that "consent is the original of all right." This directed attention to the fact of *obligation*. Political philosophy had before it the task of formulating not simply a theory of personal authority but further, a theory of personal obligation.

It was the great merit of Grotius to appreciate that task. No one could have been more disposed by his experience to plead for a settlement in Europe, and a peace, by authority; for he had been a witness to the terror of the Thirty Years'

War and was a fugitive from Holland and happy to be resident safely in France where he wrote the dedication of his book to Louis XIII. Yet scarcely anyone else in his day put so much faith in the sheer power of right, and of the human conscience, if it were properly enlightened by reason. Surveying the realm of human relations he marked how many real duties there are naturally recognized by men, duties to each other, to institutions, to Law, State, King, or God. And he called these valid and binding duties in the life of mankind,—"obligations." Now obligation in its "perfect" form, according to the tradition of Roman Law, meant a bond which had the whole force of the civil State behind it. To speak, then, of the various common duties of men as "obligations" was to convey the notion that these duties had a validity quite comparable to that of laws enforced by a civil authority. Yet Grotius did not mean to suggest by this that the obligations of men are all derived from the authority of a sovereign—he treated them as quite distinct in character, exactly as they appeared to be in the organization of society. As Christians men have an obligation of charity; as members of the civil community, an obligation to common law; as subjects to a superior, an obligation of allegiance or obedience to his commands. Indeed, even as mere individuals, men can "oblige themselves," by an act of covenant, for example, or by agreement, and this is something quite distinct from their obligation to law, where their own consent is not requisite.[1] Grotius simply described these various *de facto* obligations of human life without any doctrinaire idea of reducing them to one type, or deriving them from one authority. And this liberal view of the situation had an important consequence: if there are so many distinct types of obligation, there must be a corresponding number of different authorities. Such a reflection was a serious impediment to the drift of argument toward one supreme and all-competent authority or sovereign.

In fact, the idea of obligation threatened the preëminence

[1] Grotius, *op. cit.*, Preface XVII; Bk. I, Sect. XI, p. 12; Bk. II, Ch. XI, Sect. II, p. 280.

of the sovereign as the one possible absolute authority. For obligation was associated closely with contract. Whenever persons enter of their own free will into an agreement to do certain things they bind themselves equally to the performance of their respective engagements. This aspect of the equality of the duties and the benefits, as well as the freedom of the parties in making the contract had long commended the idea to political thinkers, who used it to emphasize the perfect mutuality of the relation between a superior and his inferiors, and to show that there were duties on both sides, the superior owing those under him his protection and care, and they, in turn, paying him their dues of willing service and allegiance. Grotius fell in with this way of thinking. Departing then from his merely descriptive account of obligations, he proceeded to explain the particular obligation of allegiance in terms of contract, instead of allowing it to stand on a distinct basis of its own. He thus accounted at one stroke for the obligation of the governed as coming from consent, and for the authority of the government. But his theory actually raised more questions than it solved. For it represented "the sovereign" and "the people" as equals, and thus lent a certain amount of encouragement to popular ideals, that the people who would be competent enough originally to make such an arrangement might be able to keep hold of the reins of ultimate power themselves, without really making over anything to a particular sovereign, that is, without alienating their sovereignty as a people. Furthermore this doctrine invited the people themselves to scrutinize the services supposed to be rendered by their sovereign and to determine for themselves what measure of protection and welfare they actually enjoyed from him; all of which seemed likely to foster an attitude of criticism which would readily become one of malcontent. But worst of all, the theory had no solution for the situation it itself seemed thus likely to create, when a people became so bold as to renounce their obligation to obey, on the ground of an imputed failure of the sovereign to play his true part:—then, apparently, only the sword could decide the issue.[1] This predicament Grotius himself saw, and he had no policy to meet it, but contented himself with general appeals to the reason of peoples and princes, and to the precepts of conscientious Christian behavior. He changed nothing as regards the claims of the parties; showed no way of determining conflicts; and therefore left sovereign authority exposed to considerable jeopardy,—all because of taking up with those disturbing notions of obligation and contract.

II

PERSONAL SOVEREIGNTY

This political theory seemed to many of that time a very feeble and doubtful thing. It opened the door to private judgment. It meant a reliance on the Christian conscience and the reason of men, both to be called into play by teachings and by books on War and Peace. Surely something better was needed. Here it was Thomas Hobbes stepped on the scene, a man with no illusions about the value of words or conscience: "The laws or rules of reason oblige merely in the inner mind, not in the external world of human affairs." [2]   Hobbes was very practical, adept in argument, and capable of thinking out a system of philosophy to support his view. He worked with single-mindedness, keeping the one purpose of all the different theories in plain view before him; there must be established an authority which is unequivocal, and indisputably supreme, and that, too, must be the authority of a person.

First Hobbes swept out of the picture of life all those invisible authorities that had competed in men's minds with the authority of the sovereign. The Greek ideals of Commonwealth and the Laws were not only confusing but also irrelevant to the exigencies of modern life, which called for ready and positive action and not merely faith-

---

[1] Grotius, *op. cit.*, Bk. I, Ch. III, Sect. VIII, pp. 64, 69, 71, 75–77; Ch. IV, Sect. II, pp. 102–103.
[2] Hobbes, *Philosophical Rudiments* (Molesworth, London, Vol. 1; Bohn, 1841), Ch. 3, Sect. 27, p. 46. Tripos, *The Elements of Law*, Vol. 4, Part I, Ch. IV; Part 10, p. 108. *Leviathan*, Part I, Ch. XV, p. 82 (Everyman Edition).

ful adherence to an established order of polity. For "the laws cannot govern, only men can govern," men, that is, who have the ability to meet unprecedented situations with intelligence and force, who can devise the laws for "reasons of State," and who have the power to enforce such laws and to make the State secure within and without.[1] Thus all the authorities, other than the personal ruler, were debarred, through being represented as incompetent to deal with actual affairs. And then Hobbes brought the vague and long-esteemed Natural Law down to earth, for he depicted the law of nature as simply the brute law of self-preservation, a law common to man with the animals, and with nothing majestic about it. Thus he managed to depreciate ideals of law and right as in any sense at all "authorities," and cleared the ground for the undisputed title of the visible sovereign as the one and only authority, the true superior, by reference to whose will all law and the State itself derived their value for the lives of men. What had been a host of competitors of the sovereign, in the popular estimation, were thus made subordinate to his absolute power.

But the confusion over authority was not yet perfectly cleared. What the particular visible sovereignty ought to be was a question at issue in Hobbes' own England. The people were in the midst of a civil war where the settlement of their allegiance was at stake. For "the government of men" might consist either of "one man or a council of men." Hobbes seems to have avoided giving too explicit an answer, perhaps lest doing so would identify him with one or the other party, and thereby prejudice his appeal on behalf of a common loyalty. Let the decision come by the sword, or by wit, or by any other means, he seems to say, but let it then be a true decision. This could be best accomplished, however, if the settlement were effected by contract, by the will of all the people, as it were: Let every man agree with every other to accept the rule of a common sovereign,

[1] Hobbes, *Philosophical Rudiments*, Preface XXII; Ch. 12, Sect. 4, p. 154. *Leviathan* Part IV, Ch. XLVI, pp. 373-374.

whether one man or a council of men, whichever one is acceptable at the fateful moment, and then all must abide by that general decision and obey all the commands of the sovereign as laws of the State. By that "social compact" the individuals would create the obligation binding upon them all, and at the same time, happily enough, they would provide a sanctioning power for their obligations, by authorizing the sovereign to enforce them even against their own will. Thenceforward their own sovereign would be in a position to see to it that they carried out every solemn undertaking or agreement with each other in the common business of life. Their sovereign would guard against any renouncing on their part of the obligation they had assumed. The sovereign would prevent any undoing of the bonds they had consented to accept. The sovereign would stop absolutely any rebellion to overthrow the régime of government that all had thus voluntarily instituted.[1] There was, too, a certain carry-over from the older theory of contract, for the sovereign was envisaged as providing security for those who obey the laws of the State promulgated under his rule, and Hobbes even allowed the possibility of the sovereign's failure to render such protection and security, in which case the individuals would be once more free to look out for their own preservation according to the law of nature. But this was well in the background of the discussion and had reference to the extreme situation when *force majeure*, that is, a force other than that of the subjects themselves in revolt, proved the sovereign to be ineffectual. Then alone did the subjects regain their liberty and private judgment.[2] But the common source of trouble Hobbes evidently considered to lie in the people themselves, especially in their temper of distrust and disobedience. He was seeking to induce them to put themselves under a discipline so as to overcome their own fickleness, blindness, incon-

---

[1] Hobbes, *Philosophical Rudiments*, Ch. 5 (Of the Causes and First Beginnings of Civil Government), Sect. 5, p. 68; Ch. 6 (Of the Right of Him Whether Council or One Man Only, Who Hath the Supreme Power in the City), Part 20, pp. 89, 91. *Leviathan*, Part II, Of Commonwealth, Ch. XVII, pp. 87–89; Ch. XVIII, p. 91.

[2] *Leviathan*, Part II, Ch. XXI (Of the Liberty of Subjects, p. 116), Ch. XXVIII, p. 165; Ch. XXIX, p. 178.

sistency, lawlessness, all of which was summed up in the term, "irrationality." He believed that a human civilization required a sovereignty above anything the people might accomplish of themselves, and that this would make them law-abiding and moral beings, rather than brutes, in the satisfying of their desires, particularly the desire for power which he saw writ everywhere in the record of human experience. Acknowledge a sovereign, then, with one accord, and let that sovereign exercise his rule without such endless questioning of right and attempted interference.

However, these arguments for the discipline of a sovereignty were against a temper which had to be reasoned with on its own terms. Hobbes was forced to bring in the notion of obligation as a moral commitment arising from contract. And he was exceedingly clever in suborning the popular ideas to his philosophy of personal sovereignty. The trick of his reasoning was this: though the individuals were dealing *with* each other, it turned out that they were not bound to each other, but *to an outside party, their sovereign.*[1] They originally obliged themselves, but only that once, for they had nothing to say afterwards about any exactions which that sovereign might make of them and to which they would then be "obliged" by him as their "superior." All participated in bringing this regimen into existence and were committed to it, but they were then obliged by their sovereign to maintain that regimen forever and to accept all the detailed obligations of their lives in the form of requirements of his command and will. That additional coercive obligation was made to appear a great merit, for the obligations of men to each other in society stand *under* something which makes them all effective, or "perfect," in the sense of Roman law. Men were free agents only long enough to subject themselves to a rule which denied them any subsequent freedom. Their competence in reason and morals was admitted only to be denied in the sequel. A pretense, indeed, of their having a continued part in the

[1] Hobbes, *vide, Phil. Rudiments*, Ch. 5, Sect. 20, p. 91. *Leviathan,* Part II, Ch. XVIII, p. 89.

affair was made by calling the sovereign, ironically, their "representative." [1] But in fact the will and good of all the people were sunk wholly in the will of that sovereign who, uniting in himself all their powers and perfections, shone with high majesty. The sovereign constituted the unity of the body-politic and therefore he actually *made* the State. He was, too, the sole law-maker. He enjoyed a perfect and an undisputed authority. So the whole duty of man resolved itself into conformity to the will of that sovereign.

Obligation was then and there dissociated entirely from the free will of the persons obliged, and related exclusively to the will of the "obliging" superior. Though the term had originally a reference to the interests of the parties in some transaction with each other, it was thought of only in relation to an outsider from whom the obligation came, as something raining down from above, and presumably having the quality of mercy. Yet all liberty and benefits for the contracting parties, save a supposed security, were suppressed from the scene. Only the enforcing agency stood out prominently, and this was an external person participating in the affair without commitments on his side, a superior who was admitted there by them but who was nevertheless empowered to compel action from them for all the future, regardless of any new interest or resolve of theirs in that indeterminate future. Hobbes had manipulated so well the notion of contract that the obligation which counted for so much in the minds of men was actually employed to fasten them more securely to their governing superiors. Obligation was represented as a mere effect of political mastery.

III

CRITICISMS OF SOVEREIGNTY

The philosopher's ideal of sovereignty was put into practice by kings. There was achieved a consolidation of central control in the dominant nations of Europe. The civil wars

---

[1] Hobbes, *Leviathan*, Part II, Ch. XXII, p. 118; Ch. XXVI, p. 142; Ch. XXVIII, p. 166; Ch. XXIX, p. 172; Ch. XXX, p. 186.

ended and war persisted only as an affair between strong
sovereign States. Royal government proved itself able to
keep a nation united as a body-politic and thus to put a
stop to the fatal disintegration to which all peoples in Europe
seemed for a time to be fatally doomed. This competence of
sovereigns to preserve their communities was warrant enough
for their title to supremacy. Consequently no lesser associations, no churches, no bodies of any sort could hold out
against them, but only enjoyed such rights as were recognized by them. All the controls over men came to be envisaged as being of the same sort as positive laws, ordinances
or commands of the political superior. As for the individual,
there seemed to be nothing else in the world for him to be
obliged to, save the will of that majestic being, the sovereign.

Yet that ideal of sovereignty did not sweep triumphantly
over all the civilization of Europe, nor did it even establish
itself absolutely in those nations that accepted monarchy.
Thus the religious sects, though they were forced to be
tolerant, would not subscribe in conscience to the opinion
of a Divine Right of Kings which was a sacrilegious theft
from their own armory, putting kings directly in communication with God, in place of the Church. Nor were the
philosophers satisfied with the absolutist system. In serving
its purpose so well, it eliminated their preoccupation with
internal peace and order and released their minds to a consideration of other values and desiderata, so that they became critical of sovereignty. The criticism was expressed
by three writers who happened to be born in the same year,
1632, and who composed their works toward the end of
the seventeenth century; John Locke in England, Bene-
dict Spinoza in Holland, and Samuel Pufendorf in Germany. These men reflected upon the premise of Hobbes,
that the basis of sovereignty is utility, that it exists to provide for security and peace in order that individuals may
then be free to pursue their own ends and enjoy their own
goods and property. But a little watching of "the mortal
god, Leviathan" had made them anxious. They saw peace
in the immediate locality, but peace without liberty. And

they noticed war still on the face of the earth, war between the sovereign States themselves and reaching to the life of humanity within every jurisdiction. The unity achieved by the sovereigns seemed really at the expense of "the general society of mankind," and therefore of humanity in every nation. The lawlessness practiced in the external relations of States was becoming the spirit of the dealings of the sovereigns with their own subjects, a spirit of tyranny going hand in hand with that of conquest. Because they were individualists at heart, the philosophers tended to become cosmopolitans. Their attitude detached them from the reigning conceptions, they reflected on their own experience and began to rewrite the theory of society so as to interpret it. Thus began a period of criticism in political philosophy which was contemporaneous with the empirical movement in philosophy from the time of Locke onward.

It so happened that the countries of which Locke, Pufendorf, and Spinoza were inhabitants offered a variety of political experience quite contrasting with that of the other nations of Europe. The Whig Revolution of 1688 exhibited a people delegating powers of government to a ruler chosen by them through their representatives. Locke was the spokesman of that policy and he wrote about it as if the people constituted a power in their own right, subsisting independently of their sovereigns and able, in crises like the present, of providing for themselves and setting up their own civil establishment just as they had already done with their Church. Then the people of Holland, where Spinoza lived, had proved themselves competent enough to secure their independence from the Spanish monarchy and to make an adventure with a republican system. Thus the situation in both Holland and England disclosed, to the observant philosophers, the reality of a common will in the people themselves and the non-necessity of assuming, as Hobbes had done, that the people never can be an entity until they have first given themselves over without reserve to a sovereign. On the contrary, their demonstrated ability to coöperate, whether in making a contract for a ruler or in revolting against oppression from above, proved that they constituted a political society in their own right, and that they were not made so by the sovereign, but contrariwise the sovereign was made what he was by them. Such thoughts contained grave reflections upon the prerogative of the sovereign.

A most striking criticism, however, came from a professor of law and moralist of Heidelberg, Samuel Pufendorf, who could not tolerate for a moment Hobbes' notion of a society existing "by force of discipline," and who was empirically disposed to make observations for himself on such a matter. He was interested in the political phenomena of his own land. The organization of the German States was looser than anything recognized as a true body-politic according to the regnant juristic theory, so that they were generally spoken of, derogatively, as "the Germanic body." Having in his veins some of the moral individualism that had caused all the modern mischief, he was not inclined to disparage such a form of society simply because it did not bear the authoritative hallmark. It was, at any rate, a form of society having the dignity of a history,—the federation. Moreover, this body maintained both a peace and the liberty of its component members without the domineering of any superior in the grand manner of monarchy. True, a sovereign existed but he was only an elective head. Such a working arrangement in the Germanic body demonstrated that genuine associations might arise distinctly prior to the active intervention or services of a governing superior and could persist without much ado on his part. Pufendorf no doubt took comfort from the remark of Grotius, too, that there is first of all in the order of events "a spirit or constitution in the people" and that this really is the primary bond of union between them.[1] With such notions in mind, Pufendorf recast Hobbes' social compact so as to explain how any society might primarily be constituted and provide the essentials of peace and security without derogation from the liberty of the individuals: every member makes a covenant with

[1] Grotius, *op. cit.*, Bk. II, Ch. IX, p. 263.

every other member of such an association to live together as one body and under one set of laws or governance, but without designating any particular governing sovereign. This compact suffices in and of itself to make the members into one body, or in the language of Pufendorf's invention, a "moral person," endowed with a will called "the general will." Before people elect their own chief they must be "a people," a generality with a will of their own. That will can, thereafter, take further action. And, in Pufendorf's opinion, such action must immediately follow the first act of covenant. For the general will cannot really exist unless it be vested in some particular and recognized authority whereby it becomes determinate and effective. The action by which the people do this is another contract, but this time it is like that described by Grotius, a contract instituting a government. Here the body-politic, already made such by the prior act of all its members, deals, as one person, with a special party distinct from that body, and confers the general right of governance upon him as a ruler. By that deed the general will becomes identified with a determinate particular will. The sovereign is the bearer, then, of the sovereignty of the whole body and he is authorized to do all the things for the community that were traditionally associated with sovereignty, and especially, to make the positive laws and enforce them.[1] The sovereign was thus allowed by Pufendorf to have ubiquity of jurisdiction, and omnicompetence as a legislative and executive power. Law in the State was nothing other than the command of the sovereign. Nevertheless, despite such deference to the person of the sovereign, Pufendorf betrayed far more inner respect for the "moral person" he had discovered, and for the "general will" of this person which he called, eulogistically, "the transcendental power" of the State.[2] By such language he recommended the general will to all men, as the truly supreme object of their allegiance. The effect was indeed to restore an au-

---

[1] Pufendorf, *Of the Law of Nature and Nations* (English Translation, Oxford, 1710), Bk. 7 (Of the Causes and Motives Inducing Men to Establish Civil Societies), Ch. 2, Sects. 4–14, pp. 507–518.
[2] Pufendorf, *op. cit.*, Bk. 8, Ch. 2 (Of the Power of the Sovereign), Sect. 2, p. 611.

thority "invisible," but it was not the old-fashioned sort, like the Law of Nature or the Republic, which Hobbes had driven off the scene by his mockery of inert, will-less powers, incapable of adjustments to new conditions,—this authority was itself a will. And the general will was superior to the will of the personal sovereign, for it and not any monarch or a Parliament really *made* the State.

This position implied that the fundamental obligaticn of men in society is to this general will and the body of the people. Pufendorf did not explicitly make this invidious distinction between the allegiances. He obscured it, perhaps inadvertently, by the sheer multitude of his distinctions in regard to obligation. For he reverted to Grotius' way of thinking and paraded the variety of obligations obtaining among men, some from the law of nature, others from covenant, and still others from the authority of a sovereign ruler. However, the obligations seemed to define themselves in two contrasting ways. "What morally inclines the will most, or ought to incline it, is obligation." This kind of obligation was not regarded as a "denial of liberty," for it is only a person who is free, and grasps the idea of a rule, that can possibly have such an obligation. On the other hand, the "obligation of law" or the "obligation laid by a superior" was deemed a real abatement of personal freedom, because it rested on some other power than the will of the person obliged. "Though law ought not to want its reasons, yet those reasons are not the cause why obedience is paid to it but the power of the exactor." [1] These two conceptions of obligation were not merely different; they were antithetical. The one form was compatible with freedom, the other not. The obligation to law was not a matter of moral right but simply a conformity to an authorized general power, presumed to be acting for good ends in every case; the obligation to a covenant, on the other hand, was a moral conformity, and a better thing. The tendencies of Pufendorf's thinking were toward an assimilating of the political obligation to

[1] Pufendorf, *op. cit.*, Ch. 4 (Of the Will of Man as it Concerns Moral Actions), Sect. 8, p. 33; Ch. 6 (Of the Rule of Moral Actions or of Law in General), Sect. 1, p. 46.

this moral form. However equivocal his language might be, he definitely refused to subordinate the moral to the political, as Hobbes had done, and to treat obligation solely as the bond laid upon subjects by the sheer power of their superior. The Whole Duty of Man (as his briefer work was translated) was not to be summed up in obedience to the sovereign. Before the sovereign there is God to be honored, the Supreme Being, and next to God the "moral person" of the people whose general will it is that makes the State, and only then come the particular persons and superiors for their dues of honor and respect. What then is the precise degree of "majesty" left to the personal sovereigns? They are not the creators of the bodies-politic over which they rule. Their own authority to give the law seems to be set in a larger jurisdiction of the people with their general will. Such were the questionings suggested by Pufendorf's writings, and these conspired, with the work of his contemporaries, Spinoza and Locke, to destroy the notion that an absolute sovereignty is vested in any particular person.

A cosmopolitan movement of the eighteenth century carried the various political ideas into every quarter of Europe. Through Bayle's great Dictionary and the discussions it aroused, the views of Spinoza received some currency, though, indeed, little real appreciation. Locke had the good luck to conquer Europe, with the help of those French writers who took up with English ideas of all sorts, whether on religion, or government, or the human understanding. Pufendorf found an able translator and an editor in Jean Barbeyrac who had likewise rendered Grotius in the French and who contributed comments of his own. He was insistent upon the need of greater clarity in the fundamental notions, and this often led him to criticize his masters, with a leaning toward the clean-cut lines of the Hobbesian theory. Thus when Grotius, thinking of the authority of the Law of Nature, seemed to insinuate that "law obliges of itself *merely as a rule*," his commentator roundly declared that "all laws derive from the superior" and have whatever validity they

possess solely from his power. When Grotius said he could
see "no reason why a man cannot oblige himself, *if laws are
covenants*," Barbeyrac retorted quickly in a note: "but laws
are *not* covenants" and ought never to be thought of by
analogy with them. In fact he inclined toward reversing
the analogy,—when men seem to be "obliged by covenant,"
or by anything not the law of a *civil* authority, they are
really obliged by the law of some superior, and when such
law is not traceable to a civil authority it must be referred to
"the will of God," from whom all the moral and political
laws come.[1] By such commentary Barbeyrac put the question of *law* in the forefront of discussion in France.

Then came Montesquieu, the true student of law, as a
phenomenon not of any special locality or of any age, ancient
or modern, but of all times and places. He achieved more
than any other writer the dignity of the scientist rather than
the propagandist for a cause, although his sentiments and
views were clearly enough liberal. He had a realistic interest
in "the laws," and considered them as if they were relations
of things, not unlike the relations studied by physical science.
This made his definition of law, as "the necessary relation
which derives from the nature of things," seem cold and
abstract to some writers like the ardent Rousseau. But it
indicated a new vein of thought. He had read Plato and
Aristotle with fresh insight, taking note of their practicality
which had been for so long denied, after Hobbes' contemptu-
ous aspersions, and he appreciated how seriously they had
reckoned with the objective circumstances of political systems, considering geographical location, climate, and various
other external conditions of the life of a nation. Of course
he saw, too, their recognition of the distinctive spirit or
character of a people, and in his own realism he counted
this as more important than the externals. But the relationships of law to both the physical factors and the national

---

[1] Grotius, *op. cit.*, Barbeyrac's notes, Bk. I, Ch. I, Sects. IX–X, pp. 6–10; Bk. II, Ch. XI,
Sect. II, p. 280n.
    Barbeyrac, *Examen du Jugement d'un Anonyme* (Leibniz?) *sur L'original de cet Abrégé*
(in same volume with Pufendorf's *Les Devoirs de L'Homme et du Citoyen*, Amsterdam, 1718),
p. 473.

character had been entirely overlooked by the moderns who had fashioned their theories in partisan atmosphere and consequently stressed the will of this or that individual or council, the monarch or the Parliament, as if the relationship to such a person or persons contained the whole significance of law. They had made entirely too much of the issuance of law by a central government. They ignored the fact that customs and morals are real in their own authority and have quite as "imperious a rule" as any royal decrees. Montesquieu undertook to exhibit, in respect to the many known social systems of the world, this double relationship to the whole people on the one hand and to their physical environment on the other. And simply to disclose such a fact that law sustained these other relations besides that of issuing from the will of a sovereign was to rob the latter relation of its exclusive importance. And further, to describe legislation as the act of adjusting people to the conditions of their life was to make it more like negotiation or contract, as Grotius had suggested, than the mere command of an authority. In any case the positive laws are but a small part of the constitution; the constitution itself is operative and effectually so, independently of the function of the personal ruler, and every ruler, no matter how absolute he seems, is actually limited in what he can do, or determine to have done, by this larger régime of the popular life to which he is subject like every one else,—"the spirit of the laws." The laws of the sovereign person who governs have their validity only through their conformity with this organic law of the nation, rooted in the sentiments, habits, and historical life of the people.[1] Such a conclusion sapped the grand pretension of the sovereign to an absolute jurisdiction. With the really valid law thus placed entirely beyond the competence of the ruler, either to make or to unmake, the sovereign *personnage* had lost another important prerogative in civil society, that of being "the law-maker."

[1] *Vide*, Montesquieu, *Œuvres Complètes* (Paris, 1866), *Considerations de la Grandeur des Romains et de leur Décadence*, Ch. 21, p. 180; Ch. 22, p. 184; *De l'Esprit des Lois*, Bk. 1, Ch. 1, p. 190; Bk. 19, Ch. 4 (Ce que c'est l'Esprit Général), p. 337; Ch. 5, p. 338; Ch. 27, p. 345.

But the sovereign seemed still of value, as being at least "the government" proper, and yet this rôle, too, was going to be denied. It was realized that the importance of the personal ruler in the function of government had been greatly overestimated. It was Locke who started this line of depreciation, in his *Civil Government*, when he assigned to the sovereign only certain specific functions. To specify power was to limit it. Montesquieu went farther than Locke, and following a suggestion found in Aristotle's *Politics*, dispersed the powers of governance among several bodies, especially separating the legislative from the executive. He pointed to the existence of such divisions of power in the various polities of history. But a lesser-known figure, Abbé de St. Pierre, had gone farther still, though his work was available to few and then largely through the divining genius of J. J. Rousseau who rescued it from oblivion (in a piece entitled *The Plurality of Councils*).[1] St. Pierre recommended a thoroughgoing administrative *pluralism*. He had observed the administration of France during a period of Regency, and reflected that the sovereign himself acted merely as a figurative unity in the government and that all real acts of governance were performed by groups of minor officials. This suggested to him a theory of government by a "plurality of councils," where each council deals with a certain phase of the nation's affairs, and is held to its place and function and prevented from transgressing upon others by the great number of other bodies of functionaries which have an interest in maintaining the whole system. The variety of the councils and their number make for the safety of the whole State against any tyrannical seizure of power or violation of justice or disturbance of the peace and good order. The bodies of men in such a scheme hold each other to the law without ever needing to invoke the coercive force of an external party or superior. They constitute a self-contained coöperative body, a group of self-governing councils. So the usual predominance of the sovereign person in the busi-

[1] *Vide*, C. E. Vaughan, *The Political Writings of Rousseau* (Cambridge, 1915), Vol. 1, pp. 397 ff.

ness of government appeared to St. Pierre not warranted by any "utility." What he proposed, therefore, was a system of government actually dispensing with the services of the sovereign as the supreme executive.

Divested of the once-held high prerogatives of *founding* the State and *making its law* and *governing* it, the personal sovereign was fast losing all "majesty." Still a deep-seated, primordial belief persisted, in the necessity of a Chief of State to provide for the security of the society and its fundamental laws, so that most writers were committed to the traditional theory of social contract which expressed the idea that for protection and peace men give over to certain persons the right to govern them. Even those who were no longer captivated by any of the glamour and prestige of the glorious monarch as the representative of a great civilization, even such men as the editors of the French *Encyclopedia*, were inclined to regard the sovereign as an indispensable chief executive, whose function it was to use the powers of the whole State to guarantee against injury all those dutiful individuals who obeyed the laws,—meaning laws "positive" and "fundamental laws" and the laws of reason or "natural right."[1] This need for social security was the primal *raison d'être* of all political authority, and it seemed quite a sufficient reason for accepting limited monarchy.

It was not a reason at all for Jean Jacques Rousseau. Disposed by his reading and by his idealization of Geneva to see glory only in the whole people, he had, in very striking essays, challenged a princely civilization reared on opportunist politics and poetic adulation. He was utterly antipathetic to the very idea of a "superior." He could not think of authorizing anyone to coerce and exercise control over other persons. Jealous of his own independence, he was alert and most critical in regard to such a scheme of giving over authority by contract with a sovereign. He was looking at the

---

[1] Diderot, *Œuvres Complètes* (Paris, 1875), T. I, *Suite de l'Apologie de M. l'Abbé de Prades*, Sect. XI, stating principles of the Encyclopedia, p. 469; T. 6, articles, Autorité, pp. 392–395; Cité, pp. 187–188; Fondation (Politique et Droit Naturel), p. 12; Pouvoir, p. 385; T. 7, Souverains, pp. 166–168.
  Cf. René Hubert, *Les Sciences Sociales dans L'Encyclopédie* (Alcan, Paris, 1923), pp. 158–159.

whole situation entirely *from the side of the subject*. He
wanted to see the precise good of any such arrangement
for the individual. Security, first of all, it had been said and
repeated, time and again; security for all men as they render
honest obedience to the laws. And whose laws are these?
Those, apparently, of their sovereign, or interpreted by
him. It is for safety under such a regimen of law determined
by an external sovereign that the individuals are supposed
to renounce all employment of their own powers for their
own private interest and to vest them, instead, in that superior who is thenceforward to take care of them and the
laws and the State. Here Rousseau proved himself as ob-
stinately logical and realistic as ever Hobbes had been.
Security is the desideratum,—is it really obtained by this
contract? What security have the individuals against the
great power of sovereignty to which they have subjected
themselves? Rousseau asked this, remembering well what
Hobbes had said, that it is always men who govern; and
another saying, too, that men are ineradicably self-interested,
and thirsting always for the power to domineer over others,
whence it happens that all their existence is made insecure
for them. To escape that savage insecurity and domination
at the hands of their equals they are here supposed to commit
themselves wholly to the charge of a superior. Yet he, the
sovereign, is a mere man, with an inevitable self-interest
and a love of dominion. The individuals conscious of their
own human weakness are supposed to be so foolish as to
overlook the fact that their ruler is a fellow-man, exposed
to the same vices and likely to behave in the same way as
themselves; and then to bestow everything that is of any
worth to them upon him. Though their intention in contracting is to obtain mutual benefits for themselves, they
actually make that outsider the chief beneficiary. After that
transaction they are bound by their deed to obey their
sovereign; he, for his part, is only bound to see that they do
it. His "obligation" is most curiously favorable to his natural inclination in the matter. All the powers of men have
been given over to him to carry out his superior will which

is very likely to be selfish and oppressive; only duties and exactions fall to their lot. But they enjoy security, do they not? Yes, a security in an equivocal sense. Theirs is a security to do their sovereign's bidding,—but nothing is vouchsafed them when they want to do their own. The individuals have no guarantee whatsoever against the abuse of all their social power by the human superior they have recognized in their contract. Surely this contract is a spurious thing. If men really seek security they never arrange for it on such terms as these whereby the life and liberty and goods of every one are jeopardized by an external power which has an absolute right of way for itself. They are all equally enslaved to a person who has nothing holding him to responsible action and justice. There is certainly no advantage in such a pretended contract, none for the parties who are "obliged" by it. Nor is it morally right. The individuals are supposed by their own free will to bind themselves, then and there, to have no other will save that of their common master. By a free deed they deny themselves a will for the future like that which their voluntary action of the present evinces. They employ their will to make an absolute surrender of will for life. Such an action is unrighteous and absurd. Freedom is the essence of humanity, and human beings cannot, even if they are tricked into the formality of doing so, divest themselves of this power to determine their own conduct in the future. Nor are they likely to be fooled into doing it by anyone, for when they once act in concert they implicitly assume that they can do so again and they will make every effort to safeguard that power of taking action in common and for their own good. This guardianship of the liberties and the common will of the people is precisely what the sovereign of old is never seen to undertake as his part in the contract. Instead he acts so as to threaten human society and the freedom of the individual. Rousseau put a question fatal to the lingering belief in a limited monarchy based on contract: Is a *secured slavery* a real ground for an allegiance to authority?

After such representations personal sovereignty seemed

to be worse than useless, a negative factor in the State, a power dangerous to the things of greatest value to humanity. The authority of kings being no longer admirable was felt to be alien and inimical. True "majesty" had disappeared, and with it went all sense of obligation. In such an aspect the sovereign was the very last thing in the world an individual could possibly be obliged to. Of course, an obedience might be rendered him perforce, but it would not proceed from the will and therefore it would be utterly different from a true and moral obligation. This momentous difference Rousseau struck off in a phrase of remarkable decision: "It is not a question of a power we are forced to obey, but only of one we are *obliged to recognize*."[1] That statement of the question was a turning point in modern political philosophy.

IV

THE GENERAL WILL

Rousseau now embarked on a genuinely new quest: What kind of power is it that men are obliged to recognize? This research involved what might be called a Copernican Revolution in politics. It was oriented from the point of view of the individuals who recognize the obligation instead of from that of a superior imposing it from above. Law and obligation were being conceived not as an effect of the will of a superior, but rather as an expression of the will of the persons who feel obliged. Rousseau was standing among equals and deciphering a social world from their experience of common duties and rights. Whereas others had made obligation subordinate to some preconceived ideal of authority, he was starting with the idea of *moral* obligation as the fundamental thing and looking for the conception of authority that would suit it. His problem was to describe a human order where it is the individuals themselves who impose all

---

[1] Rousseau, First Version of the *Social Contract*, Ch. 5 (False Notions of the Social Bond), Vaughan, *op. cit.*, Vol. 1, pp. 470, 480; Final Version, Bk. III, Ch. 10 (On the Abuse of Government, etc.), Vaughan, Vol. 2, p. 88.

The interpretation of Rousseau in this article is presented without the supporting evidence which will be made available, however, in a book in process of completion.

the bonds of their society and give themselves laws, and, in the largest sense of the word, actually govern themselves. To the charting of this new order he intended to devote a masterpiece entitled, *Political Institutions*, from which the *Social Contract* survives as a fragment.

But it took time and patient meditation of the theme, and even a second writing, to produce that essay on "the principles of political right." A certain inner work of imagination was needed to assemble into one view all the divers suggestions toward liberalism that had been made by previous thinkers, and notably by Locke, Pufendorf, St. Pierre, and Montesquieu. Each of those men had pronounced against an absolute sovereignty and had stripped the ruler of this or that particular prerogative. But these powers dislodged from the sovereign person could not be left scattered in a kind of limbo, unrelated to each other and unattached to any common subject. The earlier idea of seventeenth-century philosophy still persisted in the thinking of Rousseau, that powers inhere in some substance and that "the whole" is a very real thing. The powers of governance and legislation, though taken away from the eminent sovereign, somehow belonged together and to the whole social body. How to imagine that body-politic, its sovereignty, its legislation, its government, that was a task for a genius who could gather all the partial enlightenment of his predecessors into the clear focus of a new theory and present, in its complete form, a polity that would supplant the old rejected sovereignty.

The first step necessary was to reckon with the seeming impediments of logic. The old and accepted maxims of politics were decidedly against even the possibility of such an order of human relations as Rousseau was contemplating. They had won such currency that they were virtually axiomatic in philosophy and were consequently expressed in the most emphatic form an opinion can have, the negative proposition. Hobbes had written: "The laws of reason oblige only in the inner consciousness of man but not in external conduct," which was meant to imply that only a power external to both the men and the laws could have any force of control over them. And Bodin had voiced a similar denial: "The laws of themselves cannot oblige,— but only the power of a superior," whence it followed that "no man can lay himself under an obligation to law, if by law is meant whatever is imposed by the power of a superior." And even Grotius had joined the chorus of denying spirits: "No man can oblige himself, because, perforce, he must then be his own superior, which is impossible and absurd."[1] And an inference from this was drawn against democracy: since what holds of one man must hold of a multitude of men, and man alone cannot govern himself, it follows that a whole self-governing society is impossible. So the only possibility is a governing superior. Always that superior! This unanimity of the various opinions was enough to raise a suspicion in Rousseau's mind about their impartial logic. It seemed to him as if those writers had succumbed to the vice of philosophers described by Montaigne, that of letting their reason take its ply from their passions or interests. They all appeared to be committed in advance to an ideal of "superior power." Their maxims were framed thus cogently in order to vindicate that prejudice. Rousseau, however, had a very strong counter-prejudice for "republican principles." So he was neither persuaded nor coerced by what he called the "principles of tyranny," but was incited, by their pretense of logic, to examine them critically. In this he proved himself to have an amazing power to get behind the form of words to the real argument and the values dictating it, a critical achievement which placed him in the company of intellectuals in the eighteenth century whose questioning of all belief and reason gave it fame as an age of enlightenment.

Rousseau was a stubborn interlocutor. Why are the dictates of reason of no account *in foro externo?* Because, it had been said, the laws of reason cannot of themselves "oblige." Why not? Because they must have the will of

---

[1] Hobbes, cited above, p. 252.
Bodin, *op. cit.*, Bk. I, Ch. 8 (De la Souveraineté), p. 135.
Grotius, *op. cit.*, Bk. I, Ch. I, p. 10; Bk. II, Ch. IV, Sect. XII, p. 182; Ch. XIV, Sect. I, p. 330.

some active being behind them, the will of a "person." Why cannot that effectual will be just the will of the persons themselves who recognize those laws as their own and as rightly applying to their own conduct and life? But that, it was rejoined, is impossible, for no man can lay down a law for himself, or "oblige" himself, inasmuch as his will must then be stronger than itself,—a plain absurdity. Hence it is always necessary that there shall be in the society of men an external and superior will to give law to all alike and to oblige them to obey. This is a necessity, whether there be one man or a multitude, and it was urged that the greater number only increases the difficulty of conceiving an intelligent self-control. This was the argument Rousseau saw on behalf of the opinion that a political society must always have the form of a body of men subject to a sovereign, that is to say, the form of monarchy.

The necessity of an external sovereignty had here been demonstrated in much the same way as God had been proved to exist by the pure logic of metaphysics. This was in line with a certain way of thinking about "power" common to the philosophy of that period, whether the philosophy of the State or that of things divine. The logic of it was challenged by Rousseau's contemporary, David Hume, who had asked why everything which comes into being must have a cause for its existence *distinct* from itself and *external* to it? Usually God was conceived as a "first cause" of the world and an external mover of the world machine. And by the same pattern of thought, the sovereign was imagined as a necessary cause for the society of individuals, a power external and, indeed, a veritable deity to them. This was a political version of the cosmic arrangement represented by philosophical deism. But there was taking place at that very time in the eighteenth century one of those changes of imagination which expresses itself eventually in new theories everywhere in the realm of thought. Various philosophers, notably Bayle, Maupertuis, Hume, and Diderot had caught up from the ancients the idea of Nature as containing within herself all the powers of preservation and betterment which had been customarily ascribed to the external agency of a God. The writers of the *Encyclopedia* and others were exploring the possibilities of this "naturalism." Rousseau, moving in this atmosphere of ideas, was helped thereby to surmount, in his own thinking, the logic of the older political writers. He conceived the "natural" order in society as something analogous to the order of Nature in general; an order where the whole people themselves are quite adequate to the task of preserving and managing their own lives without dependence upon any external cause; they are self-contained and self-sovereign as a society. This was the social polity which he called "The Form of the Republic," and this conception so filled his mind that he made it the subtitle of his first version of the *Social Contract*.

This vision of the new alternative gained support in his mind from reflection upon the concrete instances which preceding liberal thinkers had cited in their works. Pufendorf had revealed the German people to be a "people" with a permanent existence of their own independently of any action on the part of their elective ruler. Montesquieu had exhibited "the invisible rule" of the spirit of the laws in every nation,—pouring masterly scorn on the writers "who see disorder wherever they do not see the Crown," and who must always have "visible chiefs."[1] And Abbé de St. Pierre had presented two very definite projects, one of a group of councils acting as a coöperative body in the administration of government, and the other of the sovereign States of Europe taking the necessary common action to preserve order and peace amongst themselves and thereby promoting the general happiness of mankind. It was quite conceivable, in these several instances, that bodies of men, or associations of any sort, might provide for their own security, their needs and their growing interests entirely out of their own resources, without subjecting themselves to any external control, or to the direction of any sovereign. It was possible to envisage very definitely a body of officials functioning as a self-governing administrative unit, and

[1] Montesquieu, *op. cit.*, Bk. 24, Ch. 6, p. 408; Bk. 29, Ch. 19, p. 478.

a body of principalities, as in Germany, managing to live together safely under a form of federative society, and even a body of sovereign States forming themselves into a solid "European republic" and governing themselves, and securing peace and justice in the international field. How immediately feasible such schemes of government might be, in the actual circumstances of the time, was entirely beside the point which was one of logic. The simple fact that these cases were clearly conceivable, without any absurdity, discredited utterly those pretentious maxims which declared such a form of association to be theoretically impossible.

Freed from the tyranny of the old phrases Rousseau explored the possibilities of this new way of life in society which had come into his view. Those exceptions to the prevailing social order might actually be made the rule for the entire range of human relationships, wherever men need permanent ties other than those of their natural affections. For administrative bodies, cities, nations, federations, and international leagues the general principle might be this, that the parties to any association are governed only by themselves or by their own laws. Yet this conception, though possible to reason, seemed still very paradoxical. It had to be worked out into a detailed theory, so as to meet every question and satisfy the imagination. To this constructive argument Rousseau devoted himself, "taking men as they are and laws as they might be."

It had been argued that "laws of themselves" cannot oblige. Certainly they cannot, if they are taken divorced entirely from all human will. They cannot then be more than what Hobbes called them—rules or entities of reason. But laws obtaining for any society of men are never in fact so separated from the active will of the men who constitute that society. It is false, therefore, to attribute a lack of power to laws *in abstracto* when they only exist in connection with human will. The real question is not as to their validity absolutely by themselves, but only *whose will it is they represent*. Now it had been further pronounced that this will cannot be the will of the persons subject to the laws. "Men by themselves" cannot impose their own laws and obligations, because they are unable to be superiors to themselves. Of course, if men are considered apart from each other and in isolation, this is true, for man in such a "state of nature" knows no law or ties. But the question is not about such fictitious, isolated beings. It has to do with people who can recognize bonds and laws. Men for whom those things have a meaning are no longer in that solitary condition but must already have joined with each other in some form of social relation. Hence it is necessary to think of them as having previously made a "*social* contract." This is a fundamental condition which must exist before there is anything like obligation or law: it is an action in which men bind themselves to society with each other. Why they do this is a matter of speculation, but it is reasonable to suppose with Spinoza and Pufendorf that the conjoint efforts of beings seeking their own preservation are of such great avail to them that they will naturally form themselves into a body in order to take a concerted action. They can achieve much more so than if acting alone or in a less organized way. For when men, who have been brought by some natural motives and circumstances into each other's neighborhood, proceed to make terms with each other, in order to live more like human beings, they create a power in their community vastly greater and more permanent than the sum of their individual powers without direction. And Rousseau perceived, from a quaint suggestion of Pufendorf's that they form a commonwealth in more than the obvious sense, not merely a pooling of goods and of physical and mental forces, but above all a pooling of their moral capacities: "some scattered seeds, (as it were), of government lie hid in particular persons, which, by means of concurrent compacts, being excited into motion, do grow and shoot forth," and appear as the sovereignty of their society.[1] So the influence of all is brought to bear on the life of every

---

[1] Pufendorf, Bk. 7, Ch. 3 (Of the Generation of Civil Sovereignty or Majesty), Sect. 4, p. 529.

individual. And this common power, acting in and through the will of every particular member of the body, is what Locke, Spinoza, Pufendorf, and Montesquieu had called either "the common will" or "the general will." Here, then, is a real *obliging* power, this general will. And the whole body or community from which it comes is, to all intents and purposes, "the superior" for each and every individual who is a member of it. Consequently it is entirely proper to say that men *oblige themselves:* "there is a vast difference between being obliged to oneself (impossible according to the maxims of civil law) and being obliged to a whole of which one forms a part." [1] "Men by themselves," if taken all together *as one body* can certainly oblige "themselves" when considered merely as so many dependent parts of the whole. And in the phraseology of the social contract this means that all the persons of any society function simultaneously in two capacities, as " sovereign " and as " subject." And this conception of what transpires in the social relationship does away with all the paradox about obligation as coming from within men themselves.

This conception of society makes it possible, too, to think of a political sovereignty which is neither alien nor tyrannous but always just. When the whole of which every member is an inalienable part acts in the common interest, it "obliges or favors" every one equally. This sovereignty gives no special privileges and makes no special exactions. To do so, would be in effect to detach from itself the party so singled out, and thereby to lose its authority not only with that individual but with every other member of the society. To be authoritative and valid the acts of the sovereign must always have this character of equality in regard to persons. Indeed, this feature becomes so important that it eclipses the old notion of superior power: "The act of sovereignty, properly speaking, is *not an order from a superior, nor a command* from a master to a slave; but an agreement of the Body of the State with each and every one of its

[1] *Social Contract*, Final Version, Bk. I, Ch. 7, Vaughan, ed., Vol. 2, p. 34.

members." [1] And law, which had been defined as the command of the sovereign, is now seen to be the will of the whole body reached by agreement with every member. "It has for its guarantee the public force and supreme power." [2] Where then is the paradox in saying that the "laws of themselves" can really oblige men? As expressions of the general will having reference to the general good they cannot even exist without enjoying an authority that no individual can gainsay. Laws need no force external to themselves to make them valid. They are, indeed, so essential in themselves that without them there is no *public* power at all, and therefore no sovereignty. The whole body obliges its parts only because its actions take the form of law, and are always just. Surely the laws, being the condition of that obligation, may be said to oblige men in their own right.

Of course there was still the puzzle Hobbes propounded, that the government of laws is impossible and only men can govern. The real power exists in the particular persons who can exercise it without let or hindrance from others. Yet, as Montesquieu showed, the actual administration is always carried on within the limits prescribed by the customs and laws of the people. No ruler wields power apart from the influence of the whole society and its constitution. If his action as an executive of the public business violates the code of procedure which the general will prescribes, it ceases to have the public force behind it and actually encounters evasion and opposition from every quarter of the body-politic. It was simply a defect of the imagination in the older writers not to have appreciated the power of the laws, and behind them, the power of the "moral person" which men themselves have constituted. "One man or a council of men" is never the mighty and independent "superior" that figures so prominently in the fancy of tradition; the governing body whatever its composition is but a lesser agent, and it is doubly subject, first to the laws and

[1] *Social Contract,* First Version, Bk. I, Ch. 6, Vaughan, ed., Vol. 1, p. 473; Final Version, Bk. II, Ch. 4, Vaughan, ed., Vol. 2, p. 45.
[2] *Ibid.*

then to the whole people whose general will is the true measure of right and utility for every body, large or small, within the society.

Rousseau was prepared by these reflections to state his theory of politics and to tell definitely what manner of power it is that men are "obliged to recognize." The true sovereign in any association is the whole body or people. The power that obliges the several members is that will for life in common which must be there if the people actually exist as a community. That general will is a power which the individuals are bound to acknowledge because it is at once their own will and a will corroborated by the wills of all those with whom they are associated. That will it is which creates the State, makes the laws, and, in the broadest sense of the term, really governs the people. By its nature belonging to all as a whole, it cannot be identified with or conferred upon any particular individual, thereafter to be miscalled "the sovereign," and it cannot act at any time in the exclusive interest of any particular person, since every sovereign act must be equal and just, that is to say, it must have the form of a law. Thus the general will is the real sovereignty. And the obligation of the individual is to an authority which reigns justly and equally, over himself and the others.

This theory of politics rounded out a period in modern thought. The first notion of an invisible authority, so drastically repudiated by Hobbes, was here reinstated fully as the only right authority. The general will of the people is in itself the very rule of right, the criterion of morality for every member of the republic, as the idea of justice had been in the *Republic* of Plato. But it is, too, an active power and not simply an impersonal idea, for the modern mind, used to sovereign functions, could not dispense with the notion of a will fully competent to perform them. The general will is such a sovereignty, the will of the whole body that adjusts it to the conditions of its social life and at the same time exercises a control over every member so as to maintain the integrity of the society. Thus

the two meanings of "superior," which had been in competition with each other throughout the modern argument,
the ideal meaning of right and the practical meaning of active power, were united in this conception of the general will.

That synthesis was accomplished, however, only at the
cost of the original premise of the argument for a supreme
authority. The search for something superior to conscience
had been made on the supposition of terrible defects in
the human conscience, manifest in men's disobedience,
division, and war. That older view implied a fundamental
evil in human nature, when left to itself and not subjected
to an external discipline. All such thoughts had been ab-
horrent to Rousseau. Consequently, when he had worked
out his alternative theory of political self-governance he
realized that he had won a new meaning for conscience, and
solid ground for a belief in the "natural goodness of man."
For conscience, it now appeared, is not merely "private
judgment," as had been thought in those days of religious
divergences and apparent disloyalty to all righteousness.
At times like that, when men are resisting evil and fighting
against external domination, their assertions of conscience
do have a rebellious and divisive character. But in its
normal action conscience is the very factor in the life of
mankind which makes for their existence in peace and community. For the conditions of the rise of a conscience in
individuals are precisely such as to make it from the start
a will in common with others and a will directed to the general good. Conscience is not what is peculiar in the individual, or idiosyncratic. It is a communicated moral power,
generated in men insofar as they are willing to be social.
Indeed, it may even be said that the high power of sovereignty engendered in the whole body descends upon every
good citizen where it shows itself as a power of self-control
in his personal life. Conscience is nothing less than the general will particularized in the decisions and conduct of the
individual. And so the thing most feared by the Renaissance was eventually exalted by Rousseau as the supreme
and only veritable authority.

V

Obligation and Contract

The general will had proved itself to be a liberating conception. Naturally Rousseau tended to make much of it, and to advance it as the key to the solution of every question. Moreover, he was a publicist, a writer for the times, anxious to make his point with people who were still used to the older ways of thinking. To those who wanted a sign he gave a sign. Some could not do without the thought of a grand authority, a sovereign, a potent will, to serve in place of the magnificent will of princes whose rule, nevertheless, they had come to believe unrighteous,—those readers were given a will in lieu of the dispossessed one, the general will, and it was represented in a grand manner. The general will inherited all the perfections once loaded on the *personnage* of the sovereign, and was spoken of eulogistically as "one, inalienable, indivisible, imprescriptible, and incapable of wrong." Others like the Encyclopedists were looking for some natural principle to account for the phenomenon of individuals living together in a society. Their first-chosen principle of "sociability" Rousseau had publicly banned in his *Discourse on Inequality*, but a principle was restored to them in the general will. Then there were moralists who desired a touchstone by reference to which men would be able to decide questions of justice and right in dealing with each other. The idea of the general will supplied this need and was exploited by both Diderot and Rousseau in their respective articles for the *Encyclopedia*, on "Natural Right" and "Political Economy." Thus many desiderata were being realized in this single conception. The general will served in one connection as a substitute for the private will of a ruler, in another as a sociological postulate, the will to live in common that is presumably obtaining among people if they have any society at all, and lastly, as an ideal norm of right, very much like Plato's Justice or the Law of Nature of earlier modern thought. The concept was becoming more voluminous with meaning than even the idea of sovereignty; and its disparate meanings were a source of confusion and danger.

Thus Rousseau could not avoid falling into a dialectic over the meaning of the general will. He found his associate Diderot interpreting it as a "will for the good of the species," supposed to be operative through the understanding of every human being, very much as instinct functions in animals. Indeed, such a will for the good of the whole organism or system was attributed by Diderot to every natural creature, so that the case of man was represented as but one in a host of others in the great realm of Nature. There is, then, a will for the general good of mankind inserted with the will for every one's private good. And this fancy inspired a fatuous optimism, a trust in the social and intellectual tendencies to work naturally toward a "general society of mankind." But Rousseau could not stomach such happy cosmopolitan illusions.[1] He was pessimistic about a civilization that comes about by the natural powers alone without human "artifice." Nor could he believe for a moment that a society of the nations will develop naturally, without heroic effort and cost. The institution of any human association is a moral undertaking, not a natural phenomenon. And the general will ought never to be thought of as a sort of biological principle in Nature that silently organizes men into an ever-increasing world-unity. Rousseau preferred to think of God in this connection, not the general will.

There was a contrary mistake, however, one destined to have tremendous effects in history. This was to identify the general will literally with the will of a nation. Being proposed as a substitute for the will of the Prince, it lent itself very readily to the opposite error of identification with the will of the people. Prince and people had been thought of for so long as in opposition that to take sovereignty from a particular chief seemed tantamount to bestowing it upon the mass of the people, designated a "person" for the sake of the legal fiction. There was no reason, however, why the will of a nation should in itself be taken as essentially more

[1] *Vide*, First Version, Bk. I, Ch. 2.

righteous than the will of their monarch. A greater rectitude may, indeed, be presumed as regards the people within the State, for the merely practical reason that if all who are affected by any decision participate in making it they are very much less likely to authorize harmful or wrong action, since they themselves will be the first to feel it. Nevertheless, they may often be mistaken even in regard to the real good of the whole group. "It is very necessary that the public shall learn to know what its true will is."[1] So the "will of all" cannot *ipso facto* be taken as "the general will," if one keeps in view the objective meaning of the latter. Furthermore their will as a people may at times be quite as particularistic, *by very intention*, as that of any single man or of a small group within the State, and in that selfish aspect it is, also, not truly the general will. And this aspect of the matter was one Rousseau could not ignore, for he himself called attention to the absurdity of the peoples of Europe setting up political institutions like the State to achieve peace and community and then allowing those States themselves to fall into a condition of perpetual hostility or active warfare with each other. Although he was often disposed to attribute such evils to the dynastic ambitions and selfishness of Kings, yet he realized there is a danger in conceiving of sovereignty as essentially national. It lent countenance to the doctrine that the Sovereign States have no law above them and so must take the law into their own hands and base their policies on the condition that there is a perpetual state of war between nations. But the general will ought never to be identified with a will that could thus do wrong, for it is by very conception a will which always intends right and the general good. In this vein of thought, with his attention on the international order, Rousseau was not disposed to identify the general will with the national will but preferred to assimilate it rather with the pure ideal of justice, or else with the final and perfect will for righteousness which is God's. Christianity and nationalism, it then appeared, must

---

[1] *Op. cit.*, First Version, Bk. I, Ch. 7, Vaughan, p. 476; Final Version, Bk. II, Ch. 6, Vaughan, p. 51.

be absolutely incompatible. That was the perplexing suggestion of the hastily-added last chapter of the *Social Contract*, entitled *Civil Religion*, a piece written ambiguously, however, as by one who is not yet sure of what is implied in the choice between those alternatives.[1] He was actually in a predicament over the meaning of the general will. It is not surprising that he made the comment, years afterwards, when he looked back upon the *Social Contract*, that it was "a book to be done over again."

The coming into prominence of the subject of international relations produced a change in Rousseau's thinking. He had long been preoccupied with these matters. The formal *Conclusion* of the *Social Contract* and the summary of it given in *Émile* show that he had contemplated an extension of his political theory to that realm. Nor was this an egoistic pretense of learning on his part or the project of an impulsive moment. From the very beginning of his career as a writer his true subject had been very wide in scope: Man and Civilization, not merely Man and the State. The Arts and Sciences had been first condemned, in his prize essay, as factors of European civilization threatening the moral integrity of the people everywhere. The political institutions typical of Europe next came under the ban, and especially the monarchical State. And Rousseau was quite as much concerned with war and its effects on mankind as with the oppressive inequalities imposed upon the subjects of every nation. It was about the time of his work on the *Origin of Inequality* that he composed an essay on the subject of *War*. His thesis was that the "state of war" is not at all "natural" to man as such but only to those sovereign States which are intended by men as "pacific institutions" but which actually follow the principle of brute force among themselves at the cost of the humanity whose concerted power they wield. War exists because the political States are not governed by any rule of right. The remedy is for men to go one step farther with their "artifice" and subject the sovereign Powers themselves to a controlling law analo-

[1] *Vide, Letters*, cited by Vaughan, Vol. 2, pp. 166–172.

gous to that which obtains among the individuals within the various States. How to establish such a régime of the law of nations was, however, too great a problem to be solved at that stage.

Rousseau turned to a practical scheme that appeared likely to serve, as at least a palliative, for suffering humanity. This is to check the power of the large monarchical States by building up the powers of the small States through confederation, which is not so wholly artificial as might be imagined. Small States have advantages of their own, such as strong internal bonds and patriotism; large ones suffer from a natural weakening of control over their members on account of their very size and the laxer ties of community; the odds against the small States are not so great as they appear—Nature tends to establish a balance of power and great statesmen need only take the next intelligent step, of uniting the small States definitely into a Confederation so as to present a strong front against outer aggression. The Great Powers will then be matched by the consolidated powers of the lesser ones. And these will be strong enough by their union to secure their own sovereignties and their rights in the system of Europe.[1] But Rousseau seemed unprepared to develop this scheme any further at the time, and he left his essay on *The State of War* an unfinished fragment, but yet a constant hint to him of a task sometime to be undertaken and carried through to a conclusion. He continued his inquiries into the meaning of the social contract, instead, and managed to complete them first. But what he learned in working over Pufendorf, in that connection, was a further encouragement to him to go on with his study of the external relations of States. He saw a double virtue in that federated "Germanic Body" described by Pufendorf and in others like it, the "Helvetic League" and the "States-General": such a type of society is too large

---

[1] *Vide,* Fragment on *The State of War,* Vaughan, Vol. 1, esp. pp. 293–300, 304–305; *Social Contract,* First Version, Bk. II, Ch. 3, pp. 485–486; Final Version, Ch. 13 (How to Maintain the Sovereign Authority), Vol. 2, p. 94. Rousseau's later work on the Constitutions for Corsica (1765) and Poland (1771–72) was inspired by the same idea and he then exalted federation as a "masterpiece of politics." Vaughan, Vol. 2, p. 470.

and powerful to be attacked by any external power whatsoever, and yet, being only a confederation without a monarchical "sovereign," it lacks the military efficiency and
wieldiness needed for successful aggression upon its neigh-
bors. One or more federations of States in that form would
make for the stability and peace of all Europe, a great bal-
ancing factor in the system.

But it was the idea of Abbé de St. Pierre that really
touched off the spark of enthusiasm and genius in Rousseau.
In his *Project for Lasting Peace* he had applied the concept
of federation to the whole of Europe, proposing a general
union of all the nations large and small, a league to secure
peace. This scheme so deeply interested Rousseau that he
took great pains to recast it, and in doing so he transformed
it, for he assimilated the project to his own dream of a social
order having "the form of the republic" universally, in the
whole of mankind and in every partial society. He spoke
of this as "the European Republic." He represented the
federation of Europe as an institution for *permanent peace
with justice*, instead of merely peace by a balance of power
between States which still continue to regard their relation
to each other as fundamentally and inevitably one of a "state
of war." His work on that project gave great impetus to his
ambitions in the field of international politics. Hence it is
not surprising to find him planning a book to surpass Grotius' *Laws of Peace and War*, where he would not truckle to
the monarchical prejudice but would honestly disclose to men
the possibilities of the new world-system on "republican principles." Of these bold projects only one was completed and
published, that on *Lasting Peace*. But when so much and
persistent thinking had been done there were bound to be
new lights on political theory in general. Of this Rousseau
himself was aware, for he said, even in *Émile:* "These investigations lead us directly to all the questions of international law (droit public) and the study of these will result
in enlightening us in regard to law and right in the State
(droit politique)." [1]

[1] *Émile*, passage cited by Vaughan, Vol. 2, p. 158.

Here, as in the earlier stage of his theory of politics, Rousseau had to overcome rooted traditional objection꞉ to the scheme he envisaged. This time the opinion of Pu.en-dorf, who had great authority over his mind, was against him. For Pufendorf had declared: "Leagues for peace add nothing to the obligation." [1] And the reason given for this disparagement of what might be done "by interven-tion of human deed, that is, by agreement or covenant," was the curious one, that this obligation exists for men in their "natural state," and therefore cannot be modified in any way by human intelligence or art. Peace is right and war is wrong. Men have a duty, by the "law of nature," to live at peace with each other and to eschew war. True, but how effective is this obligation of pure reason in the state of nature? Rousseau had learned from his study of society what a moral advantage it is for men to unite in all their undertakings and not to try honest living entirely on their own, and without the concurrence of others. He had come to see that in such unions, by compact, the consciences of men gain both in strength and in perception of the right. Through association on such terms they learn to know what is good for themselves and for the whole body, and that determines what is the true law for all who are members of the body. This knowledge of the law and right is won in common and it has the weight of the community behind it— in short, the obligation to obey becomes present and real only with the coöperative discovery of the law. If all this may be realized in the relations of men to each other within their diverse political societies, why may it not come to pass in a more general society of the nations? Thus the whole argument of the *Social Contract* committed Rousseau to a belief contrary to the older politics, that the leaguing for peace actually has *everything* to do with making peace a real *obligation*.

The new international theory had its origin in Plato's *Laws*. There it was related, as a fancy half-historical, half-propagandist, that three peoples and their kings leagued

[1] Pufendorf, Bk. 1, Ch. 2 (Of the Natural State of Man), Sect. 11, pp. 92–93.

together saying: Let us unite and make a covenant to abide
by certain laws within and without our realms, and if any
one of us attacks another or violates the laws, the third party
will come to the rescue and settle the affair, and preserve
the union and the peace.[1] This notion St. Pierre had taken
up and applied to the large scale of the European system.
He believed the scheme would work even better there than
in the ancient situation, precisely because of the greater
number of parties to the covenant. There is safety in numbers,—a modern doctrine advanced first by Bodin when he
suggested that it is an advantage to the State to have a
great many religious sects, inasmuch as they all tend to
nullify each other's domination, and thus leave the State
free to pursue its real interests, whereas two or three quar-
reling sects keep the society in a constant turmoil and civil
war.[2] So here the third party which is interested in uphold-
ing the law of nations against any aggressor or violator is
not merely one lone State coming to the aid of one other
and engaging in a contest of power but a large majority of
States, the greater part of the peoples of Europe, whose
very interest and possible coming-on-the-scene can operate
to uphold the law, without a recourse on every occasion to
force of arms. Such a confederation affords a greater guarantee of security for every State, and therefore of the peace
of the world. And the beauty of this scheme, as St. Pierre
regarded it, is that it enlists in favor of the comity of nations the very forces of self-interest which seem to be the
chief threat to general peace and unity, for the tendency
which prompts one State to take its own way, in disregard
of the law and the rights of all, works in all the others, too,
but in this manner, to draw them together much as all the
other stones of an arch would press against any one stone
that threatened to fall down, constraining that one member
to stay in its rightful place in the system. At this point in
the argument Rousseau struck off the thought in his own
mintage: the violator of the public law previously agreed

[1] Plato, *Laws*, Bk. 3, St. 684, Jowett translation, Vol. 5, p. 64.
[2] Bodin, *op. cit.*, Bk. IV, Ch. 5, p. 655.

upon by himself is there really "forced to be just" or "equitable," a phrase elsewhere turned into the paradoxical form "forced to be free." [1] That paradoxical use of the term "force" was his way of asserting how very effective the *obligation* can be in so comprehensive a society formed by a pact for peace. So long as the States of Europe make only partial treaties their "reciprocal engagements" have little validity, with the parties as with others not included in the convention. Until they "submit to common deliberations" they will never possess a "common and constant" rule by which to determine their rights and pretensions. There will be neither law nor obligation unless the association is perfectly general and on a basis of equality. But if they do thus associate themselves by a pact they acquire greater control over their relations with each other. The very conditions of bringing about an agreement on so large a scale are educative of all the parties. In conferring about the different claims and other relevant concerns, in working at a policy together, they clear up their first views of national needs or rights and discern a common interest and general rule of right or law. The process of negotiation enables them to appreciate their own good in the general good. Achieving this in common they are deeply committed to it, that is, they are *obliged*. This seems to be the trend of Rousseau's reflections upon the new system of international politics.

It is universal right, then, or justice, that men and nations are "obliged to recognize,"— not a "power." This indicates the shift of thought in Rousseau's political theory. And it is very significant that in all his discussion of federation, whether on the small or large scale, he never once mentions the general will. This idea did not fit the context of his thinking. The notion of a supreme power above the powers of Europe, as the sovereign is above the individuals within the State, was not really pertinent or imaginable. Since Europe had never acknowledged a super-sovereign, moreover, it was unnecessary to put forward the ideal,

[1] Vaughan, Vol. 1, pp. 374, 380, 390; Vol. 2, p. 36.

general will as a substitute for any false notions on that score. Nor was there any point in employing it as a principle in lieu of " sociability," for the will for general community among the nations of Europe was largely conspicuous by its absence. The only meaning the general will could have in this wider sphere was that of an ideal—a will for justice. And Rousseau seems to have preferred to speak directly of the ideal of justice, or else of the common interest of all, reverting to the language of Plato rather than strain the modern term to uses for which it hardly seemed fitted.

This change of attitude toward the general will appeared in the latter-day expressions of Rousseau's theory of the State. Most of the time he was obliged to quote *verbatim* from the original text of the *Social Contract*, inasmuch as these later discussions constituted a defense of that book; but when he was released from the necessity of a literal quotation, he used language which shows an alteration of sentiment and meaning. Thus in the summary of the theory which he wrote for *Émile* he chose to speak not of the general will but of "the will of the people or the sovereign will." This suggests that he was conscious of a distinction between a sovereign will which is only the will of a *particular* people and a will that is truly "general" and therefore perfectly "right." Again, in the *Letters from the Mountains*, there is an elaborately careful statement: "the will of all is, therefore, the true ordinance, the supreme rule; and that rule, in its general and personified form, is what I call the sovereign." Yet "the will of all " had once been distinguished from the general will—it was now accepted as sovereign, presumably because sovereignty itself is something only relative, pertaining merely to a nation and not "general." So the oath of allegiance proposed for the Constitution of Corsica ran thus: "I unite myself in body, goods, and will, and with all my power, to the Corsican nation." And similarly, in the *Considerations on the Government of Poland*, the reference was to "the will of the nation." [1] For practical

---

[1] *Vide*, Vaughan, Vol. 2, pp. 155, 201, 350, 451, 456.

purposes, then, the general will had sunk to the status of the *national* will which enjoys a sovereignty only relative to the members of the particular nation concerned. It had ceased to be a Platonic idea, and a power absolute and universal. The majesty that had once passed to it from the personal sovereign was now gone, and with this loss of imagined glory went, as always must, its perfection of authority.

But, after all, Rousseau was not interested in authority as such: "it is better to think less about authority, and more about liberty" and "the individuals." [1] In fact, his wrestling over that question of authority had been done only in order to reconcile his new principles with the traditional ideas whose hold had been so strong upon himself as well as others. And having learned from experience to treat those ideas more pragmatically, that is, to think of sovereignty and the general will as relative to a particular function, he returned from his digression, as it were, to carry on his fundamental argument. And this argument was about *moral* obligation.

"What is it that makes the State one? It is the union of its members. And whence comes the union of its members? From the obligation that binds them. We are all in agreement thus far. But what is the foundation of that obligation? This is where the various authors part company. According to some it is force; according to others, paternal authority; and still others, the will of God. Every one establishes his own principle and attacks those of the others. I have not done otherwise myself: and following the sanest party of those who have discussed these matters, I have laid down, as the foundation of the body-politic, the *agreement of its own members*. . . . Quite apart from its truth this principle has an advantage over the others, because of the solidity of the foundation it establishes, for what firmer basis can obligation have than this of being *the free engagement of him who is obliged?*" [2] So the notion of greatest value, in

---

[1] *Letters from the Mountains*, Vaughan, Vol. 2, p. 220.
[2] *Ibid.*, pp. 199–200.

political philosophy, is that of "contract," the act of agreement and free engagement. But this "social contract" is a very special type and must be conceived to fit the requirements of the case. Every one makes an agreement and undertakes to do something with reference to all who associate with him; and all are doing the same thing with respect to the individual. This makes the resulting obligation equal and just for all, and therefore solid; it simultaneously has other results in that it is the means of determining the common rules of life for all, that is to say, the rules of their society. This contract is, then, but the first act of a continual process of such mutual agreement and law-making. So long as individuals dwell together in society they must continue to deal with each other in the spirit of their original contract. We may, if we like, attribute the laws they establish by that procedure, to the agency of a general will and then personify that entity as a sovereign. But the essential thing is the "contract" in this extensive use of the term, as meaning the democratic way of life between men. All law and obligation arises from contract in that sense. When taking leave of his fellow-citizens of Geneva, in the conclusion to his *Letters from the Mountains*, Rousseau put his idea in a remarkable piece of practical wisdom for the men of his own city who were divided against one another and in great turmoil, on account of his persecution by the authorities: "Whatever part you choose to take, even if it is one bad in itself, take it together; by that very action alone it will become the best course to take; and you may be sure that you will always do what *ought* to be done, provided only you do it in concert." [1]

VI

FROM POLITICS TO ETHICS

The critical philosopher examines and defines what is already significant in the experience of men. Thus Kant was destined to reflect on the question of obligation. For

[1] *Ibid.*, p. 291.

this was a concept that had grown in meaning during the course of modern civilization. The first writers who had sought to bring about peace and order by a control of individuals from above without regard to their own will and convictions,—as it was fancied God rules man,—were compelled to recognize the idea of "contract" with its inevitable suggesting of an obligation that arises from the free commitment of the individuals themselves. Some, like Hobbes, had devoted their philosophical ingenuity to making the value of freedom seem subordinate to that of security with its promise of the satisfaction of all human desires under the aegis of an authority. This debasement of the human will was argued for by a vast magnifying of the natural powers and benefits of a sovereignty. But the more empirical-minded thinkers, like Pufendorf, Locke, and Montesquieu had disallowed the magnificent services of the sovereign and directed their attention more to the nature of law and obligation, as if these features in the situation were the more significant. This turn of thought, after many years of preparation, gained its most effective expression in Rousseau. His uncompromising denial of any glory in the existing civilization was but a preface to a politics of an ethical type, where it is precisely the laws alone that do govern and these laws are rules of conduct laid down by the people themselves who are subject to them, or obliged by them. There the obligation was realized to be a bond laid by men of their own free will, an aspect in which it seemed quite compatible with their enjoyment of freedom. But the obligation was also regarded as a social control, for every political theory had to provide such a control, and in giving the necessary prominence to this aspect Rousseau erected "the general will" as a source and authority outrivaling far, with its ideal characters, the "sovereign" of the ancient mode. In his later and more individualistic vein Rousseau stressed the intrinsic validity of the obligation that is created by contract, and he described the form such a proceeding takes, as one where men come to terms with each other by public deliberation and so make the common rules of life or laws which obtain in their community. This way of regarding the obligation made it possible to conceive of it as arising from international covenant quite as well as from the "social contract" of a single nation. The theory of obligation was thus, even in Rousseau's work, attaining a greater generality, and pointing to further meaning than had yet been realized. This was the kind of thing to interest the genius of Kant, for the philosopher is always concerned to achieve the most general signification of ideas, to make them "cosmic," as it were, so long as they continue to have meaning in their new applications. Kant was appreciative of the republican ideals of Rousseau and saw that they applied to the whole system of Europe and were the condition of a lasting peace in the world—and he very naturally went on with the argument to see the full scope of this idea of obligation based on the free engagement of the persons concerned. This might be universally valid as an ideal of life, not only true for man as a citizen, or as a member of a world-society, but for man in all the relationships of his life. So the concept was taken over into ethics in general.

What Rousseau had done was to disclose the true form of any duty, no matter in what sphere, whether in the State, or in the home, or in the silent spaces of the conscience of the individual. What is "virtue" in the citizen? The conformity of his personal will to the general will which acts for the general good. But this general will, it had also been stated, attains its end always by acting in the form of law. Here it was that Kant seems to have taken an important step of logical economy—it was to omit the general will from the account entirely, so that the prescription would read more simply: the good will in the citizen is that will which conforms to the principle of law. And so expressed this definition of virtue need not be limited to man in his political, or even his social, capacity. It tells what goodness means as ascribed to man in any capacity, although we must add, of course, that man is essentially a rational being, because only a person endowed with reason is competent to form the idea of law, and therefore to recognize, and possibly to act upon it.

By such a stroke of simplification Kant generalized completely Rousseau's conception of virtue, so that it is the virtue of man as man and not merely of the citizen. He also avoided all the problems that beset the notion of the general will as a power, and the source of obligation and law. How are men to know whether their will is truly "general" as regards the people of the community? Must they wait, before they begin their moral action, until they learn the verdict of the generality? And how, even so, are they to escape the error of following the general practice or custom, as the will of the people, only to learn afterwards that this does not really make for the good of all and that what they have supposed to be the general will is not "general" in respect to its *end?* But then, how is this good of all to be determined? By the ordinary evaluations of pleasure or satisfied desire? These questions are all very empirical, and in every particular case they must wait long for a solution. Meantime it is a fact that individuals are conscious of their obligations in such cases. They recognize their duty quite in advance of the decision of those issues about the general will and good. They do not look to see if their will is surely going to receive a corroboration from the wills of others and become "general" in that sense. Though they never spurn the approbation and aid of other men in the practice of virtue, they do not make their own action conditional upon such favoring agencies. Duty is an unconditional command for them, and it comes directly from within themselves. Nor are they determined by the consequences which they foresee and estimate to be either generally good or ill. Independently of these considerations they can be, and are, moral. How is that possible, unless it be true that men can really determine themselves to action prior to experience of goods derived, and purely from a respect for the idea of law or right? As rational beings they can envisage any course of conduct in terms of its conformity, or lack of conformity, to law as such. And this moral judgment constitutes the true obligation, for a being such as man who is not perfect but a creature of sensibility, with natural tendencies and interests alongside the interest of pure reason.

In this wise Kant disengaged the ethical meaning of obligation from all the social and political imagery with which it was confused. No more of those concrete picturings of events that never happened in history and never will happen, but which must be "supposed" in order to convey the true moral ideas—no more imagining of isolated individuals, stupid and undeveloped, meeting together, coming to terms, making contracts, acquiring a conception of law and right, declaring and maintaining public laws and institutions. Nor was it any longer necessary to wrestle over the dubious meaning of that great looming power for righteousness, the general will, which had supplanted the will of the sovereign of old. The essential idea of morality was now clear of all images: every individual possessed of reason and freedom of will recognizes the principle of law and knows that he can act from that principle, regardless of the strength of his affections and inclinations. This ideal of law, and not any social power or any natural force, is really what *obliges* the individual. Thus law is not obligatory because it is the expression of the general will which is fancied to be the real and ultimate obliging power; the general will itself is but a phenomenon of the *ideal* of law as it is operative in and through *individuals*. There is nothing more real in the realm of society or nature than the individual or person who is possessed of ideals and can lay down the law for his own life accordingly. With this doctrine arises a pure idealism in modern philosophy.

This was also, in Kant's own eyes, a pure rationalism, a view which subsequent idealists have criticized abundantly. In doing so they have rather assumed that Kant actually realized his intention of stating the sheer abstract meaning of morality without recourse to any imagery or experience. It is true that he described obligation in an abstract manner. He made no reference to the political, social, and historical phenomena of the human spirit so interesting to Hegel and others since his time. Yet this only means, perhaps, that Kant was not concrete in their way. He had imagination enough, else he would not have exercised the influence he has had upon modern thinking. But his imagination was of a different type from theirs and it drew from a different store of experience. To Kant there was something more deeply engrossing than politics and history. He had spent the greater part of his life as a thinker in trying to understand this other important phase of human experience, namely, scientific knowledge. There the question had to do with a bond or tie, the causal connection between objects, and it was not possible to escape the force of Hume's criticism that such a bond is neither directly perceived nor deducible from the nature of things and that it cannot be explained by reference to an external power because the very meaning of "power" is here in dispute. The problem of moral obligation was somewhat analogous—a tie or bond between *men* which cannot be found inherent in them in their "natural state" but which also cannot be made appendent to a supposed higher power, because the source of all "sovereign" power is itself the very thing in question. In both cases the only way to a solution seemed to be by taking the point of view of the beings for whom such relations obtain, to whom the necessity of cause and effect and the moral necessity of obligation have a meaning. In the sphere of knowledge Kant had achieved a solution,—to his own satisfaction. And what made it possible for him to conceive that *the very idea of law determines the will* of man was his belief, confirmed by study, that there is an analogous rôle of law in the sphere of human knowledge. The mind in all its workings seems to be destined to make all things, its own acts included, conform to law as a norm or ideal. It knows Nature in the form of law; when it takes to voluntary action it is true to itself only when this will realizes the form of law. Morality and science together reveal the idea of law to be a superior determinant for human reason. And so there must be a whole philosophy of pure reason, the theoretical reason and the practical reason. The vision of all this as one system of truth discovers

Kant as a great imaginative genius despite the rationalistic manner of his expression.

A *Weltanschauung*, then, is involved in Kant's theory of moral obligation. Where Rousseau in the beginning, and others at a later time, saw obligation as pertaining only to man's historical life in society, Kant regarded it in a setting of far vaster significance than politics or society. Hence it followed that the freedom of man acquires a larger meaning than the self-determination of individuals in their political societies; in moral duty man is revealed as a being free from all compulsions of Nature, both within and without himself, and free in a grand and positive sense, to legislate for all Nature. And to complete this picture,—for it is that, quite as much as anything Rousseau ever delineated,—there is the Kingdom of Ends, a cosmic republic, as it were, of the immortal souls of virtuous men, and above all, God the Supreme Being. "Postulates," these were called by Kant, but without them he could not have told the meaning of obligation in the moral life. There must be such ideals divined through imagination if human experience is to be rendered intelligible.

The intelligible world is, nevertheless, a changing world, where the change counts for something. This evolutionary aspect has become inseparable from the contemporary imagination, so that whether we intend to innovate or not, we inevitably revise the idealism of the past.

If process is essential to reality, then those processes whereby we know and deal with each other and with Nature are all ingredients of the real. Our experience is not merely "appearance"—it enters into the very essence of things. Hence we no longer expect the ideal of law, that is to say, the norm of right, to shine clearly in the "pure reason" of every individual by its own power alone: men find the ideal, in being able to meet and transact business together and come to agreement about certain things as good or right for them universally. This social process of discovery is not a mere psychological incident, indifferent to the ideal, as people oftentimes think the finding of the poet's language is to his vision. It is the democratic procedure itself which makes the law real and therefore effectual for the human beings to whose lives it applies. So idealistic ethics is committed to democracy.

"Fixed-species" is, today, an alien concept, whether it be thought of in regard to the forms of the human mind or the outward forms of living Nature. Even the categories of the human understanding seem to have an evolution and to be but relatively fixed, that is, valid only for the kind of experience which they happen to organize and reveal. As experience takes on new phases, it requires modes of interpretation suited thereto. And, in fact, it often contributes to the producing of these ways of thought, through that stimulating interaction of fact with theory of which the pragmatists have told the mutable tale. All ideas, then, appear relative to men, manners, and circumstances. And this is nowhere better illustrated than in the foregoing story of modern thinking in politics and ethics. "Authority," "sovereignty," "the general will," all have had a history, and each one, its own day and use. "Obligation" has developed in their place, and, presumably, it will sooner or later serve its purpose and become a matter of record with the other ideas. Once it was conceived only as the tie between men taking a certain action according to law, but it has come to be thought of as the *moral* bond on which all laws, institutions, and political actions must rest in order to be solid and effective. For us now, with our particular experience and history, this idea is indispensable and absolute. It is the most significant idea in modern ethics, without which we could not express to ourselves the ideal meaning which life seems to have.

The presence of this ideal character in our experience discloses, however, where idealism must take a stand. While all specific ideas, like sovereignty, the general will, and obligation, are pragmatic, the ideal form in virtue of which they have their significance and value at any time and place is itself not so. Ideals are not derived from experience, nor from the mind. They only *define* themselves there, in the history and the spirit of man. The norm of right appears to work its way in the course of events and to fix the minds of men upon this or that particular idea as important or meaningful, as, for example, "moderation" was to the Greeks, and "obligation" is to the moderns. These particular and definite ideas with which men work in the contingencies of social life and argument are things of changing value. But men cannot use or work with their ideals. Rather, they are possessed and commanded by them. Hence, in the order of human experience, ideals seem to *be* before they *exist*. They have a reality operative in affairs before they have any well-defined part in our experience. Because they are prior and of supreme meaning, we cannot but think of them as "eternal." On the other hand, we are not forgetful of the process whereby ideals *exist*,—that they have no place or value in our world apart from the coöperative thought and will and action of human persons. This means that, though men have their day and use, as all other beings of Nature, they also have, through their realizing of ideals, a future of lasting significance, which is what we mean by "immortality."

XII

THE REVIVAL OF IDEALISM IN THE UNITED STATES

R. F. Alfred Hoernlé

University of Witwatersrand

THE REVIVAL OF IDEALISM IN THE
UNITED STATES

R. F. Alfred Hoernlé

My contribution to this volume may fitly begin on a personal note. When Professor Barrett and his collaborators honored me by asking me to join in their enterprise, they said, in effect, "You are one of us." My feeling leaped to answer theirs. For, six-and-a-half years of philosophical teaching at Harvard, followed by two later teaching visits to two other American Universities, have established between many of my fellow-philosophers in the United States and myself a bond of friendship and of mutual understanding which seemed to me to justify my acceptance of the invitation extended to me.

Moreover, in writing this article on "The Revival of Idealism," I feel that I am doing a little to repay the debt which I owe to my philosophical colleagues in the United States. I reckon the years which I spent among them as, next to my Oxford student days, and my association with Bernard Bosanquet in the University of St. Andrews, the third formative period in my philosophical development. Nor is my debt confined to thinkers of one school. I am conscious of having learned no less from Realists, like R. B. Perry, W. P. Montague, R. W. Sellars, than from Idealists, like M. W. Calkins, W. E. Hocking, G. W. Cunningham. And there are others—H. B. Alexander, J. E. Boodin, M. R. Cohen, A. O. Lovejoy, C. I. Lewis: I name but a few at random—and, above all, John Dewey in his most recent books, from whom varied and powerful impulses have come to shape the course of my thinking.

Least of all, may I forget to commemorate on this occasion the fact that the earlier years of my Harvard period overlapped with the closing years of Royce's life.   Illness had by then left its mark upon him, and he was but a shadow of the brilliant self of his great days.   Even so, I felt enough of his influence to enable me to appreciate why so many of his pupils, as is shown by the personal statements in the two volumes of *Contemporary American Philosophy*, broke away from his Absolutism.   The very power of his dialectic, the very masterfulness of his mind, were a challenge to them to seek emancipation and to recover, or preserve, their own individuality as thinkers.   If Idealism in the United States has suffered a reaction, and in certain quarters even an eclipse—was not William James himself the first of the rebels?—this is due, in part at least, to the very force and distinctiveness of Royce's thinking.   Lesser men among his pupils could not effectively copy or repeat his methods, though they might regurgitate his phrases.   The stronger minds were necessarily provoked into either challenging his fundamental principles or else trying to rethink them in their own ways.   Men had to break Royce's spell in order to be themselves.

Towards the end of his life, in moments of weariness, Royce would sometimes express doubts about his own effectiveness as a teacher, because so many of the doctrines which he regarded as most distinctively original—his argument that the very existence of error implies the Absolute; his distinction of the external and the internal meaning of ideas; his use of the mathematical concept of the infinite to illustrate the structure of the Absolute; his analysis of morality in terms of loyalty and of loyalty to loyalty; his concepts of interpretation and of the beloved community; his proposal to apply the principle of insurance to the prevention of war— seemed to him to have been still-born in the sense of having been received at best with barren respect, instead of being accepted, expounded, developed.   He felt, I think, towards the end a growing isolation, as of one whose voice is still heard but is no longer listened to.   If it is death to a philosophy to become a still backwater, whilst the main stream of thought is carving out fresh channels for itself, then that

death seemed at times to be threatening Royce's own philosophy. Yet, if it is the test of a philosophical teacher to be
the cause of vigorous and independent philosophizing in
others, then Royce was indeed a great teacher in his own
generation. Nor in his own generation only: he will continue
to be a fountain of philosophical life to all who are striving
to learn the art of philosophizing by rethinking the thoughts
of a master. To any young American student of philosophy
who rejects Absolute Idealism I would say that he has no
right to dissent or condemn, unless he has first earned that
right by a thorough study and understanding of Royce.

I

A. N. WHITEHEAD AS A "NEW" IDEALIST

To speak of a "revival" of Idealism implies both that
there has been a diminution or eclipse, and that now there
is a reconstruction or restatement.

The eclipse—I am speaking with reference to the American
scene—is too familiar to require lengthy documentation.
The most alive philosophical movements in the United
States during the last twenty-five years have fought under
such banners as Naturalism, Realism, Pragmatism, Instrumentalism. However much they may have differed, one
from the others, in their opposition to some, if not all, the
most characteristic doctrines of Idealism, especially as formulated by Royce, they have been united. The concept of the
"Absolute" has been rejected by all these movements alike,
and though they have not agreed on the place and function
of mind in the universe, they have agreed also on denying to
mind the central position assigned to it in Idealistic systems.
A canvass of the names of the outstanding philosophical
thinkers of the present day in the United States, as represented by the two volumes on *Contemporary American Philosophy*, shows a mere handful who would agree to be labeled
"Idealist," and even then only on a very elastic definition
of this long-suffering term. Of self-confessed and unrepent-
ant Absolutists there is only one—Mary Whiton Calkins,

though Hocking (who does not use the word) must, I think, be classed with her. Whether Cunningham would call himself an "Absolutist," I do not know: at any rate his Absolutism is not of the forthright type of Miss Calkins, but an Absolutism profoundly qualified by a consciousness of difficulties.

The eclipse, then, may be taken as conceded. What, on the other hand, are the evidences of a revival?

By a "revival" I do not mean a mere repetition of doctrines weighed and found wanting, but a genuine restatement and reconstruction. But a reconstruction of what?

Clearly, this question cannot be answered, without saying what, for the purposes of this argument, we are to regard as essentially "Idealistic" positions, the restating or rearguing of which may fairly be adduced as evidence of revival.

I shall answer this question by concentrating on one thinker—A. N. Whitehead, and one book—his *Process and Reality: An Essay in Cosmology*. Here I find the most striking illustrations of the rethinking of Idealistic positions, all the more striking for the fact that Whitehead sets about the business of constructing a cosmology without troubling to label himself an "Idealist" rather than anything else.

1. I begin with Whitehead's magnificent and courageous defense of "speculative philosophy" (Ch. 1)—of the possibility of constructing, and the legitimacy and reasonableness of the effort to construct, a "complete cosmology" (p. vi); of the search for that "essence of the universe which forbids relationships beyond itself, as a violation of its rationality" (p. 4); or, more modestly, of the search for "metaphysical categories," in the sense of "tentative formulations of the ultimate generalities" (p. 11).

True, this is, so far, merely a defense of metaphysics in general, and not yet a defense of Idealistic metaphysics in particular. And it would certainly be a *petitio* on my part if I were, at this stage, to exploit these programmatic statements of Whitehead's as meaning that there can be no metaphysics except as some form of Idealism. Realists would be justified in demurring and claiming that they are metaphysicians too, and that the very point at issue is whether the universe is to be construed Idealistically or Realistically.

I have no intention of prejudging this issue here: I shall return to it below. My purpose is rather to emphasize the continuity in metaphysical temper between the new Idealism and the old, the striking similarity in the way in which both conceive the task and method of metaphysics. Whitehead's argument is an arresting challenge to two kinds of philosophizing which, by contrast with it, may not unfitly be described as half-hearted. There is, first, the philosophizing which is definitely anti-metaphysical and treats propositions about ultimate generalities, or the essence of the Universe, or Reality as a whole, as meaningless, or at least unverifiable. And there is, secondly, the philosophizing which, whilst acknowledging the attraction of the larger task, despairs of success in it and concentrates on problems of detail which, it claims, can be isolated and which in this detachment offer some prospect of being solved exhaustively and finally. Space forbids illustrations of the diverse nuances of this anti-metaphysical temper in present-day philosophy, in either of these two forms—the former, negative: rejecting metaphysics as such; the latter, positive: defining a more limited task.

In reasserting the legitimacy and importance of metaphysical ventures, Whitehead argues in the very spirit of the great Idealists. For, Idealists have always been metaphysicians. From Berkeley, who under the title of *Principles of Human Knowledge* offers, first, a theory of "existence" in the abstract, and then, on the basis of this, a theory of the existent Universe in the concrete as a society of spirits, to Hegel, Royce, Bradley, Bosanquet, McTaggart, and others, Idealists have stood for the faith that it is possible to think out the general nature and structure of the Universe. Even Kant's "Critical Idealism" is but an apparent exception to this rule. For, though Kant affirms that metaphysics is impossible as "theory," he also defends the acceptance of metaphysical propositions on grounds of "practical" reason, to say nothing of the hints which he throws out in his *Critique of Judgment* concerning a possible surmounting of this antithesis of theoretical and practical reason. If one surveys the history of Idealism as a whole, from Berkeley and Spinoza to the present day, it is plain that Kant is an eddy, so to speak, in the stream of metaphysical speculation—a momentary checking of the stream which is, as it were, made to turn upon itself in the form of speculation ("critical reflection") on the possibility of speculation about ultimate questions. The result has been both an enrichment and a diversification of the stream as it leaped forward with fresh impulsiveness after the critical check— an enrichment in the concentration on the systematic analysis of "categories," a diversification in the fuller emphasis on non-theoretical (=non-scientific) modes of experience and thought, with the recognition that will and feeling, too, have their principles of "reason," or, differently put, that the Universe as revealing itself in will and feeling has a logical structure no less than as revealing itself in scientific thought; that, in short, there is no mode of experience which the metaphysician dare ignore, if he would use all the available evidence in his search for the essential nature of the Universe.

Whitehead, unmistakably, belongs to this tradition. His use of "speculative philosophy" to describe his aim and outlook coincides with Bosanquet's use of the same term for the same purpose in his later years. The fact that Whitehead characterizes his "philosophy of organism" as a "recurrence to pre-Kantian modes of thought" (p. vi), should not blind us to the essential affiliations of his thinking. Whitehead's "pre-Kantianism" is, no doubt, justified by the part which Descartes' *cogitationes*, Locke's *ideas*, Spinoza's *conatus*, Leibniz's *monads*, play in providing starting-points for his own constructions. Still, it must be taken in a somewhat Pickwickian sense. For, a pre-Kantianism which can also acknowledge, and with manifest justice, great obligations to Bergson, James, Dewey; which in its "final outcome is after all not so greatly different" from F. H. Bradley's Absolutism; which, in fact, can also describe itself as a "transformation of some main doctrines of Absolute

Idealism on to a realistic basis" (p. vii), is clearly a highly
sophisticated kind of pre-Kantianism. Apart from the positive stimuli, just mentioned, the reason why Whitehead
calls himself a pre-Kantian is that he rejects "the Kantian
doctrine of the objective world as a theoretical construct
from purely subjective experience" (p. viii). But, in this
rejection, he is, of course, at one with Hegel and with every
post-Kantian Idealist, except those who, vainly, have tried
to reoccupy the "critical" position with its inherently
unstable equilibrium. If the rejection of the above doctrine
makes a thinker pre-Kantian, then all the great post-Kan-
tians are in this sense pre-Kantians—which is but a paradoxical way of saying that they are all alike metaphysicians.
Whitehead is of their company: like them, he embraces the
task of speculative philosophy with a fresh and inspiring
appreciation of the resources at the command of this manner
of philosophizing.

2. Moreover, when we turn from the defense of metaphysics, or "cosmology," in general terms to the methods
which Whitehead employs in detail, we find that he re-
affirms a number of positions the adoption of which distinguishes Idealists characteristically from Realists and other
critics.

This may be abundantly illustrated from the opening
chapters of *Process and Reality*.

Thus, we find there laid down on the very first page the
doctrine of "coherence" as meaning "that the fundamental ideas, in terms of which the scheme is developed,
presuppose each other so that in isolation they are meaningless" (p. 3). Again, "it is the ideal of speculative philosophy
that its fundamental notions shall not seem capable of abstraction from each other. In other words, it is presupposed
that no entity can be conceived in complete abstraction
from the system of the universe, and that it is the business
of speculative philosophy to exhibit this truth" (*ibid.*). A
little later, the impossibility of "tearing a proposition from
its systematic context in the actual world" is vigorously re-
affirmed (p. 15). The contentions that modern philosophy

has "been misled by the example of mathematics" (p. 10); that it is one of the aims of philosophy "to challenge the half-truths constituting the scientific first principles" (p. 13); that "the logician's rigid alternative, 'true or false,' is largely irrelevant for the pursuit of knowledge" (p. 15), all belong to the same characteristic method of philosophizing.

From this doctrine and its corollaries most Realists dissent: they make an idol of mathematical method; they hold to the principle of external relations and, therefore, believe it to be possible to abstract entities from their setting in the context of the Universe and to analyze them adequately, as so isolated; they want to accept scientific theories as the solid bases on which to erect their philosophical cosmologies.

Many of them, too, if not most, would also dissent from such a synoptic program for a complete cosmology as Whitehead outlines in his *Preface*, when he demands "a system of ideas which bring the aesthetic, moral, and religious interests into relation with those concepts of the world which have their origin in natural science" (p. vi). Or, even if they are prepared to assent to a synoptic program in principle, they would not agree to Whitehead's estimate of the metaphysical importance of religion which leads him to demand of philosophy that it should "fuse religion and science into one rational scheme of thought" (p. 21). It is not too much to say that, for Whitehead, religion is not merely one of "the data of experience which philosophy must weave into its scheme" (*ibid.*), but that it is the truth of philosophy translated into a particular way of life in which it finds appropriate emotional practical expression. This, at least, I take to be the meaning of the challenging statements that "religion should connect the rational generality of philosophy with the emotions and purposes springing out of existence in a particular society, in a particular epoch, and conditioned by particular antecedents"; and that we "require a reconciliation in which emotional experiences illustrate a conceptual justification, and conceptual experiences find an emotional illustration" (*ibid.*).

Above all, Whitehead is marked as an Idealist by his rejection of what he has christened the principle of "vacuous actuality" (*e.g.*, pp. viii and 39). The adoption of this principle is for him the root-error of all Realism. It rests on a false analysis of presentational immediacy. It is largely responsible for the misapplication, as a fundamental metaphysical category, of the concept of quality-inhering-in-substance. It commits the error of trying to conceive a *res vera* as devoid of subjective immediacy. Clearly, the rejection of vacuous actuality is Whitehead's equivalent of Berkeley's *esse est percipi* principle. I say "equivalent," because the rejection of vacuous actuality (or, put positively, the affirmation that the "actual occasions," or "actual entities," of which the Universe in last analysis consists, are "actual experiences" which can never lack the character of subjective immediacy, or "feeling," in the sense in which F. H. Bradley uses this term) plays the same part in Whitehead's philosophy that is played by the *esse est percipi* principle in Berkeley's philosophy. I do not say they are identical, for there is a world of difference between Berkeley's analysis of an experience into an act of perceiving (implying a "spirit") and an "idea," and Whitehead's elaborate apparatus of eight categories of existence, twenty-seven categories of explanation, and nine categoreal obligations. It is not for nothing that Whitehead has learned from Bergson, James, Bradley how complex actual experience is, to say nothing of the detail of logical structure which Kant's and Hegel's doctrines of categories have contributed to modern philosophical heritage. We have long lost the simple-minded innocence of Berkeley in our dealings with experience.

3. In the light of all this, what becomes of the "realistic basis" on to which, as we had seen above, Whitehead claims to have transformed some of the main doctrines of Absolute Idealism? I find it, frankly, very difficult to guess in what sense Whitehead supposes himself to be "realistic" in distinction from other Idealists. If he is a Realist, then in that sense every other Idealist is a Realist, too. And this sense

I can only suppose to be the sense in which all Idealists acknowledge a Reality the nature of which they seek to interpret, using as clues to such interpretation whatever data
their experience offers, and therefore presupposing that every
experience is a part of Reality, determined by the whole of
which it is a part and in its turn contributing its note to the
making the whole just what it is. This general principle obviously covers also those experiences which, as "reflective,"
constitute this very interpretation of the nature of Reality,
this very use of (other) experiences as clues to the nature
of the Real. It is no denial of the freshness and originality
of Whitehead's analysis of the Universe as revealing itself
in any and all experiences to say that it moves within the
general framework of such a statement as this.

But, if this is true, then it follows that Whitehead cannot call himself a "Realist" in the sense in which that term
has been used by certain contemporary thinkers to characterize the basis of their criticisms of all Idealisms as such,
and as the name for the positive counter-scheme of cosmology propounded by them. He is not a Realist, either
"New" or "Critical." He is divided from the former by
his rejection of vacuous actuality. He is separated from
the latter because in his analysis of experience existence is
not divorced from essence. I conclude that, when we give
to the terms "Realist" and "Idealist" the senses which they
bear in the familiar contemporary controversies, Whitehead is not a Realist in any of these senses. If he is to be
labeled, he must be treated as what I am treating him in
this paper, viz., a New Idealist, and a very challenging and
stimulating one at that.

Is there, then, no meaning to Whitehead's "realistic
basis"? Very hesitatingly, and fully aware that my
guess may be wrong, I venture to suggest that the phrase
may refer to the comparatively subordinate position
which, in common with many other present-day thinkers,
Whitehead assigns to "consciousness" in his cosmological
scheme.

It is interesting to place Whitehead's view of consciousness in the context of contemporary thought so as to illustrate at once its distinctive originality and its affiliations with a certain general type of theory.

Two lines of thought in contemporary philosophy are relevant here. First, there is the view that mind is a latecomer in the evolution of the Universe, an "emergent" in an up-to-then mind-free Universe. Secondly, there is the view that consciousness is a late development in the evolution of mind, being preceded by unconscious types and levels of mind.

These two lines of thought may be added to one another and treated as cumulative: consciousness belongs to a late stage in the evolution of mind, and mind belongs to a late stage in the evolution of living beings which, in turn, are late-comers in the evolution of the Universe. Or, rejecting the concept of unconscious minds and unconscious levels of minds, we may identify mind and consciousness and then treat conscious mind as the late evolutionary arrival in a previously mind-free Universe. Or, lastly, we may accept the distinction between conscious and unconscious minds or levels of mind as fundamental and, on this basis, construe the evolution of the actual Universe as an evolution of mind, or minds, in which consciousness belongs to a late phase.

This latter is clearly the type of theory to which Whitehead's belongs. Of this there can be no doubt when we substitute for "mind" the equivalent terms "experience" or "feeling" which Whitehead uses by preference. *Res verae*, or actual existents, are, for him, without exception experiences or feelings, and we shall, therefore, expect that conscious experiences or feelings are but a special group, belonging to a developed phase. Thus, we read: "The organic philosophy holds that consciousness only arises in a late derivative phase of complex integrations" (p. 226). "Consciousness is the feeling of negation. . . . Consciousness is the subjective form involved in feeling the contrast between the 'theory' which *may* be erroneous and the fact which is 'given'" (pp. 225, 226). And, finally, summing up, "(1)

Consciousness is a subjective form arising in the higher phases of concrescence. (2) Consciousness primarily illuminates the higher phases in which it arises, and only illuminates earlier phases derivatively, as they remain components in the higher phase. (3) It follows that the order of dawning, clearly and distinctly, in consciousness is not the order of metaphysical priority" (p. 227).

We must resist the temptation to examine this extraordinarily interesting theory of consciousness on its merits. Here we are only concerned with its general character as assigning consciousness to a late, or "high," level of mental development and making it an attribute of complex mental processes. The main point is that there are mental activities so primitive, low, simple, that they are not yet "illuminated" by consciousness, though they may enter as components into the complexes which are characterized by consciousness, and, as so entering, may be consciously discerned in a "derivative" manner. Thus, in this respect, Whitehead's theory is one of a class of contemporary theories which, whilst differing enormously among themselves in the way in which they distinguish the conscious from the nonconscious levels and acts of mind, yet agree in the general conclusion that consciousness is not coextensive with mind, that it is a late development, and that, though it may be first in the order of reflection, it is not first in the order of existence. It is obvious, of course, that this limitation of consciousness to certain late phases of mental development makes possible a *vast generalization of the concept of mind* (or of "experience," "feeling"), by which it can be extended not only to ranges of the natural world to which we should deny mind in the sense of conscious mind, *e.g.*, plants and inorganic objects, but by which it can also be employed metaphysically as the stuff, so to speak, or essential nature of all *res verae* or actual existents.

In this context, too, we can best understand how Whitehead reaches his concept of "prehensions" through a generalization of Descartes' mental "cogitations" or Locke's "ideas." For, there can be no doubt that, with the exception of Leibniz's doctrine of *petites perceptions* all the pre-Kantian thinkers analyzed conscious experience, and that, therefore, their cogitations, ideas, impressions refer to conscious thoughts and perceptions. Thus, conscious mental processes supply the pattern from which Whitehead obtains, by the omission of consciousness, a generalized concept of mental process or "experience."

Applying this result to Whitehead's claim to a "realistic basis," I venture the suggestion that Whitehead calls his doctrine "realistic" because it recognizes actual entities devoid of consciousness but not devoid of "subjective immediacy." Of such entities it will be true that consciousness has nothing to do with their being, or with their being just what they are. This may be compared with the Realists' criticism of Berkeley's *esse est percipi* principle. Taking Berkeley's *percipere*, as I think we must, as meaning *conscious* perceiving, the Realists deny that the being or nature of objects can be identical with, or depend on, their being consciously perceived. For an object to be "real" means, for them, precisely to be independent, in existence and nature, of being consciously perceived. Now, Whitehead, too, recognizes actual entities with the occurrence and nature of which consciousness has nothing to do, and in this sense, therefore, he appears to agree with the Realists. But the agreement is wholly superficial and indeed purely verbal. For, the Realists' principle of the independence of the object implies what for Whitehead is the fallacy of vacuous actuality, *i.e.*, it is of the essence of the Realist contention that a real object is something quite other than a feeling, experience, or mental process, whereas it is of the essence of Whitehead's contention that every actual existent is an experience or feeling, whatever else may also be true about it. Thus, behind the verbal similarity of the statements recognizing actual existences in the being and nature of which consciousness has no share, lies a profound divergence on fundamentals—a divergence so profound that on the essential point it aligns Whitehead with all Idealists and opposes him to all Realists.

II

EXPERIENCE AS THE "ULTIMATE." THE FIRST-AND-LAST, FOR METAPHYSICS

Whitehead's identification of actual existents with actual experiences suggests two problems both of which are intimately bound up with Idealism.

The first is the sense in which experience may be taken as "ultimate," and our whole theory of the Universe erected on that basis. The other is whether experience implies an experiencer, *i.e.*, whether experiences occur only as constituting the life-tissue of self-identical spirits, subjects, or persons.

First, then, experience as metaphysically ultimate: the issue here is between two ways of thinking and speaking about experience, two contexts in which "experience," and its allied term "mind," may be employed.

The one way may be defined by the task which Professor Samuel Alexander assigns to Realism, *viz.*, "to order mind to its place in Nature." It treats experience as a natural phenomenon in the context of other natural phenomena, and as conditioned in its occurrence and character by its relations to these other phenomena. The ultimate for this view is Nature, and within this context it distinguishes experiences from what are not experiences, minds from bodies, subjects from objects, etc. More precisely, it treats experiences or mental processes—sensings, feelings, perceivings, thinkings, desirings, etc.—as adjectives (predicates) of certain subjects, or, in non-logical language, as what certain bodies have or do, and other bodies lack. Thus, in this context, "experience" or "mind" are names for a natural function, or for a class of natural functions, empirically found associated with organisms of a certain structure, and qualifying certain responses of these organisms to their environment. The theory of the dependence of mental processes on physiological and neural processes fits into this scheme; and, by bringing in the evolutionary point of view, mental phenomena may be further treated as "emergents" at a late period on the basis of prior complex structures in themselves non-mental.

This treatment of experience as a natural phenomenon we may call equally well the "Realistic" or the "Naturalistic" way, for at this point Realism and Naturalism coincide. The essence of this way is to distinguish experience (or mind) from what is not experience (or mind), and to assign to the factors so distinguished their respective places within the context, or whole, within which they have been discriminated and which, in this very act of distinguishing parts within it, is taken as ultimate relatively to these parts.

The other way is to take experience as "ultimate," *i.e.*, as itself the context or whole within which all differences are found. This is the way of Idealism, as it is also the way of Phaenomenology in Husserl's sense. Thus, instead of experience being a factor within Nature, Nature will be a factor within experience.

I hope I shall not be considered to be taking a mean verbal advantage, if I quote certain passages from Professor Dewey's *Experience and Nature* to illustrate this standpoint. My excuse must be that I know in recent philosophical literature no clearer expression of the point of view which takes experience as ultimate than his. And this is not, after all, to be wondered at when we remember that Professor Dewey, though no doubt he would not call himself an Idealist, was once steeped in Idealism; and that his study of the great Idealists has left indelible marks upon his thinking, even in the very originality of his revolt against some of their principles. The passages [1] to which I refer are these: " 'Experience' denotes the planted field, the sowed seeds, the reaped harvests, the changes of night and day, spring and autumn wet and dry, heat and cold, that are observed, feared, longed for; it also denotes the one who plans and reaps, who works and rejoices, hopes, fears, plans, invokes magic or chemistry to aid him, who is downcast or triumphant. It is 'double-barrelled' in that it recognizes in its primary integrity no division, between act and material, subject and object, but

[1] Quoted by permission of The Open Court Pub. Co.

contains them both in unanalyzed totality. . . . Now empirical method is the only method which can do justice to this inclusive integrity of experience.' It alone takes this integrated unity as the starting-point for philosophic thought. Other methods begin with results of a reflection which has already torn in two the subject-matter experienced and the operations and states of experiencing. The problem then is to get together again what has been sundered. . . . For empirical methods the problem . . . is to note how and why the whole is distinguished into subject and object, nature and mental operations (*op. cit.*, pp. 8, 9)."

What Dewey here calls his own empirical method is, in spirit and principle, if not in the actual details of its execution, identical with the idealistic method, especially when one adds, from Dewey's *Preface* the refefences to "faith in experience when intelligently used as a means of disclosing the realities of nature," and to the character of human experience as "a growing progressive self-disclosure of nature itself" (*op. cit.*, p. iii). If in these utterances we substitute for "nature" simply "Reality," or even the "Absolute," they might have been written by any true-blue Idealist. Or, again, Dewey's suggestion that the distinction within experience between subject and object, nature and mental operations, must be understood and evaluated in the light of its practical effects, cannot but evoke recollections of F. H. Bradley's treatment of all distinctions within experience as "ideal constructions" which are "practical makeshifts." In other words, on the practical usefulness of these distinctions (constructions, abstractions) Dewey and Bradley are agreed, but in their evaluations of them they differ. Bradley treats them dialectically and condemns them by the standard of intellectual consistency, whereas Dewey accepts them in order to emphasize their function in enriching and improving experience itself. "To distinguish in reflection the physical and to hold it in temporary detachment is to be set upon the road that conducts to tools and technologies, to construction of mechanisms, to the arts that ensue in the wake of the sciences. That these constructions make possible a better regulation of the affairs of primary experience is evident" (*op. cit.*, p. 10). The difference between Bradley and Dewey is the difference between the detached don who, like the god of Aristotle, is engaged in "thought thinking itself" and, incidentally, finding itself wanting by the standard of its own inherent ideal, and the reformer who, demanding from thought that it make action foreseeing and intelligent, identifies himself with the dominant tendencies of contemporary civilization, and seeks through reflection at once to understand the methods and ideals of this civilization and also to raise it to new heights of achievement.

Indeed, one of the main interests of contemporary philosophy is just the way in which, from a common basis in experience as ultimate, a variety of theoretical paths can be pursued to the common aim of a deeper understanding of the Universe and of man's place in it. In principle, all these ways are metaphysical, but some are thinly dialectical (though not for that reason wholly without value), whilst others are charged with a vivid sense of the concrete meanings and values, and the conflicts of these meanings and values, in experience. "It takes," as Bosanquet used to say, "all sorts to make a world." It takes certainly all sorts of philosophizings to exhaust the self-disclosure of the world in experience.

Thus, *e.g.*, we may, Kant-wise, analyze experience into "matter" of sensations and "forms" of pure thought, with the individual percipient or thinker generalized into a "synthetic unity of apperception." Or, we may, with James and others, distinguish data, here and now apprehended, from their meanings in terms of other possible experiences to be had by appropriate action, so that the present datum, interpreted with the help of memory of past experiences, becomes a clue to future experiences and a basis for a plan of future action. Or, yet again, we may, with Bergson, contrast the Universe as conceived by the intellect with the Universe as grasped by intuition; or, with James Ward, distinguish in every experience an object and a subject and then, *via* interpreting the object as another subject, reach a spiritual pluralism as our theory of the Universe. Or, finally, we may take experience more concretely as science, art, morality, religion—each of these terms understood to be an abbreviation for the Universe as disclosed to scientific thought, as conceived from the aesthetic, moral, religious point of view. In all these, and many other, forms of philosophizing, experience is the ultimate: the total context which is taken for granted and within which all distinctions fall. And experience, thus taken as ultimate, is identical with the Universe because this term is meaningless apart from experience, or with experience delimited within it as a specialized item, a particular phenomenon among other phenomena.

This assertion will be challenged by Realists and Naturalists. Like all fundamental positions, it cannot be proved: it can only be exhibited as self-evident. Argument cannot demonstrate it, but only lead the mind to the point where the principle is intuited or seen to be obvious. As between thinkers of different schools, the difficulty of such arguments is to secure the required identity of meanings with which what is essentially an experiment in thinking has to be conducted. All that we can actually make sure of is merely the identity of the words employed as vehicles of meaning. Speech-habits and, with them, the underlying thought-habits or meaning-habits differ, and in the end the only safeguard against otherwise inevitable misunderstanding is to familiarize oneself with the diverse contexts in which the words and meanings of philosophers function. This is only the first step, avoiding actual misunderstanding. The real argument, which is a dialectical comparison of systems of meanings from the point of view of their internal consistency is still to follow. Moreover, the argument is not about the consistency of meanings in the abstract. On the contrary, seeing that the subject of the whole experiment is experience in the concrete, the meanings which are being experimented with are taken to be meanings which are realized or fulfilled in experience, meanings which apply.

To illustrate: it may be said, "Granted that all distinctions are made within a context or whole which, relatively to the details discriminated within it, is ultimate, why quarrel whether this whole is more appropriately named "Nature" or "Experience"? A rose by any other name smells just as sweet: the whole is what it is and what we find it to be, whatever name we may give it." The objection has point so long as the terms are taken in denotation. As metaphysicians, we are all discussing the same thing denotatively —the All let us say, to use the least committal term we can find. But our real differences are over the connotation— the "what," or nature, or character, of the All. And so taken, the point of the dispute is not merely verbal. Between saying that Experience is a factor within Nature, and saying that Nature is a factor within Experience, there is a significant difference in the meanings which we assert as qualifying, or claim to find fulfilled or realized in, the common subject of discussion.

Our choice between such systems of meanings must be determined by experiments in thinking which exhibit the consistency of details within the system whilst at the same time exhibiting its self-evidence as realized in experience. It is only for convenience in dialectical treatment that the system as a whole is concentrated into some one general proposition, such as that Experience is ultimate and Nature a factor within it, or that Nature is ultimate and Experience a factor within it. These statements do not carry their whole meaning within the four corners, so to speak of these words, but are abbreviations, or, better, concretions, of whole meaning-systems. The situation may be exemplified by Schopenhauer's famous statement that the whole argument of the two volumes of *The World as Will and as Idea* is the exhibition in detail of the single principle that the World is Will. Into this proposition the whole system can be concentrated, *viz.*, for those for whom the meaning of the words in which this proposition is expressed is determined by their acquaintance with the details of the whole system. Taken apart from this context, *e.g.*, in their ordinary everyday meaning, the words of the proposition are barely intelligible and their truth anything but self-evident.

The point is sufficiently important to bear repetition: Fundamental issues can be decided (and the decision will always be an individual one for the thinker making the experiment for himself) only by dialectical experiments, *i.e.*, by experiments with meanings which are tested at once in respect of their internal coherence and their realization in the subject with which thought is denotatively concerned. And the result, if the experiment is ideally successful, will be that the whole system will be seen to be self-evident in the double sense of being coherent within itself and obviously realized in ("true of") the subject of which it is the nature or "what."

Thus, Berkeley was right in method when he challenges his readers, in order to convince themselves of the self-evidence of his *esse est percipi* principle, to make some "easy trials," *i.e.*, some experiments in reflection on the meanings of the terms "to be" and "to be experienced," as applied to actual acts of perceiving objects. He is at fault, not in his method, but in the meanings with which he experiments, in that he reads into the act of perceiving at once a perceiving substance, or "spirit," and in that he treats objects as clusters of atomic sense-data ("ideas"). Similarly, most arguments between Realists and Idealists consist of dialectical experiments, whether the point at issue be Perry's ego-centric predicament, or the internality-externality of relations, or the logical independence of the meanings of "to be" and "to be perceived by a mind."

I will briefly sketch an experiment which I have found illuminating whenever I have tried it. Take any experience at random, the simpler, the better—this noise, for example. Compare the series: this noise—hearing-this-noise—my-hearing-this-noise. Denotatively, the same experience is referred to throughout; connotatively, the more complex phrase expresses a more complex meaning, corresponding to a more complete analysis of the nature of that experience. Nothing, so far, has been said, or thought, concerning what the noise is of, what it indicates, what inferences it permits (*e.g.*, the noise of a bursting high-explosive shell, presaging an attack by the enemy); nor of what "I" am and what feelings, thoughts, actions the hearing of this noise arouses in me, interrupting other feelings, thoughts, acts. Yet all this and much more might be taken as constituting the self-same experience with which we began the experiment. Anyhow, whether taken widely or narrowly, the experience, even as expressed in the ordinary language of unreflective intercourse, is clearly a complex event containing distinguishable features. Let now reflection supervene, not only making explicit the details which it distinguishes, but generalizing them at the same time. This noise becomes to be contrasted with the hearing of it; it is classed with other noises as against other acts of hearing; noises are grouped with sights and other objects; hearings with seeings and other sorts of perceivings; and, presently, it all sums up into the grand pattern of Object *versus* Subject, or Object *versus* Act.

This is stage one. Stage two is reached with a further turn of reflection: All this elaborate development, this very pattern of Object *versus* Subject, is, in its turn, the object of reflection at a higher level, so to speak. And that this is so, is yet once again an object apprehended by a yet further act of reflection. Clearly, there is no end to this process: experience proliferates—the pattern of its structure repeating itself at each new turn or level of reflection.

The lesson which I derive from this experiment in reflection is that the standpoint from which it is made is not the Naturalistic one. For, the paradigm of Naturalistic analysis is the animal (or human) body whose acts or perceiving lie for me, as spectator, equally with their objects in the same plane of observation. I see the thing at which the animal is looking, sniffing, etc., and I see the animal's looking and sniffing as a behavior of its body exactly as I see the object to which these acts are directed. I can generalize this finding to include myself by saying that what is true of the behavior observed by me is true of my own behavior in observing, and would be so verified by another observer in whose object-field I (my body) am an object reacting to other objects, in the same way as the percipients observed by me are objects reacting to other objects in my object-field. Thus, the Naturalistic analysis can be completed on this single plane of stimulus and response, in abstraction from, *i.e.*, with systematic avoidance of, reflection on my own spectatorship.

So soon as I reflect on my spectator point of view and, further, reflect on this reflection, I switch on to a different plane, or to a different point of view, where reflection proliferates from plane to plane, yielding as it does so, not an ego-centric predicament, but the recognition of the systematic abstraction practiced in maintaining the Naturalistic point of view. It brings to attention a factor omitted from view on the Naturalistic plane, but now seen to be ineliminable from the total fact called an "experience." Thus it leads to the recovery of that "inclusive integrity of experience," as Dewey calls it, which compels us to take experience as ultimate and forbids our inserting it as a factor in any context wider than itself.

It would take me too far to show here how the dialectic of "self-consciousness" in the writings of the Hegelians has grown out of this sort of experiment. But it is relevant to add an argument leading to the same conclusion by a different route. If we are in earnest about experience being, in Dewey's words quoted above, "the progressive self-disclosure of nature itself," we are committed to taking experience as ultimate because self-disclosure is, on this view, essential to Nature. We shall misconceive the nature of Nature (if I may use this phrase), if we think of it as complete in itself without self-disclosure, and regard the latter only as an occasional luxury in which Nature indulges through human minds, but which it can very well do without. Nature without self-disclosure, *i.e.*, Nature conceived in abstraction from experience, is simply not Nature complete.

I will conclude this section by returning to Whitehead's *Process and Reality*.

Into the details of his account of experience in terms of "prehensions" it is not necessary to enter for the purpose of this argument. Indeed, some of the details of his position I do not yet understand sufficiently to be able to discuss them profitably. But the principle of his position in rejecting the doctrine of "vacuous actuality," and in identifying every actual occasion or entity with an actual experience, is unmistakably identical with the position taken up in this section. It is enough, in support of this contention, to quote Whitehead's own statement of his "reformed subjectivist principle," *viz.*, "subjective experiencing is the primary metaphysical situation which is presented to metaphysics for analysis. . . . Accordingly, the notion 'this stone is grey' is a derivative abstraction, necessary indeed as an element in the description of the fundamental experiential feeling, but delusive as a metaphysical starting-point" (p. 224). This acceptance by Whitehead of experience as the metaphysical ultimate, combined with his fresh analysis of experience in which he replaces the substance-quality concept by the distinction between actual entities and eternal objects, is the best evidence for the contention that in *Process and Reality* we have a highly original working out of a position fundamentally Idealist. It may well be that Whitehead's book will do for twentieth-century philosophy what Kant's *Critique of Pure Reason* did for nineteeth-century philosophy.

III

EXPERIENCE AND A PERSONAL SUBJECT

I turn to the concluding topic, *viz.*, the problem of whether experience essentially involves a personal subject of which it is the activity.

It is a commonplace that the Idealistic systems of the past have differed, one from the other, in the metaphysical status assigned to the category of personality. Some have treated personality as the highest category, *i.e.*, as the most adequate characterization of the Universe in the light of systematic reflection on its nature as revealed in experience. Others have treated it as inadequate for this purpose and rather thought of the Universe as non-personal or supra-personal—it comes to the same in this context. The former thinkers have further differed among themselves in being either Pluralists or Monists, the Pluralists seeing in the Universe a Society of Selves of different degrees and rank, with God as the highest and, in a sense, the all-sustaining spirit; the Monists emphasizing, in their identification of the Absolute with a personal God, the singleness of the ultimate spirit in whom all lesser spirits, like human minds, are somehow included in a dependence which, in technical language, makes them "adjectival" to the "substantiality" of the all-inclusive One.

The difference between Personalists and Impersonalists among Idealists may also be described in another, and perhaps more illuminating, way by saying that to the defenders of personality, whether Pluralists or Monists, the focusing of experience in one or more individual centers, or subjects, is the highest metaphysical value, in the sense that an individual spirit, or person, is to them an "end in itself," as Kant would have said. It is through this focusing or concretion of itself in individual spirits that the Universe approves itself to these thinkers. For them, all other values, Truth, Beauty, Goodness, Love, Creativity, achieve their fullest consummation only through the part they play in the lives, i.e., the experience-contexts, of individual spirits. The other school of Idealists reverses this emphasis: individual spirits or persons, for it, rank in value according as they are the temporary vehicles of these supra-individual and supra-personal values. What matters from this point of view is not the abstract form of personality, the individuality of each focus as distinct from all other foci, but the degree in which a given individual during its existence realizes these supra-individual values in his life.

Again, it is a commonplace that these rival evaluations of personality by different Idealists rest on a basis of agreement, viz., the agreement that of all modes of experience religious experience is the most relevant to this issue. Indeed, it is, in the main, as alternative ways of using the evidence of religious experience in metaphysics that these conflicting views have been formulated. If Pluralistic Spirit-ualism stands nearest to theological orthodoxy and reflects the social organization of religion in churches, Monistic Spiritualism and the Impersonal Absolute (which regards the Universe as the realization of supra-personal values) stand nearest to the mystic temper without a strain of which religion is, admittedly, impoverished.

Now, it is when one tries to determine Whitehead's position relatively to these issues that the originality of his thinking becomes conspicuous in the way in which he transforms these time-honored problems, and effects a fresh synthesis of these familiar lines of thought.

That Whitehead accepts religion as one of the most im-portant data for metaphysics, we have seen already; and that his *Process and Reality* should culminate, in the con-cluding chapter on "God and the World," in an effort to interpret religion in the light of his metaphysical principles, and thereby, conversely, to bring religion to the support of these principles, was only to be expected. But when we come to details, it appears that the concept of individual subject, or person, plays a very minor part in Whitehead's theory. To the question, "Does Whitehead conceive God as a person?" I do not know what answer to give, and I strongly suspect that Whitehead himself would answer that the question implies assumptions utterly irrelevant to his conception of God. At any rate, according to the index, which lists "personal order," but not "person," the term does not occur after p. 225 (the whole book has close on 500 pages) and, therefore, not in the chapter on God. In this, the index is at fault. For, at the very end of the chapter, on p. 496, there occurs this passage: "Each actuality in the temporal world has its reception into God's nature. The corresponding element in God's nature is not temporal actuality, but is the transmutation of that temporal actual-ity into a living, ever-present fact. An enduring person-ality in the temporal world is a route of occasions in which the successors with some peculiar completeness sum up their predecessors. The correlate fact in God's nature is an even more complete unity of life in a chain of elements for which succession does not mean the loss of immediate unison. This element in God's nature inherits from the temporal counterpart according to the same principle as in the temporal world the future inherits from the past. Thus in the sense in which the present occasion is the person *now*, and yet with his own past, so the counterpart in God is that person in God."

The language of this passage, with its obvious echoes of Bradley's terms, does not suggest either a society of spirits or a personal God. It conveys rather an impersonal Absolute in which persons are "completed" and "perfected" by "transmutation." It does not seem to me that we can find here any use of personality as the highest category: we find only an illustration of Whitehead's metaphysical principles by application to human persons. Whitehead does not say that the Universe is an all-inclusive person or a society of persons: he merely says that human persons and God exhibit the same metaphysical principles. Personality is not one of his fundamental categories.

None the less, all that Whitehead says about God is instinct with deep and genuine religious feeling: no attentive reader can mistake this. At the same time, it is feeling which, thanks to philosophy, has emancipated itself from traditional theology, whilst remaining colored by traditional terminology. God remains God denotatively: connotatively, however, Whitehead's God is conceived very differently from the traditional way. No summary can do justice to the freshness or the sincerity of what Whitehead has to say, and I shall therefore confine myself to a bare discussion of a few points which will support my contention, above, that Whitehead shows the originality of his thought in this field by the way in which he makes the old difficulties drop out of sight by the new pattern in which he arranges familiar elements.

Fundamental, as I see it, is the position taken up in the following passage: "God and the World stand over against each other, expressing the final metaphysical truth that

THE REVIVAL OF IDEALISM   325

appetitive vision and physical enjoyment have equal claim
to priority in creation. But no two actualities can be torn
apart: each is all in all. . . . God is the infinite ground of
all mentality, the unity of vision seeking physical multiplicity. The World is the multiplicity of the finites, actualities seeking a perfected unity. Neither God, nor the World,
reaches static completion" (p. 493).

So far—the qualification is important, for there is a
further step to come—Whitehead's position is clearly
Spinozistic. If God and the World are each all in all, then
we can say with Spinoza, *Deus sive Natura*. And if, within
this fundamental identity, we still wish to maintain some
connotative difference between the terms, we can only do
so by taking each as characterizing the All but with a difference of complementary emphasis—like Spinoza's *Natura
naturans* and *Natura naturata*—according as we throw the
weight for the moment on unity or on multiplicity, on permanence or on flux, on harmony or on discord. This shift of
attention from one aspect to its complementary, especially
when intensified by the impossibility of saying all things
at once, may give rise to the illusory appearance of an abstract sundering of what is meant to be merely discriminated
within a concrete unity. This remark applies more particularly to the distinction between the "primordial" and the
"consequent" nature of God, these terms understood not in
a temporal, but, again Spinoza-wise, in a logical sense.
God's primordial nature, as "the unconditioned actuality
of conceptual feeling at the base of things" (p. 486), is the
ground of God's consequent nature, as the concrete realization, or embodiment, of conceived possibilities in "physical
feelings." Either side, taken in abstraction from the other,
is less than the whole fact to be understood.

What is non-Spinozistic in Whitehead's position is the
further and, for him, most fundamental contention that
"creative advance into novelty" is the ultimate metaphysical ground (p. 494). Thus Whitehead's God is no static
Absolute, eternally self-complete and enjoying everlastingly
the contemplation of its own perfection; his experience is

not Roycean *totum simul* in which past and future are but enrichments of an infinitely extended specious present. At this point Whitehead is a modern of moderns, incorporating in his metaphysical vision the lessons which he has learned from James, from Bergson, from Samuel Alexander—from all, in short, who have felt that the Absolutes of the older Idealists did less than justice to the character of inexhaustible novelty and creative fecundity in the Universe. A summarizing phrase must be generously understood if it is not to be misleading, but, subject to this caution, one may not unfairly say that Whitehead substitutes a creative Absolute for the static Absolute of his Idealist predecessors.

"There is nothing here in the nature of proof," confesses Whitehead himself (p. 486). And, earlier, he warns us that, in reflection on the plane, "however far our gaze penetrates, there are always heights beyond which block our vision" (p. 484). Still, if in trying to render in rational reflection the lessons of religious experience concerning the nature of the universe, Whitehead has to push thought to the limits of the thinkable, he once more but illustrates his kinship with the efforts of the great Idealists and indorses their final findings. In his theory, the theories of his Idealist predecessors achieve what he himself would call their "objective Immortality," and thereby a new and vigorous reincarnation.